LEANINGS 3

First published in 2014 by Motorbooks, an imprint of Quarto Publishing Group
USA Inc., 400 First Avenue North, Suite 400, Minneapolis, MN 55401 USA

Motorbooks titles are also available at discounts in bulk quantity for industrial
or sales-promotional use. For details write to Special Sales Manager at Quarto
Publishing Group USA Inc., 400 First Avenue North, Suite 400, Minneapolis, MN
55401 USA.

To find out more about our books, visit us online at www.motorbooks.com.

ISBN-13: 978-0-7603-4642-6

Library of Congress Cataloging-in-Publication Data

Editor: Zack Miller
Senior Art Director: Brad Springer
Cover Designer: Simon Larkin
Book Designer: Diana Boger
Layout: Helena Shimizu

On the cover: Photo by Cycle World
On the back cover: Photo by Cycle World
On the back flap: Top photo by Peter Egan; lower photo by Cycle World

Printed in the United States of America

10 9 8 7 6 5 4 3 2 1

LEANINGS 3

*On the Road and in the Garage with Cycle World's **Peter Egan***

Contents

Foreword

O Brother, Here Art Thou

Before ever meeting Peter Egan, I felt a rare brotherhood with him, a connection forged through common experience and interests unlike any I'd ever felt. He somehow brought to life all these vague but very real feelings and ideas I had when riding and working on my motorcycles. Man, it was like he knew exactly what I was experiencing and had just been on the same ride I had.

Thing is, he does that to everybody who reads his work. And that's the power of Peter Egan. Our monthly date with *Leanings* and his other pieces in *Cycle World* over the past three decades is like that great meeting you have with an old friend to talk about the things that really matter—your friend who gets to go places and do things that most people never do.

When I first subscribed to *Cycle World* as a 13-year-old, I wasn't really cognizant of the staffers who did the writing I so eagerly devoured. Still, it didn't take long to figure out this Egan fellow wasn't your typical moto scribe.

For me and so many others, it was through his writings that I actually learned how to become a motorcycle enthusiast. I learned the subtleties of feeling and experience that formed the core of a rich motorcycle life, got thoughtful glimpses into two-wheel history and developed a better understanding of how motorcycles worked.

And it's all been delivered in world-class storytelling. Peter picks you up beautifully at the beginning of a story, carries you along nicely and sets you down ever so wonderfully at the end, revealing inalienable truths about life and motorcycling along the way.

We are lucky that his "flimsy vow of retirement" from writing *Leanings* every month in *Cycle World* has been just that: flimsy. He's still filing the occasional column, essay or feature, while restoring Norton Commandos or similar and generally enjoying the motorcycle life he's so ably shared.

I've been fortunate to work with Peter at *Cycle World* since 1999. During that time, we've become good friends, playing guitar in his shop and examining closely the many great motorcycles (and cars) he's had there during my visits. And we've shared a few fine beers after a long day's ride. He's that same cool guy in person that he is in writing, and to know him on the page is to know him.

It's that truth and authenticity in his work that has drawn us all here together in *Leanings 3*. So I'm going to make a long pour with a motor-oil-hued English ale, sit back and step out of the way. Here's to Peter, our brother on the road. Cheers, and thanks for making the world of motorcycling a better place.

Mark Hoyer
Editor-in-Chief, *Cycle World* Magazine

SECTION 1

The Columns

01

Ever More Upright

IBELIEVE THE TREND FIRST STRUCK ME ABOUT TWO YEARS ago, as the Slimey Crud Motorcycle Gang wended its way through the green hills of Wisconsin toward an overnight stay at the little village of Alma on the Mississippi. As we rode along, I pondered the bikes on the road ahead of me, and those in my mirrors as well.

There were about 15 of us strung out along the twists and turns of Highway 33, and I gradually became aware that nearly everyone I could see in both directions was sitting relatively upright in the saddle, with his feet beneath him and his elbows slightly out, dirt-track style.

I, on the other hand, was leaned well forward into the bars of my Ducati ST2, and only two other riders—both on Airhead R100RSs—were seated in similar, if slightly less radical, riding positions. For perhaps the first time in years, there was only a single committed sportbike with clip-ons and rearsets—a much-modified old Moto Guzzi LeMans. Otherwise, there was little evidence of the classic café-racer riding position so prevalent in the group not long ago.

Instead, the bike of choice was the Cagiva Gran Canyon. There were at least six of these adventure/tourer/whatever Italian V-Twins in the group. Add in a couple of Ducati Monsters, a BMW R1100GS, and a Suzuki Bandit 1200 with wide, comfortable Superbike-style bars, and you have the complete picture. My ST2 and the Guzzi were beginning to look like a pair of low, rounded submarines traveling in a fleet of square-rigged sailing vessels.

Which is all a long way of saying that it has not escaped the notice of a really sharp guy like myself that nearly all of my lifelong, sportbike-riding friends are gradually metamorphosing toward a more upright riding position, some slightly taller and more modern version of the peg-bar-seat relationship found on my ancient 1968 Triumph Trophy 500, one of the original "dual-sport" bikes of the Triumph line.

This transition has begun to remind me of one of the old "Ascent of Man" illustrations that show the human species evolving from Australopithecus, or

one of those little knuckle-dragging, lemur-like hominids with no chin or forehead (sort of like your freshman photo in the high school yearbook), upward to a slightly stooped Neanderthal who looks like Charlie Watts and onward to a Cro-Magnon who walks perfectly upright and looks, essentially, like a modern human except for his lack of Dockers and a cell phone.

At the time of our group ride to Alma, I'd made it about halfway up this sliding evolutionary scale—stooped, yet not quite down on all fours—but a lot of my riding buddies have graduated into the post Cro-Magnon era. Mike Mosiman in Colorado, for instance, bought himself a BMW R1150GS and has called several times to tell me it's the best-handling, easiest-to-ride motorcycle he's ever owned. Fellow Crud Lew Terpstra recently joined the Gran Canyon brigade and told me it's "as close to the perfect motorcycle as anything I've ever had."

And the trend continues this year. A couple of Cruds have just picked up Ducati Multistradas (Multistradi?) and are presently attempting to transform their seats, via the aftermarket, into something that can be sat upon. Also, a couple more BMW GSs and a standard R-model have been added to the club.

And now, even I (yes) have moved experimentally more upright, having traded my ST2 for a black KTM 950 Adventure, which seems to remind all my friends of a praying mantis–like insect. One said, "I notice all the cicadas have gone silent or left town since you bought that thing," and another described it as "looking like a large, fearsome insect that eats its young." In any case, the riding position is strictly dirt bike, hardly any different from that of my KTM 525 or Suzuki DR650. You ride with your feet underneath you, elbows slightly out and faceshield at a right angle to the ground.

So what's going on here? Are my colleagues and I simply getting old?

Well, yes, of course we are. But it's more complicated than that.

First, you have to remember that nearly all of us *d'un certain âge* (as the French so tactfully describe that middle ground between vibrant youth and looming death) grew up on Triumphs, Hondas, Nortons, etc. that had their handlebars and footpegs arranged pretty much like those Gran Canyons and GSs—and much as they had been (by general agreement on the norms of human comfort) since the turn of the previous century. Outside the café-racer movement in England—and real roadracers who needed that extra three or four mph on the main straight—it seemed not to have occurred to anyone that you would want to ride around with your head lower than your butt.

That all began to change in the mid-1970s with mild—and still pretty comfortable—café bikes like the Honda 400F, BMW R90S, and Kawasaki Z-1R, which gradually metamorphosed into the more committed, eminently track-worthy sportbikes we have today—the 999s, RC51s, and R1s of this world.

These are bikes I still like and admire, both technically and for the roadracing tradition they represent, and I like nothing better than a track day with a real, hardcore sportbike.

But I think my days of voluntarily riding them on the street are over.

For public roads and longer distances, I simply go faster and ride more confidently and comfortably when I have better leverage at the handlebars and a wider field of vision.

The template of my favored range of riding positions these days seems to begin with, say, a VFR Honda and arc slowly upward to the adventure-touring stance of the KTM.

Neither of which, incidentally, has a riding position quite as perfectly evolved as that of the Vincent Black Shadow I once owned, a bike from the age of mastodons and cave paintings, when the Cruds were, quite literally, still learning to walk upright.

02

The Fine Art of Planning to Crash

L AST SUNDAY, ON A BRIGHT, FROSTY AUTUMN MORNING, BARB and I sat in a café in the small town of Mount Horeb, Wisconsin, drinking coffee and hovering over the steam. We were gripping our coffee mugs with both hands, in the fashion peculiar to chilled motorcyclists and torpedoed sailors who have just been rescued from the North Sea.

"We should have dressed warmer," I told Barb. "It was supposed to get into the seventies today, so I thought blue jeans would be warm enough. I should have worn my leather pants, the ones with the kneepads and shin guards."

Barb nodded through the steam, and I rubbed the thin denim that covered my bony right knee–an Egan genetic trait inherited, no doubt, from generations of Celts who didn't have to kneel on anything harder than a peat bog.

"And, under the circumstances," I added, "it wouldn't be such a bad idea to have some knee protection, anyway."

The "circumstances" of which I spoke were tacitly understood by both of us.

Just the night before, we'd gone to the hospital to visit our friend Greg, whose right knee was about to be reconstructed by a team of orthopedic surgeons who gathered around his X-rays like football coaches plotting a double-reverse play at the Super Bowl.

On the previous weekend, seven of us had gone on an all-day ride through the gloriously red and orange autumnal backroads of southern Wisconsin. Late in the afternoon, Greg and I had traded bikes so he could take my KTM 950 Adventure for a short test ride.

Uncharacteristically (this is a guy who's fast and smooth and hasn't crashed in 30 years), he went too deep into an off-camber, decreasing-radius corner, ran out of road and traction simultaneously, and disappeared into the woods.

Greg and the bike flattened a small grove of saplings and came to rest between two much larger trees. A woman motorist called 911 on her cell phone, and EMTs arrived within minutes.

We pulled the bike off Greg and—to our great relief—found him lucid and essentially uninjured, except for a dysfunctional right knee. He was carted off to the hospital, and six of us lifted the bent and battered KTM back up onto the highway.

Amazingly, I was able to start it up and ride home, though my dealer now says the frame and triple clamps are tweaked, and the 950 is probably a goner.

But it's just a bike, and we're all deeply grateful Greg's injuries weren't any worse. Big trees are unyielding things, as several celebrity skiers have fatally discovered. His helmet was cracked in two places and his armor-clad jacket was scraped up, but he had no injuries beyond the damaged knee beneath his blue jeans.

Meanwhile, back at the café, Barb and I soaked up heat from our coffee and pondered all these things. It was interesting, I noted, that less than a week after Greg's crash, Barb and I were riding our big Beemer around the leaf-strewn, deer-infested, gravel-plagued backroads of rural Wisconsin with nothing over our vulnerable kneecaps but the reassuring cotton weave of Levi's denim. Through which—if you hold it up to the light—you can almost read.

We had full-face helmets, jackets with body armor, gauntlet-style leather gloves, sturdy touring boots and...jeans. What were we thinking?

I've been riding dirt bikes quite a bit the last few years, and I would never consider riding off-road without knee and shin protectors just above my Frankenstein-quality motocross boots. And why not?

Because I know I'm going to crash.

Okay, I don't crash every time I go dirt riding. Just every other time or so. And I know, with absolute certainty, that every time I drop the bike I'm going to land hard on at least one knee. And probably an elbow, too. It's inevitable.

Riding a dirt bike without body armor is like playing football or hockey in street clothes; you can get away with it for a while, and then it's time to contemplate those interesting patterns in the acoustic tile on the ceiling of your local emergency room, while you wait around for an intern to tell you the eternally amusing "donor-cycle" joke.

Okay, so I look like Wayne Gretzky when I go dirt riding. Yet I generally hop on my streetbike with almost no lower body protection, even though I have a closet bulging with so much gear I can barely close the door. I've got roadracing leathers, two-piece street leathers with knee cups, and a nicely armored Aerostich suit. But off I go for a day of riding, more often than not, in my trusty blue jeans. Why? Well, there's heat to consider. On a hot summer day, jeans are cooler. And then there's "appropriateness" of dress; I always feel a little odd sitting in the dentist's chair in a full set of leathers. Also, the creaking of body armor can be distracting at movies and dinner parties.

But mostly I wear jeans on days when I don't plan to crash.

If I do think there's a high likelihood of a get-off—going on a fast sportbike ride with friends, for instance—I wear my full street leathers or Aerostich suit.

Same with helmet selection. Open or full-face? Do I feel lucky today? On "safe" rides, I often take the open one, despite full-face helmets having saved my chin and teeth from the tarmac grindstone in two roadracing crashes.

All of this is total lunacy, of course. Most of us aren't very good at predicting when or if a bike will go down. Accidents happen randomly, despite our best efforts to choreograph fate. We can't see the future; if we could, we'd stay home that day.

Or wear everything we've got.

Barb and I rode home from the café that Sunday morning without incident, our denim-clad knees unharmed once more. Barb decided to weed her flowerbed, while I took off on a long solo ride toward the Mississippi.

The fall day was warming up nicely, but I changed into full leathers before I left anyway. It seemed like a good idea, even though I wasn't really planning to crash.

03

On the Trail of the Mighty One

RANDOM SNOW FLURRIES SLANTED ACROSS MY HEADLIGHTS LIKE SMALL javelins, but inside my car the CD player glowed warmly.

"Donde esta la estacion de ferrocarril?" a male voice asked me, ferociously trilling every *r* in the Spanish word for *railway*.

I quickly repeated the phrase twice, my tongue clicking against the roof of my mouth like a pair of castanets. I sounded just like him.

Yes, folks, I was reviewing what little Spanish I'd retained from high school, and had bought myself some instructional CDs. They purported to be the same ones used by our State Department and CIA. Who better to learn from than Yanqui spooks, who have been meddling in Latin America since the early days of James Monroe?

Why these sudden language lessons?

Well, two reasons, really.

First, I'd just returned from a 1,000-mile, off-road trip through Baja and had felt let down by my poor language skills, vowing to improve them when I got home. And, second, I'd come home from Mexico just in time to see a movie called *The Motorcycle Diaries*, based on communist revolutionary Che Guevara's famous travelogue by the same name.

For those of you who haven't already seen it, here's the basic story: In 1952, young medical student Ernesto Guevara Lynch and his buddy Alberto Granado set off from their native Argentina, two-up on a 1938 Norton 500, to tour South America. Granado called the bike *La Poderosa*, or "The Mighty One." The pair makes it all the way south into Patagonia, across the Andes, and halfway up the coast of Chile before their much-abused big British Single finally disintegrates. They complete the trip hitchhiking through Peru, Bolivia, Columbia, and Venezuela by flatbed truck, train, raft, and airplane.

Both buddies later published diaries of the trip. Granado's account was called *Traveling with Che Guevara: The Making of a Revolutionary*. Scenes from both their books were used to make the movie.

And an excellent movie it is, I think.

I should interject here that I have never been much of a Che Guevara fan. One of my roommates in college had a big poster of the guy on his wall, but I've always cast a jaundiced eye on politicos who don't like freedom of speech. Also, shooting your critics without trial always sets a bad tone in government. Good things almost never happen after that.

Other than those few glaring, fatal flaws, of course, Guevara had many admirable traits. He was highly intelligent, a born romantic, absolutely fearless, and an intrepid world traveler, despite a lifelong battle with asthma, right up until he was captured and executed in Bolivia in 1967.

And, at the time he wrote his *Motorcycle Diaries*, at least, he was very funny. The book is full of dry, hilarious comments and droll understatement, without too much proselytizing. And so is the movie.

There are rumblings of the forces that would later turn Che Guevara into Fidel Castro's second-in-command, but it's mostly a beautifully filmed, well-acted road story about two young men on a motorcycle adventure in the 1950s.

Which I guess is why I've seen it twice. So far. Simply put, the movie makes you want to run out of the theater, fly to South America, grab a motorcycle, and start touring, preferably through the Andes and Patagonia. The scenery in the movie is that stunning.

Hence the Spanish lessons. And the pile of books now sitting next to my reading chair.

I just re-read my hardcover copy of *Motorcycle Diaries*, which was given to me by my friend Diane Almond when it first appeared in English back in 1995. I'd forgotten how well-written the book is; Guevara could have spent his life as a travel writer, and we'd all have a shelf of his stuff.

In fact, he could have written a whole second book on an earlier trip he took in 1950, riding his bicycle—with a Ducati Cucciolo engine mounted on it—on a 2,400-mile tour of northern Argentina.

Che rides the first Ducati! Maybe he could have been saved. "You have nothing to lose but your chains" would have acquired a whole new meaning.

After reading all that, of course, I had to run out and buy Granado's book, which gives a slightly different perspective of the same trip. (Granado moved to Cuba to join his old friend Che after the Revolution, and is still there.) That, in turn, caused me to pick up yet another volume on the subject, published in 2000, called *Chasing Che: A Motorcycle Journey in Search of the Guevara Legend*.

American author Patrick Symmes retraces the old Guevara/Granado route with his BMW R80GS, camping where they camped, stopping where they stopped, and commenting on the legacy of Che Guevara. Symmes is a terrific travel writer, and this book alone will make you want to quit your job and tour South America, never mind Che and his Norton.

A more harrowing account of riding into Latin America is provided by Glen Heggstad's *Two Wheels Through Terror*. Heggstad made it into the mountains of Columbia before he was kidnapped by communist rebels of the ELN. He survived five weeks of beatings, starvation, and marching through the jungle before he was released in a truce/prisoner exchange. Friends in the United States sent him another Kawasaki KLR650, and he continued the trip. This guy is not a quitter.

A fine book and—with obvious reservations—more inspiration to explore the hemisphere to our south. Something I've never done.

This reading binge, and its attendant Spanish lessons, may have been set off by *The Motorcycle Diaries*, but when you read some of the more modern travelogues you are left with one small irony: it's the violent godchildren of Che Guevara—the merciless ELN and the psychotic Shining Path guerrillas—who are the biggest threats to your health and survival these days.

I guess the trick is to go anyway, and ride around them. As history seems to be doing.

04

Sustainable Trailer Towing

"**H**ERE'S A QUESTION YOU MIGHT CONSIDER IN YOUR COLUMN," a motor-cycle dealer said to me a few weeks ago. "Why am I selling so many bike trailers? I used to sell only one or two a year, but now the number is way up. Why do people suddenly need to haul bikes on trailers?"

I have to admit I was momentarily stumped. This doesn't happen very often, unless I'm pondering a unified theory of the physical universe, or wondering if I should spring for synthetic oil at $8.99 a quart in my KTM or just get a premium brand of mineral oil for $1.99. And if synthetic oil isn't made from "minerals," what's it made from? Tree sap? Distracting questions, all of them.

But back to trailers.

"I don't know why there are more trailers around," I said. "Maybe the answer is specialization. I have a bike trailer, and so do a lot of my friends. We use them for track days or dirt bikes, or just for hauling motorcycles to Daytona in the winter. Also, a lot of people haul their sportbikes out to the Rockies or the Blue Ridge, where the curves are. Saves the tires until you need them.

"Also," I added as an afterthought, "a lot of touring bikes now are pretty big to wrestle into the back of a van or pickup truck when you need to transport them. Trailers are easier to load."

All coherent reasons, I suppose, but it occurred to me later (just last night, actually) that the probable reason for more trailer sales is simply increased wealth.

I've been reading a book, you see, called *The Progress Paradox* by Gregg Easterbrook. He points out that, for all our grousing about the economic stresses of modern life and our nostalgia for the good old 1950s, nearly all Americans with jobs are materially much better off than they were even a decade or two ago.

We have bigger houses, more cars per family, cell phones, bass boats, SUVs, RVs, PCs, ATVs, CDs, DVDs, etc. —tons of things our parents didn't dream of owning. We talk poor, but have an enormous and unprecedented amount of stuff.

I was glad to read this, because now I feel a lot richer. Never mind that I'll probably spend my retirement years living on peanut butter and crackers because I've blown all my money on motorcycles, old British car restorations, and vintage electric guitars.

And trailers. Actually, I haven't spent quite enough money on trailers recently, and that's the crux of a current problem.

I usually haul bikes in the back of my Ford van, but there are occasions when an excess number of passengers and/or motorcycles forces the use of a trailer. The one bike trailer I own is a weather-beaten, light-duty, three-rail rig I bought 14 years ago. It was clearly built to hold no more than two spindly dirt bikes or one streetbike, but the poor thing's been flogged to Daytona and back three times, hauling pairs of 500-pound streetbikes. It also gets loaned out constantly, so it's been through more wheel bearings than I've had hot meals. Those little 12-inch wheels spin like twin turbos, and you always drive down the highway with one ear cocked for the siren sound of bearing failure, half expecting a wheel to pass you in the fast lane. In short, something heavier duty would be nice.

This past fall, Rob Himmelmann and I made a "ranch run" to the South Dakota cattle ranch/dirt bike paradise of our friend Randy Babcock. We took his ATK 605 and my KTM 525 to ride on the ranch, but also brought along our dual-sport Suzuki DR650s for exploring the backroads of the Badlands.

We put two bikes in my van and then loaded the other two on Rob's trailer, which has 14-inch tires and much larger axles and hubs than mine. It's a heavy-duty steel trailer, with a drop-gate ramp, flat bed, and a rail running all the way around it—you could use it to haul snowmobiles or riding mowers, if you'd accidentally spent your money on the wrong sort of vehicle.

This thing worked fine, but reduced the van's mileage from 18 on the highway down to about 11 mpg. Pretty dismal, with current fuel prices. Our all-too-frequent fill-ups were costing $60-plus.

As Rob and I are both "economy minded" (which sounds a lot better than "cheapskates"), this outrageous expense set off a long discussion on what the ideal, most efficient, long-term combination of tow vehicle and trailer might be. This question is especially germane to both of us, because Rob is recently retired and living on a fixed income, and it's my fondest hope to retire someday myself and do a lot of riding, preferably several months before I drop dead.

Rob's vote was for a diesel truck or van, pulling an all-aluminum trailer. "That new Chrysler box van with the Mercedes turbo-diesel is supposed to get about 30 mpg on the highway," he said. "Combine that with a light aluminum trailer, and you'd have a pretty efficient combination."

We no sooner got home from the trip than Rob ran out and bought an aluminum trailer from a friend who owns a Suzuki shop.

"It's exactly like my old trailer, but it weighs 250 pounds instead of 500," he told me over the phone. "I used it to haul my brother's R1100GS back from Virginia this week and got 42 mpg with the trailer empty and 30 mpg loaded."

"What on earth were you towing it with?" I asked incredulously.

"My old turbo-diesel Beetle."

My eyes narrowed and I exhaled through my teeth, like a caveman watching a space launch. Could this be the future of towing in a world aflame over oil reserves? A de-escalation of mass, in which lighter loads automatically allowed the use of lighter tow vehicles?

"Do you have the phone number of that Suzuki shop with the aluminum trailers?" I asked Rob.

I decided to do one thing at a time. Trailer first; a diesel car or truck could always come later.

My dad, of course, somehow got through life without either one. But then he didn't have two slightly different dirt bikes to worry about. Or any vintage electric guitars, either.

05

Infamous Drawers
of Useless Dead Weight

WHILE STANDING AROUND MY GARAGE THE OTHER NIGHT WAITING for spring, I decided to kill some time by mounting the new license plate on my Ducati ST4S. I took the plate out of its envelope, approached the rear of the bike, and realized I'd failed to perform a time-honored ritual.

Stuck between the saddlebags on the rear fender of the Ducati was a heavy, steel license-plate bracket, bolted over a steel strap whose sole purpose was to hold two small, plastic side reflectors. The reflectors are invisible with the bags in place, and were no doubt bolted there grudgingly by Ducati workers to meet some arcane federal law.

This would never do. Never has.

So I grabbed some wrenches from my toolbox, removed both brackets, and hefted them in my hand. Heavy. Surprisingly heavy. I then drilled two small holes in my license plate and mounted it directly to the rear fender with small, gold-anodized 6mm bolts. Now you're talking. Elegant minimalism.

After a moment of quiet admiration, I scooped up the cast-off parts and carried them over to a red Craftsman storage cabinet whose large bottom drawer is used exclusively for superfluous parts taken off motorcycles over the years.

As I laid the license-plate frame to rest in the drawer, I looked down and noticed there were three others exactly like it. Each had come off some Ducati I'd owned in the last 15 years (900SS, 998, ST2). I always saved these "original parts," planning to bolt them back on the bike if I ever sold it, but I always forgot and the new owner never seemed to care.

Or maybe I saved these things because I always picture some outraged museum curator far in the future saying, "I can't believe this idiot threw away the original license-plate bracket and reflectors!" Sort of like the Indian Chief fenders everybody tossed 50 years ago because they were so heavy and weird, and now everyone likes them because they have a period charm, like the tailfins on a '59 Cadillac.

In any case, the Ducati brackets went into my special drawer, which is the official Elephant's Graveyard of weighty, useless parts.

Looking deeper into the drawer, I noticed that most of the other pieces had come off my Suzuki DR650. These were substantial: license-plate holder, inner rear fender liner, right-side mirror, passenger pegs, fork reflectors, bar-end vibration dampers, and passenger grab bars.

One night, just before a dual-sport trip to the South Dakota Badlands last fall, I'd gone nuts and stayed up into the wee hours, stripping all this excess mass from the DR. I'd thrown the parts into a box and weighed it on our bathroom scale (the scientific way, with me holding the box and then not holding it) and found it to weigh just over seven pounds. This doesn't sound like much, but when you heft the box it feels like a lot of extra weight to accelerate, stop, and turn. It's like having our cat, Duffy, as an unwanted passenger. And Duffy eats a lot of cat food, when he isn't sleeping.

Since then, weight removal from the DR has been a work in progress. I've acquired a set of tiny, faired-in turn-signal lights and a virtually weightless LED taillight. One of these nights I'll get out my soldering gun and put all this stuff on. The next and most obvious step, of course, would be to find a lighter aftermarket exhaust system.

The weight of most stock exhaust systems, whenever I've removed them from a bike, is astounding. They feel like the submarine-shaped lead Linotype "pigs" I used to cast at my dad's print shop when I was a kid.

I'm not quite sure where this compulsive need to remove weight from machinery comes from. Some of it originates with roadracing and off-roading, of course, where the benefits of light weight are immediate and obvious. But mostly, I think, it's just a gearhead's state of mind, an instinctive way of looking at the world.

It's always seemed to me that there are two types of motorcyclists: those who remove things from bikes, and those who add stuff. Some of us will spend $200 on a carbon-fiber front fender to remove a few ounces of unsprung weight, and others will spend that same $200 on chrome-plated eagles. Some rejoice over using titanium license-plate bolts, while others add flag holders designed for the sterns of motor yachts.

And then there are those of us who can entertain both these concepts, schizophrenically, within the same brain. A few years ago my garage contained both a Road King (whose designers apparently had not lost one moment of sleep over the weight issue) and a Ducati 996 slathered with carbon-fiber, so there you go. I guess it all depends on the spirit and purpose of the bike.

Still, I've never bought a chromed eagle, and I would like to have lightened even the Harley, if it hadn't been such a daunting prospect. So I guess I'm still firmly in the weight-reduction camp.

Even as a kid, I was always taking the fenders, chain guard, and reflectors off my bicycle, stripping it down. And the Harleys and Indians of my 1950s boyhood always looked better to me as bob-jobs. I would have been the first to throw away those art-deco Indian Chief fenders.

So the beat goes on, and now I have a deep storage drawer, filled to the top with Suzuki parts and old Ducati license-plate brackets.

I suppose you can carry this weight-reduction thing a little too far, however. I recently showed my wife, Barbara, the very trick and lightweight LED taillight I'd bought for the Suzuki, at no small expense.

She hefted it in her hand for a moment and said, "So, why didn't you just skip lunch?"

So now I don't know whether to go jogging this evening or get out that soldering iron. My bike lost 7 pounds last fall and I gained 10 this winter, so maybe I should do both. Spring is always a good time to lose a little sprung weight.

06

Riding the Ortega

FEW WEEKS AGO, BARB AND I FLEW TO CALIFORNIA for a short vacation from Wisconsin's idea of springtime, which was largely unblemished this year by the traditional signs of radiant warmth. But it was sunny in California, and we spent a week visiting my sister Barbara, who lives conveniently close to *Cycle World*'s offices in Newport Beach.

We packed helmets and jackets, of course, in the event that *CW* might have a bike we could borrow. And, happily, they did: a new BMW R1200RT. Perfect for a two-up re-exploration of some of our favorite roads from the decade we lived in Southern California.

Climbing aboard the new RT on a Monday morning, we automatically did what we have always done, which is head south from Newport Beach on the 405 Freeway, exit at San Juan Capistrano, and take California Highway 74, better known as the Ortega Highway, over the Santa Ana Mountains to Lake Elsinore.

Yes, this is the once-sleepy little retirement town featured in *On Any Sunday*, home of the historic Lake Elsinore Grand Prix, with Messrs. McQueen and Smith sliding through the streets.

The Ortega Highway is named after Jose Francisco de Ortega, an early Spanish explorer, but ace California historian Allan Girdler assures me that Ortega himself never traversed this difficult route. "The road was built as a WPA project during the Depression," Allan told me. "The canyon was too rugged for horses and wagons. You can tell how modern a highway is," he added, "by what it can disregard."

And the Ortega Highway disregards a lot of daunting steepness. It's a 25-mile stretch of mountain road that climbs sinuously up San Juan Creek to emerge on a mountainside pullout (home of the Lookout Roadhouse Café), offering a spectacular view of the San Jacinto Mountains and the lake below. It's a great motorcycle road. It's also the first place I ever rode in California.

In January of 1980, having just arrived for my new job at CW from Wisconsin in a totally rusted-out Volkswagen Beetle (picture Jed Clampett, but with less furniture), I asked then-Managing Editor Steve Kimball for advice on a good weekend ride.

"Take the Ortega Highway over to Lake Elsinore," he said, "then go south to Temecula and take De Luz Road through the mountains to Fallbrook. Then you can ride down to Oceanside and come home along the coast."

I was instantly amazed at how little traffic there was on this beautiful road, so close to the pulsing organism that is Greater Los Angeles. There were a few café racers and random tourists in rented convertibles, but the road was otherwise empty. And there didn't seem to be any cops. Anywhere.

This road quickly became my Standard Weekend Ride, the quickest way out of suburbia and a direct escape valve into the mountains and the open, dusty world of the Old West. I made many early-Sunday trips over this route on my old bevel-drive Ducati 900SS, often riding with my buddy John Jaeger and his BMW R90S.

We'd ride over the mountains, stop at The Lookout to warm our hands on coffee, then descend the serpentine road into Lake Elsinore for breakfast at a Main Street café. We'd tank up on coffee to the point of nerve damage, jitter out of the place, and streak back home.

On one return ride, John and I had a little speed contest on a long downhill straight, and we both hit a dead-even 135 mph (indicated) on the Ducati and BMW. As we crouched behind our windscreens, all glassy-eyed with speed euphoria, two cars emerged out of the distance, coming toward us. At closer focus, they turned out to be police cars. Lights and sirens came on.

John and I sat upright and pulled over.

The cops kept going and didn't turn around. They must have had larger fish to fry. John and I looked at each other and shrugged, then quickly rode down to the freeway and split for home, before they had time to set up a roadblock. It was one of those rare lucky moments in life, like being hanged and having the rope break. Over a fast-moving river.

Barb and I also made a lot of Sunday-morning breakfast rides over the Ortega, usually on our Kawasaki KZ1000 Mk. II, riding at slightly reduced speed. Which, eventually, we had to.

As the decade of the 1980s wore on, more and more people moved to Lake Elsinore. It became a bedroom community for people who commuted to jobs on the coast. The cops and increasing numbers of civilians began to take a dim view of the Racer Road concept. You were no longer riding through the middle of nowhere, but between two versions of somewhere. The wild times were over.

And on this recent trip, Barb and I rode the Ortega again. There was too much traffic to make passing worth the effort, so we merely cruised. Stopping for our obligatory coffee at The Lookout, we gazed down upon many square miles of new subdivisions in the valley.

Riding into town, we found Lake Elsinore's once slightly seedy old Main Street freshly redecorated with red brickwork, flowerbeds, and vintage streetlights. Our favorite old restaurant was gone, but a new, slightly classier one had opened two doors down.

Over breakfast, Barb said, "There sure is a lot of traffic on the Ortega now, and so many new homes."

I nodded. "Things change in 25 years. But the road is still here, and so are we. And it's a nice day. It's probably snowing right now back home."

We grinned and clinked our coffee cups in an unspoken toast.

On our way back to the coast, the traffic was so heavy I didn't bother watching for cops. No speed was possible, so we just relaxed and motored along, taking in the scenery.

It was a nice ride, but no longer the merciful escape from regimentation we once enjoyed. To find the Old West now, you have to go farther east.

07

In Praise of Cop Bikes

I MUST SAY THAT OUR WEEKLY MEETINGS OF THE SLIMEY Crud Motorcycle Gang here in Madison, Wisconsin, are much nicer in the summer than in the winter.

We can sit outside at our favorite beer garden and actually gaze upon our cluster of bikes in person, rather than brood indoors at the bar and merely talk about them. In the winter, we might as well be a Crimean War discussion group, with no visible tie to the subject at hand. It's hard to feel like a motorcycle gang when there are no bikes nearby; everything becomes theoretical.

Anyway, this week's meeting was pure bliss. We'd all ridden our bikes to the meeting and were sitting outside, inhaling the blossom-scented air, watching heat lightning flicker across distant clouds, and looking fondly at our smorgasbord of motorcycles—Honda 400F, Hawk GT, and street-legalized XR650, a couple of Ducatis, various Beemers ancient and modern, Harley FLH, KTM 950, Triumph Sprint, Suzuki DR650, Cagiva Gran Canyon, and two old Guzzis.

I had ridden my posh BMW R1150RT, as I'd been running errands in the city that afternoon and it has more cargo capacity than my car.

As I hoisted a stein of something called Black Bavarian, the guy next to me—a visitor to our group named Aaron Fisher—looked at my BMW and said, "I've always liked cop bikes. And I've almost always had one myself."

I took a sip of my dark Teutonic elixir from nearby Milwaukee, internalized that comment for a moment, and said, "Hmmm, I guess I have, too."

"I find that the virtues that make a good police bike," Aaron continued, "also make for a very useful, all-around daily motorcycle—comfort, a good riding position, luggage capacity, wind protection, low maintenance, longevity . . . practicality. If the cops use them, they're probably pretty good."

I nodded in agreement. I'd never had an actual police bike—solo saddle, radio rack, crash guards, and the rest—but in a lifetime of riding I'd owned several motorcycles that were used by the police forces of the world.

The BMW R100RS, for instance, was employed by both German police and French Motorway Patrol gendarmes during the 1980s, and in 1990 I finally bought one myself and rode it for 10 years.

And then there were Harley FLHs and Kawasaki KZ1000s. Back when we lived in California, the Highway Patrol just shifted from Shovelhead FLHs and Guzzis to KZ1000s, and my main bike for most of the 1980s was a KZ1000 MKII. I once got ticketed by a cop who had, essentially, a white version of my own bike, with windshield and radio. Not to mention the screaming siren option.

Later, about the same time the CHP went back to Evo Harleys, I bought myself a Road King, a civilian version of your standard Harley copsickle. During the 1990s, I also owned both a Honda ST1100 and a Moto Guzzi 1000SP, which were used as patrol bikes in England and Italy, respectively, and probably a few other places as well.

And now I've got a BMW R1150RT, which seems to be appearing all over the world in police livery—Germany, Italy, California, etc. I was in Italy last fall and saw no fewer than 30 of these beauties lined up at the Colosseum to patrol a Maserati rally arriving in Rome. Apparently, Guzzi lost the local polizia contract. This would never have happened under Mussolini.

No angry letters, please. Just kidding.

Actually, I do miss the national flavor of police forces riding motorcycles from their own countries. Italian cops just look better on Guzzis, and Harleys always look right in American motorcades. And back in the heyday of British Twins, England was full of Triumph 650 police bikes (another one I've owned in civilian guise), and even Norton 850 Interstates (ditto) were used. The imagination reels at the tragically short—but highly entertaining and charismatic—highway pursuits that must have taken place. And your heart goes out to the motor pool mechanics.

Anyway, I seem to have accidentally owned at least seven motorcycles in the past 40 years that have also done duty as police bikes. There's no secret, psychological wish-fulfillment at work here—I don't have any mirrored sunglasses or jodhpurs in the closet—and I've never wished to be a motorcycle cop, at least not in adulthood.

I don't have the mental organization or the force of personality for the job. I can't even get close friends to listen to my casual suggestions—like going to see *Dust to Glory* a third time—let alone make total strangers with lots of tattoos and large biceps keep their hands on top of the hood and spread their feet. No, police work is not for me.

Although it would be fun to tear up my own speeding tickets. . . . Or arrest Pierre Terblanche before he strikes again. . . .

Anyway, I guess I've owned this series of cop bikes for the exact reasons my friend suggested. They make good, honest, real-world companions for travel, running errands, picking up parts for less reliable bikes, and generally hauling the goods.

Looking back on this list of loyal and useful motorcycles, however, it also occurs to me that there are only a few of them I would have wanted as an Only Bike. The Kawasaki, R100RS, and SP1000 would work (and did) but some of the others are a little too grand or relaxed in their deportment to stimulate the full use of one's adrenal core. With some of them you need something a little more wild and crazy at the other end of the spectrum to counterbalance their seductive comfort and practicality—and as compensation for missing out on all those high-speed chases, crack-house raids, and SWAT-team shootouts.

A two-stroke Triple, perhaps. Or maybe a street-legal version of something Duhamel and Mladin might race at Daytona. Or any Ducati.

Cop bikes are all well and good, but you have to give the police something to chase. It's a sacred part of the social contract.

08

Towns of the Blue Highways

IT WAS REALLY TOO EARLY TO STOP FOR THE night when I came riding into Effingham, Illinois, a few weeks ago on my way home from the Honda Hoot in Tennessee. I pulled over into the shade of a tree and looked at the clock on my Beemer's instrument panel. It read 18:07.

I grinned and shook my head. Was it really necessary to use military time on a motorcycle clock? Did any rider ever seriously wonder if it was three in the morning or three in the afternoon? A 12-hour clock works fine on motorcycles. We aren't coordinating the D-Day invasion here.

Anyway, in civilian time it was a little after 6 p.m., with about three hours of good summer daylight left. I looked down at the Illinois map on my tankbag and realized I could easily make it to Springfield before nightfall. But I was hot and a little tired, having ridden since 5:30 in the morning. That's O dark early, military time. Twelve and a half hours in the saddle, with stops only for fuel, fluids, and a fish sandwich in a fast-food joint with a terrifying clown on my drink glass.

Stop for the night, or keep rolling?

I decided to cruise around Effingham and see if it had the Three Essentials for an early stop: a clean motel, a decent restaurant, and a movie theater.

Most likely it would have the first two, because it's a big town at the junction of two interstates. The theater might be another matter.

Turning off Highway 33, I headed downtown to the square around the courthouse, and there—lo and behold! —was a movie theater. Not just that, but a genuine, neon-festooned downtown movie palace called The Heart Theater. On the marquee was the third and last of George Romero's excellently creepy zombie trilogy, *Land of the Dead*.

Perfect. Effingham had everything.

I got a room in a nearby Mom and Pop motel, but Pop had forgotten to fix the air conditioning (the air coming out felt exactly like hot dog breath), so I checked out and got a room in a modern box out by the Interstate. By then it was too late to look for a restaurant before the 7 p.m. movie (1900 hours) so I decided to dine on popcorn and Junior Mints. A classic meal.

Fun movie, great popcorn, good mints. I rode back to my blissfully chilled room, slept like the dead (better, actually, than the guys in the movie, who seemed restless), got up early in the a.m., and hit the road.

As Effingham disappeared in the mirrors, it dawned on me how few towns on my 1,700-mile, four-day trip had been this inviting. I'd gone from Wisconsin to Knoxville and back almost entirely on what author William Least Heat-Moon called "blue highways," those meandering roads that never go directly between two major cities. In doing so, I'd seen perhaps a hundred towns of all different sizes. By the time I hit Effingham on the way home, it occurred to me that America has metamorphosed into a country with, essentially, three kinds of towns: 1) dying towns; 2) medium-sized towns that are holding their own; or 3) big, growing towns that have way too much traffic and sprawl.

Towns of the first class, the dying, are easy to spot. Their main streets are mostly closed and boarded up, and the only place to buy groceries is at a convenience store/gas station. There are no sit-down restaurants, theaters, or motels. If any businesses remain open on Main Street, they are most often bars, a tattoo parlor, a tanning spa, and a video rental.

It escapes me why a town without a hardware store or a grocery needs a tattoo parlor, but there you go. The one well-kept, neatly groomed business in town is usually a nursing home. Which, of course, absorbs the stored wealth from another era, rather than producing it. Lastly, there's almost always a magnificent stone bank building in town (the kind Baby Face Nelson might have robbed), now used as something else. The old brick high school is closed or turned into cheap apartments.

At the opposite extreme are large, growing cities. Many of these are probably good places to live, if you've been there a while and know your way around. But from a cross-country motorcyclist's point of view, they have little to offer but clogged freeways, sprawling suburbs, and what my friend John Lamm calls "the architectural sound loop." Home Depot, Office Max, Circuit City, Best Buy, etc., over and over. Stoplights, dripping radiators, and frustrated suburbanites waiting for the four-second left-turn arrow. On bike trips, I avoid these places like the plague.

Somewhere in between, we have the Effinghams of this world. Medium-sized cities that retain the critical mass of population needed to support a few good restaurants, a movie theater, some motels, maybe a bookstore, and at least one bar that makes a decent martini and has dark beer on tap. And, ideally, that crown jewel of commerce, a motorcycle dealership. Or two or three.

These places have traffic and visible human activity, but not the overheated, Malthusian kind that drives you nuts. They also usually have a working downtown that has somehow resisted the predations of the big-box stores. Essentially, the same features that make a traveling rider stop for the night also make "regular" people want to live in a town, or move there. And stay.

I grew up in a small midwestern town of 1,500 people that, in the mid-1950s, had four grocery stores, three hardware stores, four restaurants, two dime stores, two clothing stores, two furniture stores, a local newspaper, a dairy, an old hotel, a new motel, Ford and Chevy dealerships, a train station, and a beautiful old brick high school on the hill. And a nice movie theater.

I went back last spring and found that nearly all of that is gone now, and the movie theater is for sale. It's still a nice place, but much of its kinetic force and spirit are gone, along with so many of the people who made it all work.

I often wonder if I take motorcycle trips now just to look for that town, as it was in 1955.

Sometimes I find part of it, and stop for the night.

09

King of the World

ON A RECENT ROAD TRIP, I FOUND MYSELF THINKING about our late and much-missed Editor-at-Large, Henry Manney III.

Henry was what you might call a cheerful curmudgeon. He had a darkly humorous view of the human condition, and often prefaced his corrective anecdotes with the words, "If I were King of the World . . ."

For instance, he'd walk into your office, ease himself into a chair, toss his tweed cap onto his knee, and say: "If I were King of the World, motorists who block the fast lane on the freeway would be instantly vaporized with large ray guns mounted on overpasses."

Or: "If I were King of the World, people who write checks in the Cash Only line at the supermarket would be turned over to the Barbary pirates and sold as palace eunuchs at the slave market in Al Qatrun."

His imaginary punishments for bad behavior were always hilariously specific and harsh, yet apparently well-deserved.

Henry's been gone now for 16-years, but this phrase of his comes back to haunt me all the time, simply because it's so useful and cathartic. I used it just last month, in fact, on the first day of a 4,000-mile trip Barb and I took through eastern Canada and New England on our 2004 BMW R1150RT.

We made the mistake of leaving home with the stock seat, you see, and realized about three hours from home we'd made a Terrible Mistake. Barb climbed stiffly off the bike at a restaurant near Green Bay and regarded the bike sullenly.

"I can't believe BMW would put a seat this bad on a bike made for two-up touring. What were they thinking?"

"I don't know," I said, climbing stiffly off the bike, "but if I were King of the World, the person who designed this seat would be swatted to death with his own hat, then spend eternity riding the Iron Butt Rally in Purgatory."

I realize that sounds severe, but I was not happy at the time.

As the trip wore on, however, I eventually cheered up again, mainly because this train of thought kept me amused for many miles of our 12-day journey and helped take my fevered mind off the chronic discomfort of the Beemer's seat.

Here are just a few samples from those many miles on the road as I contemplated the many advantages of absolute power:

If I were King of the World, Ducati management would be held in a dungeon with nothing to eat but bland Scandinavian food, such as lutefisk, until they hired Massimo Tamburini back as head designer.

Anyone who sells a touring or adventure-touring bike without heated grips to a person living north of the 36th Parallel (or in mountains higher than 5,000 feet) would be forced to hold two cans of ice-cold Budweiser at a late-season Vikings game while I go off to search for his lost gloves in the parking lot. And maybe shop for some cool souvenirs in the heated gift shop, after I find the men's room.

The president of the company that made my last pair of "rain pants" would be forced to address a stockholders' meeting at the Waldorf Astoria with no podium and his crotch totally soaked in ice water. The spotlight would be aimed low and follow his every movement.

The designer who put that kink in the new Triumph Bonneville's exhaust system would be given a straight edge and forced to draw the shortest distance between two points, over and over again, until I finish translating all nine volumes of Euclid's Geometry from the original Greek, or whatever language those funny letters are.

Business executives who buy legendary racetracks and then name them after a product or a faceless corporation would be forced to have their own names legally changed to Zippy T. Carbuncle or Adolph Hitler, Jr. Anything to make introductions at cocktail parties more awkward.

Any motorcyclist who holds up a line of automobiles on a winding road would be required to sell all fringed accessories, buy some plaid pants, and take up golf.

Companies who use legendary zenith-of-performance names like "Sportster" and "Bonneville" on the slowest bikes in their product line would be forced at gunpoint to make them at least as quick as a Ducati 620 Monster.

Any designer who hides an oil filter or battery under bodywork that takes more than 10 seconds to remove would be forced to disassemble all the air-conditioning ducts on my '53 Caddy Fleetwood and find out what that funny dead mouse smell is all about.

Inventors of "reality" TV shows about guys who badmouth each other while building choppers under fake deadlines would be made to watch *Andy Griffith* reruns, so they could see how humans used to behave, and how good television once was.

Any motorist who turns left in front of a motorcycle with its headlights on and says, "I didn't see it" would have his or her eyes examined with a klieg light left over from Stalag 17.

All streetbikes would come with centerstands, real tool kits, and helmet locks that actually work. Those that didn't would be airfreighted back to the manufacturer, overnight C.O.D.

Any engineer who designed a dual-sport bike with a seat height greater than 35 inches would be forced to clean our rain gutters while I hold the ladder.

Owners of motorhomes who fail to use turn-outs on winding mountain roads would have their AARP memberships canceled and be denied access to Wal-Mart parking lots.

Cops who set up speed traps on empty, deliberately under-posted roads in the middle of nowhere would be required to do 200 hours of volunteer police work of actual benefit to society. Like catching the kid who ran over the King's rural mailbox last week with a pickup truck.

Kids who run over the King's mailbox with their pickup trucks would be turned over to the Barbary pirates and sold as palace eunuchs at the slave market in Al Qatrun, then vaporized with large ray guns. And then I'd give them my rain pants, and the seat from my BMW.

Cruel, yes, but I think Henry would approve.

10

Old School Triumph

WHAT WE HAD HERE WAS A CLASSIC CASE OF full moon, big campfire, beer in hand, and firelight glinting off the chrome of motorcycles. A balmy mid-September breeze rustled dryly in the trees, bringing down a random leaf or two. Dogs barked in the village of Bridgeton, Indiana.

Most of that reflected firelight was bouncing off the chrome of Moto Guzzis. This was a Guzzi rally, after all, a low-key, friendly little event put on for the past six years by Ben and Brenda Jackson.

It's always held in the same place, a grassy, shaded field next to the old red-brick Bridgeton High School. A family lives in the school building now, but they allow campers to use the old Boys Room and Girls Room and the showers for the gym.

If you open the wrong door while looking for the Boys Room, you are presented with the emotional hit of a perfectly preserved basketball court, complete with bleachers and a wood floor, right out of the movie *Hoosiers*. You can almost hear the lingering echoes from the last home game, decades ago.

But I hadn't come to this Guzzi rally simply to be struck dumb by the march of time and its inexplicable losses. I'd come to pick up a motorcycle, an old Triumph.

An old Triumph at a Guzzi rally?

Let me explain. Last summer I rode my BMW down to Knoxville, Tennessee, for the Honda Hoot. While I was there, a local enthusiast named Fred Sahms kindly loaned me his 1969 Triumph 650 Tiger to ride on our *Cycle World* Rolling Concours. It was a clean, nice-looking bike with a cheerful but historically incorrect blue-and-white paint job, and it ran perfectly all day.

Fred had owned the Triumph since 1988, when he rescued it as a project bike from a local repair shop. It'd had a 1969 Tiger frame and cycle parts with a '67 Bonneville engine, no instruments, and a skinny rear wheel. Fred installed a correct wheel and tires, new instruments, and a Boyer ignition system. He did a fresh valve job on a single-carb Tiger head and installed it on the Bonneville bottom end. What he ended up with was a sweet-running, good-looking "bitsa" bike, as the British would say, with mismatched numbers.

But I don't care much about matching numbers anymore. I just like stuff that runs well. I've owned and restored "matching number" bikes that were never quite right after reassembly of their obsessively polished and powder-coated parts, as if their molecular memory had been disturbed. Fred's Tiger wasn't like that. It was a smooth and happy motorcycle. So of course I told him, "Let me know if you ever think of selling this bike."

This is always a mistake. A few weeks ago he sent me an e-mail and said he might sell off a few of his old bikes to buy something modern—maybe a brand-new Triumph Tiger. And unfortunately his asking price for the old Triumph was so reasonable I couldn't refuse without having someone commit me to an insane asylum. Also, Fred said he could deliver it halfway to Wisconsin, at the Guzzi rally in Indiana.

So two days ago I loaded my ramp, tent, and sleeping bag in the blue Ford van and headed south. My friend and total vintage motorcycle nut Rob Himmelmann went with me. We left early on a Saturday and reached the campground by mid-afternoon.

Bridgeton is a charming little village on a river, and it has a working gristmill. The surrounding countryside is famous for its covered bridges—there are 35 of them in the county—so the area draws a lot of rallies, swap meets, etc.

When we arrived, the Triumph was sitting under a tree. Fred signed over the title and I took off for a ride on a beautiful fall afternoon, following part of the famous covered bridge trail. The bridges are linked by twisty rural roads like something out of a storybook. I rode for at least an hour, soaking up the Triumph's lovely exhaust note, light weight, and agile handling and listening to the smooth, castanet-like clicking of the valvetrain.

I suppose everybody has one bike of which this can be said, but when I am on a late-1960s Triumph Twin, I always think to myself, This is exactly who I am. A couple of other bikes have this effect on me, too, but not with the absolute certitude of Triumphs.

Rob and I put up the tent and camped for the night, enjoying a grilled chicken and Italian sausage dinner around the campfire. While we were eating, two dogs got into a vicious fight. Both dogs, it turned out, were named "Harley," so the owners were pulling them apart and shouting "Harley! Harley! Har-ley!" Fred turned to me and said, "Only two Harleys at this Guzzi rally, and a fight breaks out." The rest of the night was peaceful and moonlit, with a million stars, and we all stayed up late and told many unbelievably truthful stories around the campfire.

In the morning Rob and I said our good-byes, tanked up on coffee, loaded the Triumph in my van, and headed for Wisconsin. We got home late in the afternoon and unloaded the Tiger in my driveway. Barb came out of the house and said, "You're just in time. The Onoskos have invited us to come into Madison for dinner and to watch a DVD of the new Bob Dylan documentary, *No Direction Home*. We're bringing wine and dessert."

"You take the car," I said. "I have to clean up, and then I'll be along in little while with the Triumph."

On a beautiful autumn evening when you've just acquired an old Triumph, you can't very well drive a car to see an early Dylan biography. I would brave the 50 miles of rural darkness and deer with my Lucas headlight, living dangerously, in the fatalistic spirit of those times.

Just before leaving, a small light went on in my brain (very small, as usual). I went back into the house and dug out my faded "Highway 61 Revisited" Triumph T-shirt, beat-up, old cowboy boots, and ancient Bell open-face helmet.

When you get wooden bridges, an old schoolhouse, a '69 Triumph, and a Bob Dylan documentary in one weekend, you have to show some respect for history, not to mention the march of time and its inexplicable losses.

GPS VS. the Classic Map

IT WAS FIVE DEGREES BELOW ZERO HERE IN WISCONSIN this morning, so I cleverly decided to drink coffee and read the paper instead of taking a ride.

After the mandatory scan of motorcycle want ads (slim pickin's in winter), I found myself reading a column called "Tech Smart" (quite beneficial to those of us who are "Tech Stupid") and ran across a product review of a new portable GPS unit.

It said this small, hand-held device contained not only a satellite navigation system, "but also a built-in music player, photo viewer, US travel guide, audio-book reader, language translator, currency converter and more."

I set the paper down on my lap and stared into space. Who would build such a thing and not include an electronic guitar tuner?

I mean, if you're going to replace every appliance in your house, why not go all the way and help the customer tune his Rickenbacker 12-string?

Just kidding, of course.

As one who can barely program the radio/alarm clock in a Motel 6, I'm always leery of these multitasking devices. After all, the word processor on which I am writing this column is the least reliable thing I've ever owned, including my first Norton. It shuts down, changes its mind, reformats, crashes, and suddenly asks incomprehensible questions ("Would you like to destroy all existing files or just set your keyboard on fire?") seemingly at random. If my old Olivetti portable typewriter had given me this much trouble, I would have thrown it off a bridge.

In other words, I don't trust computer chips to do even one thing correctly, let alone six or seven. Nevertheless, I have to admit that the GPS unit in the newspaper story caught my eye. Why?

Well, I consider the Global Positioning System to be an outright miracle of human ingenuity.

Like manned flight, it's something our ancestors dreamt about, through all those centuries of astrolabes, sextants, reading ocean currents, struggling to compute longitude, watching the stars, and leaving trails of bread crumbs. Right after "Why can't I fly?" the second most common question in history has probably been "Where the hell am I?"

This very question came up, urgently, a couple of years ago, when my buddy Pat Donnelly and I were exploring Baja on our Suzuki DR-Z400s.

We were on a remote trail, west of Gonzaga Bay, struggling to get over the mountains to Catavina. Late in the afternoon it started to rain, and we skidded into a little abandoned settlement called Mine Camp (which I mirthfully dubbed "Mein Kampf.")

Our map showed a single trail leading west out of these ruins, but, in real life, there were three trails, all spreading out in a westerly direction. I picked the one that "felt right," but soon it swung north into the middle of nowhere. Pat—who'd brought along the first hand-held GPS unit I'd ever seen—stopped on the trail and frowned at his small lighted screen in the gathering darkness.

"The GPS says we're off the track," he said. "We should have taken the middle trail."

So we backtracked and took the middle trail, which turned out to be right. A few hours later we found the main highway and headed north, reaching our hotel in Catavina at about 10 p.m. Cold, wet, hungry, and tired.

We probably wouldn't have died out there in the mountains without the GPS, but we could have run out of fuel, and I've never really enjoyed hiking in motocross boots, even with a good flashlight.

So that night I became a GPS fan.

And last year, I actually bought one.

Barb and I got a Garmin GPS unit for our occasional sailing trips on upper Lake Michigan. We'd been able to navigate without it, but there's something very nice about checking that little screen to make sure you are really headed into Escanaba harbor at night, and not into something that looks like it. Especially with the wind rising and lightning crackling on the horizon.

So the GPS has become a useful tool, but I must admit I'm still a classic map and chart kind of guy. In fact, I'm addicted to maps. The paper kind, with printed lines, blue rivers, and shaded mountain ranges.

In an upstairs filing cabinet, there are two drawers packed with state and national maps, and an entire shelf in my office is filled with nothing but road atlases. I also have all the old FAA air charts from a Piper Cub trip Barb and I took around the United States, and I still have a military chart of Ninh Tuan province in Vietnam, which I carried on my knee during many helicopter flights. If I had any more maps in the house, our dogs would have to sleep outside.

And on the wall next to my desk is a huge Rand McNally wall map of the United States and southern Canada. All I have to do is turn and look at it (as I did just now) and I get this strange rush, an odd mixture of hope and foreboding that harkens back to something a Viking might have felt when stepping into a longboat. Or, in my case, an Irishman stepping into a curragh.

It's a vision that blows the walls off your house, zooms you backwards into deep space, and makes anything seem possible. Looking at a map is the seed of adventure.

GPS screens don't do this to me.

But they're still useful tools, and I'll probably always have one. Along with a good paper map for backup, and for the Big Picture, when I need to see it.

Much as I like the GPS, I'm privately troubled by the huge infrastructure of satellites, military budgets, and semiconductors that make it all possible. It reminds me of fuel injection on adventure-touring bikes—great as long as it works, but it can't be repaired in the mountains west of Gonzaga Bay.

The GPS unit, like fuel injection and my home computer, remains symbolic of a vast technological dependence on others, while maps—like carburetors and typewriters—still represent a certain level of freedom and independence.

No wires, no batteries. Unplugged.

12

It's Hard to Beat a Motorcycle

I SUPPOSE BY NOW VIRTUALLY ALL HUMANS—INCLUDING THE TIMID FOREST People of the upper Wombezee—have heard the old nautical saying that the two best days of boat ownership are the day you buy it and the day you sell it.

This is a universally understood concept, and I've heard it used on airplanes, cars, marriages, Victorian houses, vacation cottages, and certain brands of vintage motorcycles—whose Druidic country of origin I won't mention here.

In fact, this "two best days" phrase came up just the other night at our monthly Slimey Crud Motorcycle Gang meeting, which was held at my recently swept garage workshop.

Yes, I always go all-out when hosting these affairs. I knock all the cobwebs off the Steve McQueen Great Escape poster, vacuum most of the dead flies off the window sills, make a huge batch of corrosive Tex-Mex chili, and put some blues music on our garage band's PA system. Then I turn on the "mood lighting." This consists of colored light bulbs installed in my drill-press and bench-grinder sockets, which give the place a kind of opium-den-meets-bike-museum aura, with Mississippi Delta juke joint overtones.

Anyway, there we were, listening to Albert King, sipping a few beers, and eating chili when someone said to me, "Hey, where are you storing your sailboat this winter?"

"We sold it last summer," I said.

"Sold it! I thought you and Barb were having a great time sailing around Lake Michigan."

"We were," I said. "But it got to be too much. We had to drive for five hours to get to the boat, and then we'd spend part of the weekend cleaning and fixing it. Some weekends we'd get there and it would be too windy to sail, or too calm. Also, we had to rent a slip for the summer and have the boat hauled out in the fall and stored in the winter. Too much monkey business."

Several Cruds nodded thoughtfully. At least four had owned—and sold— sailboats or inboard power boats. They knew.

"The two best days of boat ownership . . ." someone said, without finishing the sentence.

Truth be told, selling the boat was not one of our best days. Barb and I had great times sailing the thing, and parting with it felt like the end of an era. But there was also (I have to admit) an element of relief. One less thing to worry about in a complex world.

About 12 years ago, I'd felt almost exactly the same mixture of regret and relief in selling an old airplane—a 1945 Piper Cub that Barb and I had owned for many years.

A fine old aircraft, but, like the boat, it needed winter storage, professional maintenance, licensing, a time-consuming drive to the airport, careful preflight examination, and good weather.

And it also required you to spend a perfectly good sunny summer weekend doing something other than riding your motorcycle. And there was the rub.

Many times I'd walk out of our house into a perfect summer morning on my way to the airport and think to myself, What a great day for a motorcycle ride.

Not that I didn't want to go flying, but riding was more . . . accessible. Less hassle. More immediately inviting. Less regulated and more free.

Exactly the same thing happened when we owned the sailboat. We'd be loading the car with food and supplies for a weekend of boating and I'd glance at my bikes sitting there in the garage. I'd look up at the sun, feel the warm breeze through the trees, and shake my head. What a great day for a motorcycle ride.

And, as we sat around in my workshop the other night, I leaned back in my festive plaid lawn chair, gazed fondly at my nearby DR650, and said, simply, "It's hard to beat a motorcycle."

Fellow Crud Toby Kirk reflectively jingled the ice cubes in his usual glass of Old Offenhauser and said, "It really is the perfect sport."

Toby, incidentally, has an old sailboat that is becoming one with nature in his backyard. It looks like a boat sculpture, done in moss, lichens, and pine needles.

So, as we sat discussing these things, our little gang of vehicle addicts gradually came up with an informal list of advantages the motorcycle has over other equipment-intensive pastimes—such as flying or boating—which I'll enumerate as follows:

Motorcycles have no wingspan, draft, or mast height, so you can keep them at your own house, and you never have to rent a hangar, slip, or warehouse.

When the engine stops, you can pull over and put your foot down, instead of doing a dead-stick landing in a cornfield. Or getting towed to port.

When the weather turns really violent, you can retire to a place called "Al's Nibble-Nook" and order a cheeseburger instead of sinking or crashing.

There are no mandatory and costly annual inspections.

You don't need permission from a control tower or harbormaster to visit the men's room, refuel, or eat lunch.

During a big storm, you don't have to lie awake at night and picture your motorcycle bashing itself to pieces on some rocks.

Your selection of motels, restaurants, and acquaintances is not limited by shorelines or airports.

You can leave right from your garage and return to it without filing a flight plan. No one needs to be notified of your intentions.

Your "navigation system" fits in a back pocket or under the clear plastic of your tankbag. A compass is optional.

Your passengers generally don't require Dramamine.

And so on.

I don't mean to be too dismissive of other sports here. I still love boats and airplanes—I've got them in my blood—but they will always be second-tier activities for me, for all the reasons listed above.

Motorcycling, as Toby says, really is the perfect sport. You have pistons and wind combined by alchemy into a compound of pure freedom.

13

Return of the Scrambler

DID YOU EVER HAVE ONE OF THOSE WEIRD DAYS where cosmic chance repeats itself and you hear three different people use the word "Abyssinian"?

That's kind of how my whole month is going, but in this case the magic word has been "Scrambler."

A few weeks ago, you see, I was invited out to California to write the *Cycle World* story on Triumph's new 900 Scrambler, which takes its inspiration from a long line of Trophy Twins, the bikes that dominated desert and enduro racing for much of the 1950s and 1960s.

To brush up on a little history for this assignment, I walked over to my office bookshelves and pulled out all my Triumph books, which are legion. In fact, their absence made my bookcase look like a boxer with his front teeth knocked out.

My favorites are *Triumph in America* by Lindsay Brooke and David Gaylin, and *Triumph Racing Motorcycles in America*, a solo effort by Brooke. These volumes are as well-thumbed and worn as Pat Robertson's two favorite Bibles.

For a few evenings I immersed myself in these books again, then went out to my mildew-scented Wall of Ancient Motorcycle Magazines on "what used to be a perfectly nice sun porch" and dug out all the old road tests I could find on Triumph scramblers from the 1960s. While searching, I also paged through the magazines, looking at ads, articles, and other road tests.

It reminded me once again that this really was the era of the street-scrambler. Every manufacturer had one—or many—in the lineup. Most motorcycle companies built a scrambler in every single displacement category—all the way down to 50cc.

Some were attempts to make real dual-sport bikes, while others were just trendy styling exercises with high pipes, knobbies, and braced handlebars slapped on a streetbike.

It's hard to imagine, for instance, that anyone took the scrambler version of the peaky-fast Suzuki X6 Hustler very far off-road. Yet it's that high-pipe version I remember best, probably because there were so many around. And it looked cool.

Some scramblers you wouldn't suspect of having great off-road competence did surprisingly well. A fearsome CW-sponsored Norton P-11 Scrambler ridden by Jerry Platt and Vern Hancock finished 18th overall in the first Baja 1000 in 1967, despite a devastating nighttime crash and lengthy repairs.

And a Honda CL350 won the 1968 Baja 1000 outright! Never mind that it was breathed upon by Long Beach Honda and ridden by the talented duo of Larry Berquist and Gary Preston; it was still based on the all-purpose street-scrambler you could buy at your local Honda store.

I should confess here that one of the tragedies of my young life was that I went through this whole era without owning a scrambler. As an impoverished student, I felt lucky to have any bike at all, and bought my first three motorcycles because, like Mount Everest, they were there. Also cheap.

But the bike brochures taped to the wall above my desk, as I drudged through high school homework, were all scramblers. Mainly, the Honda 160 and 305 Scramblers, high-pipe Triumph, and the exquisite (but reputedly troublesome) BSA 441 Victor.

What was the appeal here?

Well, what these bikes had going for them were romance and versatility.

There was—and is—something especially appealing about being able to climb on a bike and think you might go almost anywhere on earth (okay, anywhere in your own hemisphere) right from your garage. That notion might have been largely illusory—as a teenager, you probably weren't going to Peru— but there were dirt and gravel roads right at the edge of town, and you could head out into the country and explore them. The compact size of most of these bikes, along with "trials universal" tires and wide bars, made that prospect not only possible, but inviting.

The racing connection helped, too, with all those pictures of Ekins, McQueen, Mulder, et al. bounding through the desert. In this respect, street-scramblers were a perfect expression of the impulsive, slightly reckless mood of the times. Sliding and jumping were much admired, fatalism rampant.

The popularity of the general, all-purpose dirt/streetbike gradually faded, probably about the time the Honda CB750 Four took a fork in the trail marked "fast, heavy Superbike." You could make a scrambler out of a road-going Norton 750 or Triumph 650, but the Honda 750 was hopeless in that regard. As was the Kawasaki 900 or Triumph Triple.

Meanwhile, light, street-legal bikes like the 250cc two-stroke Yamaha DT-1 developed into much better dirt bikes than the average street-scrambler had been. Specialization set in.

But now those forked roads seem to be converging again. BMW's R1200GS is its best-selling bike, the new Ulysses is (in my opinion) the best Buell yet, and Husqvarna is making all its enduro bikes street-legal this year. And in my own garage are a KTM 950 Adventure and a Suzuki DR650.

Twenty-first century street-scramblers, you might say.

Or are they?

The bikes mentioned above (other than the Suzuki) are rather tall, heavy, and expensive for the average street rider with a mildly adventurous streak. A bit too hardcore, perhaps.

Each of those traits takes a little fun out of the picture for someone who just wants to hop on and ride around, or make a quick run to the corner store. The big, modern adventure-tourer lacks what you might call "casualness," that inviting sense of accessibility and nimbleness that comes with smaller size. Beginning riders shy away from them, sensing too much seriousness and not enough simple pleasure. Or enough traditional style and finish.

Enter the Triumph Scrambler, modern on the inside, 1960s on the outside.

Maybe it'll be much-copied, just as its ancestors were. All the way down to 50cc.

14

The Fine Art of Riding Your Own Bike

GONE ON A PRESS TRIP LAST WEEK, I RETURNED home to Wisconsin to be greeted with the astounding news that I'd missed a warm winter day on which it was virtually possible to ride a motorcycle, if you didn't mind the road salt eating your rims.

Yes, it was all of 51 degrees, so you can see that "warm" is a relative term here in the upper Midwest. Loosely translated, it means "not so cold that you'd die right away if you locked yourself out of your car."

Family picnics, badminton games, and watermelon-eating contests are not part of the picture. No one has a mint julep on the veranda. The ground is still frozen.

Nevertheless, several of my friends went for rides while I was gone. One even found time to crash.

Actually, the miracle is that he didn't really crash. He just went straight off a 35-mph corner at about 70 mph—having wisely thrown in the towel on further leaning—and took a high-speed trip over a ditch (airborne), then across a snow-covered field full of dips and hummocks without actually dropping the bike. Nice riding!

Now, this is a guy who never makes mistakes like this. He's been motorcycling for 40 years, and I ride with him all the time. He's quick on a backroad but always seems to know when it's time to go slow and live. The very picture of maturity.

"So how did you happen to misjudge the curve?" I asked, intrigued by this anomalous event.

"Well, I was riding with a couple of other guys," he admitted, "and following a really fast rider on his new sportbike. I just went into the corner too fast."

"Ah," I said, the light bulb lit brightly at last, "a group ride with a fast guy. That explains everything."

And it did. I've been riding for 43 years and have observed that nearly every solo crash within my experience has been caused by one of two things:

Drinking a bunch of beer.

Trying to keep up with—or ahead of—someone else.

Sometimes those factors combine, of course, and then you've got real trouble.

In this case, however, my friend doesn't drink—never has. He was simply trying, by his own admission, to keep up with someone else.

And this is the problem with group rides, which are both one of the true pleasures of motorcycling and one of its great hazards at the same time.

I actually ride in small groups all the time—usually with two or three close friends whose riding habits I know quite well. This helps a lot. We all like to go about the same speed, and ride within the same narrow band of talent (if "talent" is the right word for not having any).

I would call our sportbike rides "reasonably swift without the threat of imminent death." We're all older than 50 and see motorcycling as the sustaining infatuation that will take us blissfully into our retirement years. Also, we've all seen the insides of ambulances and don't like them much. But I've been on many rides exactly like the one that took my friend on his recent off-road adventure. In fact, I've ridden with so many competitive groups where you have a mismatch of adrenalin, courage, and skill that I can now almost predict tragedy during the first five minutes of a ride. I'll leave a parking lot in a group of six or seven sportbikes, observe the riders around me, and say to myself, with some certainty, "This day will not end well."

How do I know? Because I get infected with the same red mist as anyone else, and I can sense the tension in the air around me. There's an almost-palpable electricity in the atmosphere, and it soon starts to manifest itself in sparks off mufflers, missed apexes, crossed centerlines, and twitches in steering. Nowadays, when I feel this happening, I back off a notch.

Keeping up with someone who's slightly faster or smoother than you is admittedly a great part of the sport, because it helps you improve. But struggling to keep up with a rider who's a lot better—or insaner—is an exercise in futility.

Riding over your head to lead a group can be a problem, too. It engenders a "Watch this!" mentality, where the thing people usually end up watching is a big crash. I think the clinical term for this is "showing off."

Either way, the symptoms are easy to spot: sudden cold sweats, a tightening of neck muscles, and a tendency to shout expletives in your helmet that would get you ejected from a decent restaurant. Or swatted by your mom.

Some years ago, I was on a group ride with my friend Bruce Finlayson, who was one of the best natural riders I ever knew. He made speed look easy. When the two of us rode together, he calmed himself down to my level, just out of politeness, but in a large group of fast guys he liked to run at the front.

Why? Because he could, and most of us hate to follow riders who are markedly slower than we are. It's almost painful. We are most comfortable dropping into our natural spot in the Great Mandala, and, in Bruce's case, that spot was generally in the lead.

Anyway, at a rest stop on this fast-moving ride, one of the guys (who I will call Bob) walked up to Bruce and said, "You've gotta slow down, man. You're gonna get someone killed."

Bruce looked at the guy thoughtfully for a long moment, then put his hand on his shoulder and said, "Bob, ride your own bike."

That phrase has stuck in my mind ever since. Even now, when I get pushing too hard to stay with another rider and things get a little loose, I calm the situation down by saying to myself, "Egan, ride your own bike."

Naturally, no one really likes to admit being slower than someone else, at least not in a group of friends off for a sportbike ride through the countryside. But, as age and enlightened self-preservation (i.e., mortal fear) set in, I've developed a psychological defense for that problem, too.

When someone pulls away from me these days, I just shrug and say, "So what? He's still slower than Rossi."

Humility, in our sport, starts in second spot on a GP grid and works its way down, one hero at a time.

15

Dangerous Liaisons

HEARD AN OLD JAZZ SONG ON THE RADIO THE other day called "I Fall in Love Too Easily." I don't know who it's by—you have to wait a long time (usually shortly after your own death) for DJs to back-announce their songs these days—but I can certainly identify with the subject matter.

Normal people probably see this as a tune about romantic entanglements, but I immediately spotted it as a motorcycle song. When it comes to bikes, falling in love too easily is the story of my life.

This past weekend, for instance, my wife, Barbara, and I flew down to Saint Augustine, Florida, for a big charity motorcycle concours called Riding into History, where 250 people suffered the grave misfortune of having me as guest speaker while they were trying to eat dessert or flag down the waiter for more wine. You can hardly blame them for drinking.

Nevertheless, Barb and I had a wonderful time. We were houseguests of Bill and Valerie Robinson, who helped organize the event, and 305 classic bikes showed up at the concours. On Sunday a bunch of us took a ride into historic old Saint Augustine, and Bill let me ride his 1982 Honda CBX.

Some of you (the grayer ones, with great accumulated wisdom) will remember this as the last version of Honda's amazing transverse-Six, a pearl-white GT bike with a sport-touring fairing and hard bags. I actually wrote the CW road test on the silver version of this bike in 1981 and am pictured on the cover of our July issue, waltzing the glamorous, wide beauty down a mountain road in California.

Building a GT version of this bike with a fairing and saddlebags was, at the time, an effort by Honda to widen the appeal of a bike whose sales had been disappointing, despite the obvious visual splendor of that twin cam Six. Shoichiro Irimajiri was the brilliant, young engineer who'd designed the ethereal six-cylinder 250cc Honda racebike (among others), and he'd also done the big 1047cc CBX, injecting an element of race-bred credibility.

Despite these bloodlines, the CBX didn't sell all that well. It was fast, great-looking, and had a lovely wail to the exhaust note, but it was also wide and a little heavy at 662 pounds with half a tank of gas. It was in about the same performance envelope as Kawasaki's KZ1000 and the Suzuki GS1000, but those bikes were cheaper, more agile, easier to maintain, and better on the racetrack.

So, after the CBX run ended in 1982, Honda still had leftover bikes and started discounting them. Heavily. The sticker on the handlebars went from $5,495 all the way down to about $2,695, and at that point I considered buying one myself. I was looking for a good, all-purpose road bike that Barb and I could use for weekend touring in California, and I recognized the CBX as an unbelievable deal.

But . . . still . . . there were all those valves—24 of 'em —with buckets and shims. And six carburetors, all huddled tightly together. I'd owned Honda 400Fs and 750 Fours with gummed-up carburetors and knew that cleaning (or replacing) jets in these big banks of carbs was no treat. So I passed on the exotic CBX and bought a leftover 1980 Kawasaki KZ1000 MKII instead. Or, more accurately, Barb bought me one for my birthday. And so it happened that the KZ was our road-burner for the rest of the 1980s. A near miss on CBX ownership.

But riding Bill's bike last weekend reminded me how much I like CBXs, visually and aurally. Also, they're amazingly comfortable, with a low, flat seat and perfectly placed handlebars. Barb liked riding it as much as I did. "I could go anywhere on this bike," she said.

So now I've fallen in love too easily again and returned from Saint Augustine with CBXs on the brain. The old brochures are scattered around my bedside stand like autumn leaves.

Fine. But what about old BMWs?

Old BMWs?

Yes. Last month, my buddy Rob Himmelmann and I hauled a couple of dirt bikes out to South Dakota to go trail riding on the cattle ranch of our friend Randy Babcock. Randy has, among other things, an old BMW R75/5 in the barn. It's a well-worn nail with 205,000 miles showing on its now-broken odometer, but it runs like a clock.

I took this thing for an afternoon ride on the nearby gravel roads, and this was yet another mistake. Here we have a simple, plain, basic, unadorned, sensible motorcycle that ticks down the road with a wonderfully relaxed gait. Two carburetors, four easily adjusted valves—all sticking out into mid-air. Looks good and handles amazingly well. So I came home from the ranch all fired up about BMW Slash-5s from the early 1970s. Got out all my books; read all the old road tests; started looking at the want-ads. I've been keeping my eyes open.

And now this CBX ride.

Two marvelous old motorcycles, poised like bookends of the 1970s, sitting at opposite ends of the engineering spectrum, appealing for totally different reasons, but compelling nevertheless. Pragmatism versus exoticism, with no clear winner.

There's a 1971 R75/5 in our local paper today with only 22,000 miles on it. On the other hand, a friend of mine in D.C. has a beautiful '81 CBX for sale. Like the one I rode on the cover.

Still, it has all those carburetors. And all those valves. Twenty-four of 'em, with buckets and shims. . . .

Funny how the very things that make us nervous and shy also seduce, even after 25 years. And sensible things never stop making sense.

16

Time Travel

*T*HERE'S AN OLD SAYING IN THE MILITARY THAT WAR consists of hours of boredom punctuated by moments of terror. When things happen, they tend to happen all at once, and as our old sergeant once said (after cleaning up his speech for a family magazine), "You don't know whether to spit or go blind."

Civilian life seldom produces much terror, but it's quite common for multiple things to happen all at once.

Last week, for example, I came home from an overseas press trip just in time for two carloads of relatives to come up the driveway for a family reunion in the middle of a crashing thunderstorm. As they got out of the car, our two impeccably trained dogs began flinging themselves against the kitchen door and howling like crazy, and at that moment the phone rang. Maybe our roof was on fire, too; I can't remember.

Anyway, I answered the phone and it was a man named Mark Sliwa who said he was calling from a rest stop on the Interstate near Madison, Wisconsin. He explained that he was touring the entire United States on his 1981 BMW R80G/S and used to work for my old friend Bob Smith at his motorcycle shop in Pennsylvania. Would we mind if he stopped by for a visit?

I looked out the window at our in-laws disembarking in the sudden downpour and for one pivotal second there I almost told Mark, "I'm sorry, but this isn't a very good time." But then I quickly remembered Egan's Second Law of Party Science, which states, "There is virtually no social gathering that isn't improved by having more guests."

I can't remember what the first law is, but I think it involves nacho cheese–flavored Doritos and a drink blender.

Anyway, I'm quite convinced that when you bring a couple of extra people along to a party or a dinner, things automatically liven up. The most unlikely people will make friends and talk to each other all night long, and everybody has a good time.

So I told Mark, "It's a little crazy around here right now . . . but, sure, why don't you stop by."

"Be there in about twenty minutes," he said cheerfully.

Long story short, he showed up, turned out to be a great guy and we ended up inviting him to stay for our very fancy dinner, which consisted of burgers on the grill. He'd planned to camp in a nearby KOA campground, but it was threatening more rain so I talked him into "camping" in the carpeted garage-band corner of my workshop (what with our guest rooms all full) and putting his bike in the garage. We found him a large air mattress and a real pillow.

Over breakfast the next morning, we learned that Mark had, at the age of 43, quit his job as a Porsche mechanic in the Washington, D.C. area in order to take his BMW on a long-anticipated six-week lap around the United States. He'd ridden down to Key West, across the Deep South and Southwest, up the West Coast, and back across the Northern Rockies and Great Plains. And now he was only about two days from home. He had two saddlebags on the G/S and a tidy tent and bedroll in a waterproof duffel across the luggage rack. The bike had the big Dakar tank and no windshield. He'd camped most of the way, or stayed with friends.

When he left our place at mid-morning, I waved goodbye and watched him roll down the driveway with a mixture of fascination and outright envy.

For many years, I've wanted to take a long, long motorcycle trip like this but have never found the time. A two-week trip is feasible in my working life, but six weeks or a couple of months is nearly impossible. That'll have to happen after I'm retired.

Retired, you say? On what?

Good question. Having frittered away most of my "savings" on motor-cycles and restoring useless, old British sports cars, I am not exactly poised for a life of golden-age leisure by the infinity pool in Saint Tropez. But I do allow myself to envision an imaginary distant future with an epic motorcycle journey or two.

As a matter of fact, the two-week, 4,000-mile trip Barb and I took to the Gaspe Peninsula in Canada last year was a kind of dress rehearsal (at least in my mind) for the touring life as it might shape up during our Social Security years. And it was an eye-opener, in which we learned one essential lesson: touring without a tent and cooking gear is very, very expensive. Motels with defective neon now cost about $60 a night, while nice places are often over $100. And unless you eat every meal at McDonald's, it's hard to get two people out of a café for less than about $20. Really good dinners in romantic places that look out over the ocean and have wandering waiters with big pepper grinders can cost multiples of that amount. If they serve anything with a balsamic reduction sauce, look out.

Obviously, this is an unsustainable way of traveling for extended periods of time, especially if total indigence is not one of your long-term financial goals.

The answer, of course, is camping and cooking your own food, as Mark did. And staying with friends who live around the country. This is the way I traveled when I was younger, and it was pretty good.

Food tastes better when you cook it in a mess kit over a fire or a Svea stove. Coffee tastes better in the morning when you have to wait for the water to boil while standing in a grove of pine trees. Nights with stars are better than nights with 57 channels of cable TV. And burgers over a grill or spaghetti and cheap Chianti with old friends is better than any restaurant meal, at any price.

I remarked in a column years ago that I'd never forgotten a campsite or remembered a hotel room. The same might be said of home-cooked meals in friendly kitchens versus restaurants.

I thought about all this after Mark rolled down our driveway toward home, and that evening I went upstairs to the storage closet and dug out our giant cardboard box of camping gear.

For some reason, I just wanted to lay my hands on my old army mess kit. The one with "US" stamped in the handle.

17

First Imprint

"**W**ELL, AFTER WHAT I DID LAST WEEK, MY PLACE in heaven is assured," Rob Himmelmann announced at our Slimey Crud Motorcycle Gang meeting last week.

Several Cruds raised one eyebrow and looked at Rob curiously, ever alert to the remote possibilities of virtue and salvation. Someone in the group finally stopped eating peanuts and deep-fried cheese curds long enough to say, "How's that, Rob?" Or at least that's what it sounded like.

Rob, who is now retired and spends much of his time restoring, buying, selling, and trading old, orphaned bikes and parts at his rural Wisconsin retreat, explained that he'd made an odd "barn find" a few weeks ago. It was a largely complete and unmolested 1960 Ducati Bronco, which is a nifty little 98cc pushrod ohv four-stroke rated at 6 hp, with a top speed of 53 mph. He bought the bike for $50, thinking he might clean it up and be able to sell it at a swap meet for around $300.

But he'd no sooner set it out in front of his vendor tent at a Farmington, Minnesota, swap meet when a man riding by skidded to a halt and said, "I must buy that bike! It was my first motorcycle. I got one when I was 11 years old and rode it on my uncle's farm until it wore out. I've been looking for another one for 40 years! I'll pay anything you want for it."

Rob, who regards karma as the most powerful force in the universe, told the man, "I paid $50 for it, and I'll sell it to you for that. You should have this bike."

Done deal. The happy man took it away.

Funny what an indelible image the memory of one's first bike leaves in the mind. That's assuming you're fixated on motorcycles, of course, which apparently is not true of everyone.

Once or twice a year, I'll be at some kind of social gathering—a large family reunion, say, or a Christmas party—and someone will come up to me and say, "I hear you work for a motorcycle magazine. I used to have a motorcycle when I was in high school."

"What kind was it?" I always ask.

"Well, I think it was a Honda. Or maybe a Suzuki. No, I think it was a Honda 105 Scrambler. It was red."

You hardly know what to say. It's like hearing "I used to be in the Marine Corps. Or maybe it was the Air Force. . . . Anyway, we had a lot of big battles in Vietnam or Korea or someplace. I can still remember that the wood on my rifle was brown. . . ."

There's a lack of specificity here that usually calls for a change of subject. Like "How about those Brewers?" Or that great Walter Brennan icebreaker, "Was you ever bit by a dead bee?"

Most of us, however, don't have quite so much trouble remembering our first bikes. Seems nearly every lifelong motorcyclist has one bike like that Ducati Bronco, a single model so rare or full of symbolic resonance—or both—that it might stop you in your tracks. One bike that would make you open your wallet or checkbook, unconditionally.

For me, that one bike would be my 1964 Bridgestone 50. Yes, the legendary Model 7 Sportster.

I spent so much time staring at that thing—first in the showroom window and then in my parents' garage—it probably left permanent physical indentations on the surface of my eyeballs, like the mold for a sand casting.

This model first appeared in the window of Lee Hardware on Main Street in my hometown of Elroy, Wisconsin. A lot of small bikes, including Hondas, were sold through hardware stores and sporting-goods stores then, as the Japanese manufacturers were trying to get away from the dark, oil-stained atmosphere of traditional motorcycle shops. And Gib Lee, a friend of my dad's who ran the hardware store, had taken on a lineup of Bridgestone 50s.

The first one he got in was a step-through model, which I admired at great length, but it was eventually bought by the town's only beatnik, a strange and interesting guy who wore a beret and was known to have bicycled through South America. Very cool. My motorcycle-crazed buddy Pat Donnelly and I took this as a good omen.

That bike was replaced in the store window by the Sportster model with a proper saddle tank, a real hand clutch, and a three-speed transmission. The brochure rated the engine at 4.2 hp at 7000 rpm and said the bike would deliver "over 200 mpg." Top speed, the copy claimed, was a bicycle-beating 45 mph. Now we were talking.

I had to sell my Mossberg .410 shotgun to come up with the $100 down payment and borrow about $175 from the bank. My dad made me take a second job—outside my "college fund" employment in our family printing office—to pay off the loan. Actually, I got two other jobs, mowing the Catholic cemetery and fueling planes at the local airport.

By the time I finally got my hands on the Bridgestone, however, Gib had sold about six of them, and the town was literally buzzing with two-stroke

Bridgestone 50s, day and night. Old people complained, and young people bought more Bridgestones. My friend Pat finally turned 16 and got one. Darned things were everywhere.

But not anymore. I sold my bike when I went away to college and bought a Honda S-90. Each time I came home from college, there were fewer Bridgestones on the streets, and after a few years there were none. The Bridgestone company itself quit making motorcycles altogether in 1970 to concentrate on tire making.

I don't know where all those bikes went. I guess they just got worn out and junked, or left in barns.

In any case, I haven't seen one anywhere in about 40 years. Not at a swap meet, a garage sale or a farm auction. Not one.

So I could easily identify with Rob's Ducati Bronco customer. If I were to cruise past a tent at a swap meet and spot a 1964 Bridgestone 50 Model 7 Sportster sitting there, complete and in good condition, I too would skid to a stop and open my wallet. Unconditionally.

Everything else is negotiable and has a price, but your first bike is priceless.

18

Project Repellent

THERE'S AN OLD SAYING THAT YOU SHOULD BE CAREFUL what you ask for, because you just might get it.

This is an expression you hear most often when people are talking about marriage or war. They say things like "I bet that attractive gal drinking double shots of tequila would be a fascinating date" or "It sure would be cool to fire a 30-caliber machine gun out of a helicopter door!"

The next thing you know they're in big trouble. In over their heads.

It can happen with motorcycles, too. Just a few weeks ago, I became a victim myself.

Seems I mouthed off and told all my friends that I wished fervently to find an example of my very first motorcycle, a 1964 Bridgestone 50. I'd written about this recently ("First Imprint," Leanings, page 58), which brought distant memories of the zippy little two-stroke to the fore.

Well, about three days later, I drove to a shop called Country Sports in Wisconsin Rapids to pick up a new aluminum motorcycle trailer. Naturally, the shop owner, John Montgomery, had a 1964 Bridgestone 50 sitting there. A red Model 7 Sportster. My first bike, exactly. The first I'd seen in 40 years.

"There's your bike," my friend Rob said. "Let's see you put your money where your mouth is."

I think you'll agree there was no backing down. I need another old motorcycle like I need a good dose of swine flu, but I'd painted myself into a corner.

The Bridgestone was in pretty good condition, though the right footpeg was broken off and the taillight lens was gone. John had already started to restore the bike in his spare time. The red vinyl seat had been expertly recovered, and he had a new taillight assembly in a box.

"I don't really have any emotional investment in this bike," John said. "I never had a Bridgestone 50 when I was young, so you should own it."

I nodded, trance-like, and he generously sold it to me for a few hundred dollars, which was probably less than he'd spent on parts.

"Do you have a title?" I asked.

"No," he said, "but I'll make out a bill of sale, and you can get one through an out-of-state title service."

Hoo, boy.

I'd recently tried to re-title my junkyard-rescued Honda Spree in the state of Wisconsin and had run into a stony wall of bureaucracy that made North Korea look like a beacon of friendly efficiency.

Nevertheless, I resolutely loaded up the bike and headed for home. A Bridgestone 7 owner again for the first time in 42 years.

I felt vaguely like some Darwinian creature going backward in time, developing gills and a vestigial tail. Ontogeny recapitulates phylogeny, I think is the scientific term. The organism retraces its biological roots from the dawn of life. Nerd-like youth, recaptured!

A noble concept, but there was one downside to this whole transaction: After a couple of bad experiences several years ago, I'd absolutely sworn in blood on a stack of Bibles that I would never do two things again as long as I lived:

1. Buy any vehicle that doesn't run.

2. Buy any vehicle without a title.

And now I'd bought this Bridgestone, which neither ran nor had a title.

"Oh, well," I said to myself aloud, tilting the mirror of my van so I could gaze upon the bike, "if I can't make it run, I'll mount it on the wall in my workshop. It's just a memento from my youth, after all, like my old baseball glove. It's enough just to look at the thing; I don't have to use it."

Fancy talk for a guy who can't leave any mechanical device alone—or tolerate a motorcycle that doesn't run.

So of course I've wasted countless hours in the past few weeks fiddling around with the Bridgestone. I cleaned the gas tank with anti-rust treatment, found a useable petcock at a swap meet, and then discovered the carburetor is just dangling on its worn-out phenolic sleeve, sucking air. I installed a new battery, but no electricity flows to any terminal. Probably a bad ground.

The original tires are checked and aged.

The air-cleaner sleeve, too, is broken away from its filter.

I'm still getting rust out of the gas tank.

The word *quagmire* comes to mind.

Yesterday, my old friend and former *Cycle World* Managing Editor Steve Kimball called and asked how the project was going.

I told him the whole saga of the Model 7's missing parts, lost electrons, and misplaced title.

Steve, who can be counted on for detached logic when all around you (including you) have lost their heads, said, "Well, look at the bright side."

"Yes, and what might that be?" I asked.

"What you've got there is what I call 'project repellent.' If you didn't have the Bridgestone sitting in your garage, you'd just have some other semi-useless old bike, and it would probably be a lot more expensive. The 50 will simply keep you from buying something else. One old bike that doesn't run is as good as another."

"Uh huh," I said, letting that train of reason sink into my brain.

"You have a long history of making the same mistakes over and over again with orphaned motorcycles," he said, "so you might as well be working on a worn-out $200 Bridgestone as a $3,000 worn-out Triumph or Norton."

It's great to have friends like Steve. Now I don't feel so bad.

The crazy thing is, he's right for once. I went to the big Davenport swap meet in Iowa a few weeks ago and had exactly as much fun looking for Bridgestone parts as I usually do scrounging for old British stuff. More, maybe, because the parts are cheaper and the search is more mysterious and arcane, like looking for pieces of a lost treasure map.

It occurs to me that maybe the appeal of old bikes is just a dream, a flow of current through the neurons, and one dream really is as good as another.

Especially if it repels other dreams and occupies garage space.

Flying on the Ground

LATE AUTUMN IS USUALLY THE BEST TIME FOR RIDING in the upper Midwest—dry, clear, and sunny. It's cool enough to enjoy wearing a leather jacket, but not so cold that great sheets of ice cover the North American continent and drive our local mastodon herds relentlessly south. It's a time of ideal balance.

Not this year, though.

October was pretty much a washout for riding. Granted, we had a beautiful first weekend for the Slimey Crud Motorcycle Gang's fall Café Racer Run—about 1,000 bikes showed up—but after that things went downhill fast.

On Monday morning, low clouds moved in like an armored division and brought with them an endless convoy of bad weather—wind, cold, freezing rain, and snow showers. Nearly four unbroken weeks of it. I parked my bike and, until yesterday, didn't ride at all. Pretty grim.

Luckily, I found a novel way to make it through those dark and difficult weeks without giving up my usual quota of banked turns, skids, slips, hair-raising miscalculations, and grateful homecomings.

I took flying lessons.

Yes, after a 15-year absence from flying, I'd decided to get back into it, to see if I could be taught to fly again and update my license. I took an FAA physical (alarmingly thorough, it seems, when you're 58) and signed up for flying lessons at a place called Morey Field in Middleton, Wisconsin. My instructor, an unflappably calm and patient man named Richard Morey, is the grandson of the airport's founder. A third-generation flight instructor. His grandfather, an aviation pioneer and barnstormer, flew with Lindbergh.

It may have been too cold for riding—at least by my exacting and self-indulgent standards—but not for flying. Airplanes don't mind a little sleet or dry snow blowing around. They have heaters. So I flew twice a week for four weeks and finally finished up last Tuesday.

On this final lesson, we flew to nearby Sauk Prairie Airport so we could take advantage of the fierce crosswinds and see what I was made of. Never a good idea, but we somehow survived my crosswind landings without serious injury. So Rich—in a mood of life-affirming gratitude, no doubt—signed off my ancient and crumbling log book (first entry, 1964). I was good to go. A pilot again.

And the next day, as if by magic, the bad weather skulked off to the east, high pressure moved in, and our classic fall riding weather returned. It was a sunny 65 degrees yesterday, and I took my big KTM 950 out for a good backroad flog through the russet-colored hills with leaves swirling across the road and the dry smell of corn-harvester dust in the air. Carved pumpkins grinned at me from farm porches. Glorious stuff.

And, while riding again at long last, inevitable comparisons crept into my partially trained journalistic brain and I started thinking how closely related motorcycling is to flying.

Okay, they aren't exactly the same. When you climb out of a Cessna after an hour of crosswind landings, driving anything on the highway at moderate speed seems absurdly easy, and you wonder briefly how anyone ever manages to have an accident—especially in a car.

There are no critical instruments to scan (other than your speedometer, if you so choose). No rate of climb or stall speed to worry about. Your altitude and heading are pre-determined by the road. You don't have to radio ahead to Barnes & Noble and tell them you're coming into the parking lot from the west on a heading of zero-niner-zero. There are no other vehicles above or below the road surface. If your engine quits, you pull over.

Another difference is that flying—once you've mastered the basic motor skills—is more of a cognitive process than riding and less of an athletic act. You always have to think about where you're going, where you'll be 20 minutes from now, and how you're going to make it all happen. The actual steering is not so crucial, except in landing.

Riding, particularly dirt riding, roadracing, and fast backroad riding, is more physical and immediate. Your plans are much shorter in range and duration, corrections more frequent and imperative. Expletives of doom arrive with greater regularity.

But the two sports are still related. You tilt the horizon and forces act through your own personal vertical axis. Bank, accelerate, zoom. Grin. Your inner ear is hard at work, as it is nowhere else. In full flight, with either bikes or planes, all your senses are engaged and you become hyper-alert.

Maybe that's the link: The thing flying and motorcycling have most in common is that you simply must pay attention. Your life depends on it. Both sports, you might say, are naturally riveting.

Of course, the same may be said of mountain climbing, whitewater canoeing, sky diving, bicycle racing, downhill skiing, and mountain biking. (Notice how all these sports involve a rapid elevation change. A form of falling, as it were, skillfully arrested.)

In any case, it's that paying attention thing I like best.

Winston Churchill once remarked that nothing is more exhilarating than to be shot at and missed. Well, pilots and motorcyclists are shot at quite often, figuratively speaking, and called upon to arrange their own near misses.

Which is a good thing, in my opinion. Life is full of perfectly nice activities that don't require this kind of concentration, but most of them seem to me only half-interesting.

As I've discovered at many parties and social gatherings over the years, I'm never really comfortable—or completely awake—around people who are unacquainted with the invigorating joys of mild panic.

20

The Accessibility Factor

WHEN MY WIFE, BARBARA, AND I MOVED FROM CALIFORNIA back to Wisconsin 16 years ago, we came up with a list of reasons to explain the move to those who were baffled. For instance, "You can cool your beer just by setting it outside the door in the winter" or "I need at least five months of arctic hibernation so I can finish restoring my Norton."

All in good fun, in a bleak sort of way, but two of our reasons for moving were actually quite serious:

We wanted to be close to a couple of restaurants in Madison—Paisans, our favorite pizza place, and Smoky's Steakhouse, winner of many awards as one of the best steak houses in the United States.

And all these years later, we still go to both places at the drop of a hat. We often use Smoky's as a way of celebrating significant milestones, such as birthdays, buying another Ducati, or finding a lost Snap-On 10mm socket under the workbench. In fact, we go there so often we've become friends with a member of the family that owns the restaurant, Tom Schmock, son of the original Smoky and his wife, who founded the place in 1953. Sometimes Tom even buys us a martini or sends a bottle of wine over to our table.

Yes, it's official. I am now so old that real restaurant owners actually know me by name, instead of throwing me out for being a hippie.

It helps, of course, that Tom is an avid motorcyclist who's become a regular at our Slimey Crud Motorcycle Gang meetings. He rides a Ducati ST2 and has a Suzuki DR650 dual-sport bike exactly like mine. And, just last month, Tom bought himself one of the new Triumph Scramblers, the high-pipe variation on the Bonneville 900 Twin.

And now we see him everywhere.

Go to Border's books on a cold autumn night with snow flurries in the air, and in walks Tom, wearing his insulated Gore-Tex enduro jacket. "Are you riding on a night like this?" you ask.

"Yeah," he says, "I'm on the Triumph. I can't stay off that thing."

The other night, Barb and I went to Smoky's for dinner (to celebrate my recent purchase of new guitar strings for the Strat), and we asked the waitress if Tom was in the building. "No," she said, "he's out riding his new motorcycle."

I looked at the waitress and said, "It's pitch dark and twenty-nine degrees out there."

She just smiled and shrugged helplessly. Barb and I were, frankly, a little disappointed because there was no one to buy us a free drink.

But a few minutes later Tom walked in, wearing a neck-warmer and his motorcycle jacket. He came over to our table, radiating cold (if that's possible) and carrying some wine glasses.

"Out on the Triumph tonight?" I asked.

"Yup."

"You're riding that bike a lot."

Tom frowned thoughtfully and said, "It's so inviting and easy to ride. You just hop on it and go. There's nothing to discourage you from riding, if you know what I mean."

I knew exactly what he meant.

I've had a lot of bikes over the years and enjoyed them all for different reasons, but some have been ridden a lot more than others. And those have all shared a trait you might call "accessibility." They're motorcycles you ride on a whim, rather than in fulfillment of a plan.

There are a lot of small, subtle things that make a bike whimsically inviting to ride, and they make a wonderful testament to the widespread condition of human laziness—at least in my case.

For instance, if a bike is too tall, clumsy, or heavy to back out of the garage easily, it doesn't get ridden as often. Also, I've found that a sportbike with severely dropped handlebars and high rearsets may be wonderful on a pre-ordained Sunday ride with friends, but it seldom gets used for a trip to the post office or the bookstore, or just a quick evening cruise to soak up the last hours of summer light.

Many of my sportbike friends are mystified at the continuing popularity of Harleys, but I always try to explain it with the simple phrase "They're easy to ride." Low cg makes them easy to maneuver in the garage (or at a gas station), various forms of windshield keep the bugs off, and you can put both feet on the ground. Start it up and go, easy as a golf cart. They make no unreasonable demands.

I see the same thing in my own garage. My main bike for the past several years has been a KTM 950 Adventure. Once this thing is out of the garage, warmed up, and rolling, I love it. But I often choose my Suzuki DR650 for short, impulsive rides because it's just a little lower, lighter, and easier to maneuver between the car and the lawnmower. More of a no-brainer to park and hop off of, too. Tom's new Triumph is easier still. It throws up absolutely no defense—real or imagined—against being ridden.

The world is full of other examples outside the realm of motorcycling. My neighbor Lyman recently told me he's doubled the amount of bicycling he does since he replaced his old roadracer with a hybrid. "I don't have to change shoes," he says, "and I don't get a crick in my neck looking for traffic."

I have a book on buying used sailboats in which the author says, "For every 5 feet of length and complexity you add to a boat, you will sail it half as often."

You could see the same syndrome with test cars when I worked full time at *Road & Track* during the 1980s. When it was time to drive to lunch, everyone gravitated toward the Honda Civics of this world, while the Lamborghini Countach sat in the parking lot. Beautiful and exotic, but hard to see out of and too much work in town. A great weekend car, but not so good at Burger King.

Exotica, in other words, can be very rewarding, but so can honest simplicity. In the ideal garage, there's sometimes room for both.

Which reminds me, our local Triumph shop, Sharer Cycle Center, has a leftover 2006 Triumph Scrambler on sale right now. Just like Tom's. It probably wouldn't hurt anything if I wandered over there later this afternoon, just to say hi.

21

Your Life in Harleys

THE POET T.S. ELIOT CLAIMED HE HAD MEASURED OUT his life with coffee spoons, which I suppose is fine, in an introverted, shut-in kind of way, but only last week I discovered a slightly more colorful medium for marking the passage of time: Harley-Davidsons.

Yep. Through a set of convoluted relationships in which I rode to Milwaukee with a friend who has a buddy who used to know a guy in high school, I was granted a rare opportunity to walk through that Upper Room of American motorcycle lore, the Harley-Davidson Archives on Juneau Avenue.

This is the place where Harley stores not only its entire paper trail—production records, catalogs, owner's manuals, etc. —but also a representative sampling of motorcycles, most of them brand-new and right off the assembly line, stretching back to 1903.

Most of these historic bikes are destined for the new Harley-Davidson Museum in downtown Milwaukee next year, but for right now they are crowded, cheek by jowl, into the upstairs of a red-brick building at the old factory, accessible only to those engaged in serious research—or to some lout like me who accidentally tags along with his buddy.

Nevertheless, the man in charge of the Archives (who asked not to be named so his phone doesn't ring off the hook with people wanting to know if the green headlight wire should be routed to the left or right of the steering head on the 1947 Knucklehead) was very gracious and friendly, and he guided my friends and me on a stroll through the caged collection of bikes for most of a cold and gray winter afternoon.

Harley-Davidson is probably alone in all the industrial world for having set aside a sampling of its products going back for more than 100 years. I'm told Coca-Cola has a similar museum, but—let us face it—that shapely six-ounce bottle you got at the gas station in the 1950s just doesn't have the same mojo as a perfectly preserved Hydra-Glide.

Luckily for those of us who are easily confused, Harley has lined up its archival bikes chronologically with a model-year plate on each front fender. So you can walk down the row and say to yourself "There's a bike you could have bought the year America entered World War I" or, "Here's a Harley from 1927, the year Lindbergh flew the Atlantic. . . ." and so on.

Historically interesting, to be sure, but I found myself moving pretty quickly through those early years of production. To be perfectly honest, one Silent Grey Fellow looks pretty much like the next to my under-trained eye. I have to force myself to soak up the differences in mechanical detail, like someone studying for an exam.

But then I came to 1948 and suddenly stopped in my tracks. A red Panhead.

"See something you like?" our curator asked.

"Came out the year I was born. . . ."

"An important year for Harley," he noted. "First-year Panhead, last of the old springer forks."

We moved slowly through the 1950s Panheads, and I said, "All the first bikes I saw when I was a kid looked like this. Our landlady's son had an FL when I was five years old, and I used to stand in the driveway and watch him work on it. I just soaked up the whole look of the thing."

I stared at one now and realized that somewhere in my brain there's a file drawer marked "Roy Rogers holster with rhinestones; Dad's 1951 Buick; Les Paul & Mary Ford guitar music; Harley Panhead with two-tone windshield." They're all melted together in there somewhere.

A little farther down was the first Duo-Glide, the 1958 version that finally got a swingarm. One of these was the first bike I actually rode on, at 13. Got picked up while hitchhiking to a junkyard. Climbed on the back and knew within five miles that I had to have a motorcycle and nothing else would do.

Stroll up to 1965 and there's the first Electra-Glide and the only electric-start Pan. Came out the year before I graduated from high school. Harleys were too heavy and conservative for me by then; I'd lost interest. They didn't win desert races. I was a confirmed Triumph guy. With a used Honda.

In 1967, we see a touring-oriented, electric-start Sportster, the XLH. I rode through Canada in the cold autumn rain with a guy who had one of these. Air Force vet, just out of the service, off to see the four corners of America. I grudgingly admitted it was a lot less hectic at 70 mph than my Honda 160.

Ah, we are on to the bad graphics of the early 1970s. But in 1977 we see Willie G's stunning XLCR Cafe Racer, the first Harley I really, really wanted. Later bought one, too. Pure charisma on wheels.

And, good Lord, here's the 1981 Heritage Edition FLH in vintage green and orange with fringed buddy seat and saddlebags. Harley's first intentional nod to its own past. Barb and I rode one up the shoreline of California when I first worked for *Cycle World*, for a story called "Shooting the Coast." Wonderful trip. "Can you still find these?" I ask our guide.

"Yeah, they turn up. And they aren't too expensive." Information filed.

Suddenly we're in Evo country. There's Barb's 883 Sportster, my FLH Sport, and green and black Road King, all in a row. A big part of my 1990s, flip-side of the Ducati addiction. This is your life, pal. And there's my Twin Cam Electra-Glide Standard in black. Nearly froze to death on that baby, riding home from Nashville in late October.

Now we're into the new 96-inch bikes and Sportsters with rubber-mounted engines. Haven't ridden them yet. Might have to.

End of the line.

And here we are in the present, right now, on a cold winter day at the Harley factory. I'll be 59 next month. But right back there, in the shadows farther down the row, is that '48 Panhead, unfazed by the passage of years.

You can keep the coffee spoons, T.S. When I want to measure time, I'll just go back to Milwaukee.

22

Just an Old Green Book

SOME OF MY FRIENDS SEEMED WORRIED LATELY THAT I'D grown increasingly morose over the lack of riding during this long, dark winter, and maybe even suicidal. But the fact is I wasn't really planning to drink that gallon of acrylic enamel reducer—I was just reading the contents on the can.

Still, it lifted my spirits considerably when the mail arrived the other day.

With snowflakes falling out of the leaden sky in desultory fashion, I slid down our icy driveway on the edges of my boots and arrested my descent at the mailbox with a classic stem turn right out of the Hans Tanner Ski Manual.

And what to my wondering eyes should appear but a package from someone named Mr. Patrick Haley of LaCrosse, Wisconsin. I did a standard herringbone climb back up to the house and opened the padded envelope.

Inside was a green, 127-page volume titled *John Surtees' Motor-Cycling Book*, published in 1961. Inside was a nice note from Mr. Haley saying I might like to add this book to my collection, if I didn't already have it.

Well, I didn't.

But if I'd seen this book in 1961 (when I was 13 years old), you can bet that several dollars of my lawn-mowing money would have gone to its purchase. The year of this book's publication coincided perfectly with my own TNT-like explosion of interest in bikes—followed soon by my first copies of *Cycle World* bought from the drug store in Elroy, Wisconsin.

Which is another way of saying that John Surtees is one of my original motorcycle heroes. When I discovered the sport, he was already the world's most famous motorcycle roadracer, just recently retired, making room for a rising, young star named Mike Hailwood.

Yes, while I'd been busy mounting playing cards in the spokes of my bicycle, Surtees had been out there running factory Manx Nortons at the Isle of Man and winning world championships with the fabulous MVs. He won his first 500cc GP title for MV in 1956 and then won every 350 and 500 championship from 1958 through 1960. Seven world GP titles.

I don't know about you, but I haven't won seven of anything in my whole life—including chances to sign up for a free aluminum-siding estimate—let alone world GP titles. When I hit this sport, John Surtees was The Man.

And later, when he switched to F-1 cars and won a world championship for Ferrari in 1964, he became the only man ever to win GP titles on two and four wheels.

All this was a long way from Elroy, Wisconsin, of course, so I didn't actually see Surtees in person until 1971, when his twin racing careers were over and he was campaigning F-1 cars as director of Team Surtees.

I'd just gotten home from Vietnam the previous autumn and was too restless to go right back to college, so I flew to Europe and bummed around Paris for most of the winter. In the spring, I took a 1,000-mile bicycle trip from Paris to Barcelona with my buddy Bill Steckel so we could attend the Spanish Grand Prix at Montjuich.

When we arrived at the circuit to watch practice and qualifying, we were amazed to find almost no security around the track. The Spaniards, apparently, were all off at a bullfight. Bill and I were free to wander around the paddock unchallenged.

And one of the places we wandered to was the Team Surtees pits, where a white-haired John Surtees was directing things. I stood right next to the man (like Woody Allen's Zelig, inserted anomalously into a historic tableau) while he talked to his mechanics. I was too shy to say anything—or maybe afraid of drawing attention to myself and being thrown out of the pits—so I just watched and listened.

I might also have been afraid to talk to Surtees because I'd recently read a book by Robert Daley called *The Cruel Sport* in which he portrayed Surtees as a cold, silent man who could harbor a deadly grudge against another driver. What if I said hello and he had me arrested for insolence?

Years later, I worked at *Road & Track* with Phil Hill, who drove for the Ferrari team and became America's first F-1 champion in 1961. Phil, who is a shrewd judge of character, not given to false praise, told me Daley got it completely wrong. "Surtees is a wonderful guy," Phil said, "and a great gentleman."

And so it turned out.

A couple of years ago, I was invited to a dinner at Road America, where Surtees was guest of honor at the Brian Redman International Challenge vintage-car races. I maneuvered things so Barb and I got to sit at the same table with Surtees (only a few people were injured in this scuffle), along with his children and charming wife, Jane.

And the John Surtees I met was the one Phil described. A true gentleman, lively, articulate, good-humored, and still infatuated—after all these years—with motorcycles. He restores and works on bikes as a hobby, including his own original racebike, a 500cc Vincent Gray Flash.

You don't talk to Surtees long before you realize you're dealing with a racer who has the soul of a mechanic and craftsman, with a deep, abiding love for machinery and its place in history. He's one of us.

Or, with luck, we are one of him, inasmuch as we are able.

And this past cold winter weekend, I sat down and read *John Surtees' Motor-Cycling Book* cover to cover. A well-written, fascinating look at riding and racing in the late 1950s.

When I finished the book, I set it down and went out to the workshop, turned up the heat, and spent some time dusting off my three hibernating bikes. Suddenly, all my riding synapses were firing again, and spring didn't seem so far away.

Funny how energy and enthusiasm can travel across decades, like an echo whose resonance doesn't diminish with distance or time.

This old green book was like something I'd been waiting for without knowing, and it provided that rarest of all things, a good day in winter, when the driveway is frozen and snowflakes fall silently out of a dark sky.

23

The Locus of Karmic Perfection

"**I**'LL MEET YOU IN MARFA, TEXAS," I TOLD MY friend Mike Mosiman, "if I can ever get out of Wisconsin."

It wouldn't be easy. We'd had two blizzards in three days, and my driveway was sculpted in drifts and hollows like some frozen treat from Dairy Queen. Nevertheless, I fired up my Suzuki DR650 and slithered through the deep snow into the van. Success. I was on my way to Texas.

And after that, Mexico. We'd cross the border at Presidio, then down to Copper Canyon, for seven days of mostly off-roading through old mining towns in the rugged deep valleys.

But first I had to get to the border.

So on that wintry Thursday afternoon I drove south to Pekin, Illinois, where I transferred my bike onto a trailer belonging to Mike's brother, Bob, and tied it down alongside his big new BMW R1200GS. We then climbed into Bob's new Toyota Highlander hybrid (which had lots of power but got an unremarkable 12 mpg) and towed both bikes all the way to Texas in two long days of fast driving and fast food.

At Marfa—famous as the place where the 1956 movie *Giant* was filmed— we hooked up with Mike and his buddy Dave Scott, who drove down from Fort Collins, Colorado. Mike brought his KTM 640 Adventure and Dave had a BMW R100GS Paris-Dakar model, the one with the huge 9.3-gallon tank. We would soon be calling this the "Mother Ship." And many other things, as well.

After the usual border hassles—tourist permits, vehicle permits, Mexican insurance, etc. —we rode into sunny Mexico at last. Warm weather and clear skies. Blooming jacaranda everywhere. Nice people, great food, surprisingly good paved roads and a different sense of time. I love old Mexico. Don't expect both faucets to be hooked up in the men's room sink, though.

We rode through the big city of Chihuahua and on to Cuauhtemoc, where we found a good motel along the highway just before dark. The motel was owned by Mennonites, part of a large colony that moved to Mexico from

Germany. Mennonite farms are responsible for most of the great Mexican cheeses we sprinkle on our tacos. We ate at a Mennonite restaurant, which, sadly, served no beer or margaritas. Or tacos. Still a nice place, though. I told Mike the Mennonites are so helpful and friendly, they're in danger of giving organized religion a good name.

We had lunch in Creel the next day, then finally turned off the pavement and headed down into the canyons for four long days of off-roading.

And two things immediately became apparent: 1) The roads were steeper, rougher, and rockier than we'd been led to believe; and 2) unless you're some kind of Paris-Dakar superhero rider, BMW GS Twins are way too big and heavy for serious off-roading in Copper Canyon.

We had one bad day in the wilderness. Picked too long and difficult a route—with one pretty deep and wide river crossing—and found ourselves after dark having to cross a mountain ridge with miles of rocky switchbacks.

Dave ran flat out of energy on his P-D, so we traded bikes and then I ran out of energy an hour later as we crested the ridge. One of those new, street-legal KTM 525 EXCs was looking pretty good at this point. Dave crashed my DR650 twice getting to the top. Bob hammered his way to the crest with his massive R1200GS, then parked the bike and said, "I quit. I'm walking the rest of the way down to Batopilas."

We had been riding for 13 hours and were very, very tired. Not to say a little brain-dead.

This energy crisis was resolved when a Mexican pickup truck pulled up and offered us a ride down the mountain. We found a hotel and then hired another pickup the next day to take us back up the mountain. Our motorcycles were still there—despite silent prayers that certain large, well-insured bikes might be stolen—and it was a much easier ride down in daylight, after some sleep and a good breakfast with plenty of chorizo.

The rest of the trip was great—and even the hardships added their charm, retrospectively. They don't call this "adventure" touring for nothing.

And there was one strange moment on this trip that was so right, it probably qualified as one of those personal epiphanies you hear so much about.

We were winding down a cliff-hanging road above the town of Urique, motoring through a canyon of huge rock spires, falling streams, and green foliage, when the road opened up on a spectacular view of the chasm below and the distant mountains. On a spur of land in the foreground was a small farm with burros roaming and apple blossoms blooming. The beauty of the spot was surreal. We shut off our bikes and just sat for a while.

Then I had one of those odd shifts of focus and looked down at my bike, and my dusty, worn gloves on the handlebars. We were in the greatest place in the world, but what had it taken to get here?

Quite a bit.

Learning to ride, getting a driver's license in high school. Acquiring tools, learning to change flat tires and clutch cables. Gaining dirt experience and going to dealerships to shop for the right bike. Installing knobbies and handguards and a skidplate. After years of youthful indigence, moving through a series of jobs that finally allowed you to afford a truck or a bike trailer. Learning to read maps and cross rivers in deep water. Finding helmets and enduro jackets and motocross boots that fit. Getting a passport, paying your bike registration, learning a smattering of useful Spanish. . . .

And living long enough to have friends who were crazy enough to do all these things, as well. People you could count on who'd gone through the same lifetime of motorcycle connections that had brought us to this perfect spot in time.

As I put my helmet back on, it occurred to me that you are never more completely the sum of everything you've ever been than when you take a slightly difficult motorcycle trip into a strange land. And make it back out again.

24

Too Much Bike, Not Enough Road

WHILE MOVING MY VINTAGE BRIDGESTONE SPORT 50 AROUND THE garage yesterday so I could sweep the floor, I unconsciously found myself picking up the entire bike by the handlebars and the back of the seat and scooting it closer to the wall.

Interesting sensation, picking up an entire motorcycle, and one I haven't enjoyed for a while.

This set me to wondering what the Bridgestone weighs. I thought about fetching our big doctor's-office-class bathroom scale (where I daily monitor the wondrous effects of beer and enchiladas) and dragging it down to the workshop, but I soon realized it would be easier to roll the Bridgestone up to the house.

In the end, of course, common sense won out and I simply looked in my old 1964 Bridgestone brochure and noted that the bike has a claimed "unladen weight" of 149.6 pounds. Close enough. In any case, it's nice to have at least one bike that's lighter than you are.

Back when I owned a Bridgestone 50 as my first bike, of course, my main problem in life was that the bike was too small. On the highway, I had to cling to the shoulder of the road at a shrieking 39 or 40 mph while pickup trucks full of milk cans swerved around me. I wanted to ride from Wisconsin to California, but when I looked at a map of the greater United States, I realized that what we had here, essentially, was too much road and not enough bike.

Now, of course, that problem is often reversed.

This thought has struck me a couple of times in the past month. The first time was right before three buddies and I left for a dual-sport ride in Mexico (the one I wrote about in my last column). Expedition planner Mike Mosiman sent me an inspirational DVD of *Long Way Round*, a documentary of the world tour done by actors Ewan McGregor and Charley Boorman.

I'd already read the book, but it was fascinating to see the film. It was a grand adventure, and you have to give these guys credit for hanging in there. But about halfway through the movie—after watching the exhausted McGregor and Boorman struggle for the umpteenth time to pick their bikes up out of the sand and muck—I actually shouted at my TV screen, "Your bikes are too bloody big!"

As if they hadn't already noticed.

They originally had KTM 950 Adventures (exactly like mine) in mind for the trip, but KTM pulled its sponsorship at the last moment. McGregor and Boorman were crestfallen (oddly, they seem not to have considered buying their own bikes), but BMW bravely stepped in and loaned them a pair of R1200GSs.

Frankly, I thought both the KTM 950 and the R1200GS (two of my favorite all-purpose road bikes) were too big for this rugged trip, and I couldn't help thinking how much more fun they could have had on BMW F650 Dakars or KTM 640s. Or anything smaller and nimbler. The concept of going seriously off-road on a 400-pound-plus bike is simply baffling to me, like renting a B-52 to take flying lessons or opening a bag of Cheetos with a howitzer. More machine than you need.

Yes, I know the great Paris-Dakar champions have soared over sand dunes on these big trailies, but I ain't them. And not many people are.

A week after watching this movie, of course, I was in Mexico, riding down the steep dirt roads of Copper Canyon with three other guys. And two of them were on—guess what? —BMW GS models. An R1100GS-PD and an R1200GS.

Like our friends Ewan and Charley, they toughed it out and made the trip—with a little help from their friends—but they could have spent a lot more time grinning and relaxing on smaller bikes. I watched Dave struggle up a stretch of steep, boulder-strewn canyon road on his big, wallowing P-D, and said to Mike, "Too much bike, not enough road."

I'd almost brought my KTM 950 on this trip, but at the last moment I saw someone's website photo of a dirt road in Copper Canyon and said, "Hmmm . . . Looks pretty gnarly. Think I'll throw some new knobbies on my DR650 and take that."

I was glad I did. The KTM would have been too tall and heavy for me to hold up on our one big river crossing, and the battery (which lives inside the skidplate) would have been under water. Not ideal. The bike would probably still be down there, drying out its electrics.

As it turns out, my Suzuki DR was a good choice for the trip. Bob and Dave returned from Mexico vowing to keep their big GSs for daily use and Alaska-type trips on "well-graded gravel roads," but to buy much smaller bikes for their next encounter with true dirt.

I hesitate to sound like some kind of evangelist (and, no, I am not under secret contract to Suzuki), but I have to say that the trusty, sometimes under-rated DR is toward the top of my list of recommendations.

Why?

Well, with a 324-pound dry weight, it's not exactly a gossamer concoction, but at least it carries its weight low and you can put your foot down when you have to (and, believe me, you often do). The seat height is only 34.8 inches, and you can easily lower it another 1.6. This is a very good thing, at least for most of us earthbound mortals.

Also, it has an electric starter, and it's inexpensive, simple, air-cooled, durable, dead smooth at 70–80 mph on the highway, agile enough to steer a tight trail and torquey enough to blast effortlessly up steep mountains. There aren't many other bikes out there with this combination of traits—although I see the new-for-2007 BMW G650 Xchallenge shares some of these virtues and is in the same weight class.

Maybe Ewan and Charley can try that 'round-the-world thing again and have a little more fun this time, with lighter bikes. I'm sure they're anxious to attack Siberia's Road of Bones again during mosquito season. Should be a piece of cake.

And a good reminder that lightness, in nearly all things, is just another form of freedom. It's those alluring extra molecules we buy that are always the trap.

25

A Trip to the Barber

WELL, THIS CERTAINLY ISN'T HOW I'D HOPED TO ARRIVE.
For years I've imagined a sportbike ride from Wisconsin down to the Barber Vintage Motorsports Museum near Birmingham, leaning this way and that through the shaded green hills of the South, dressed in full leathers, and dialing on the throttle in a road-narrowing rush of speed.

Instead, I arrived on four squishy, wide whitewalls in my huge green 1953 Cadillac Fleetwood, wearing cowboy boots and a big white Stetson.

Yep.

Last week, you see, I was on a cross-country trip with this fine automobile, doing a *Road & Track* feature story about Hank Williams' final road journey from Alabama to West Virginia. Luckily, Hank's old route passed only about seven miles from the gates of the museum, and the Cadillac unaccountably veered in that direction like a compass needle detecting a major iron deposit (or another Fleetwood) when we got close. It was fortunate, too, that my co-driver, Richie Mayer, is a lifelong motorcycle fanatic, so he was not averse to this short diversion. In fact, I think his exact words were, "If we don't stop at the Barber Museum, I'll kill you with this tire iron."

So our big Fleetwood glided into the expansive Barber parking lot and wafted to a halt in front of the museum. I'd been down here several years ago, when the racetrack and new museum were still under construction—and the bikes were housed in downtown Birmingham in the old Barber dairy truck building—but had never seen the finished product.

By now, you've probably already seen pictures of the museum with its 650-plus bikes and fabulous surrounding racetrack, or have been there yourself and are well aware that it's an impressive place. It's brilliantly realized on a vast scale, as if Dr. No or some other Bond villain had suddenly rejected the dark side and put all of his boundless energies into Doing Good—as we understand that concept.

I met George Barber a few years ago and found him to be a calm, polite, and charming gentleman, but when you look at the track and the museum, you know there's a lot of voltage humming through the man's soul. The whole facility is a tribute to the ability of a single human will to make life a lot more interesting for the rest of us on this planet.

Richie and I parked the Caddy and ambled into the museum's air-conditioned coolness. We were greeted at the door by Jeff Ray, executive director of the museum. He shook my hand and grinned, "Your old friend Brian Slark has been trying to get you to come down here for two years, and when you finally arrive he's gone to his son's college graduation. But I'll be glad to show you around."

Brian Slark—an expatriate Brit who used to ride on the Greeves ISDT team—works full time for the museum, acquiring new bikes and managing their restorations, and we talk on the phone weekly about his latest adventures.

Yes, somebody has to drive all over the country attending auctions and sizing up classic old bikes in barns to see if they belong in the world's most dazzling motorcycle museum, and Brian is the guy who bears this cross.

"Let's start on the top floor and work our way down through the other four," Jeff said.

So we took a glass elevator up past tall columns of motorcycles suspended from aluminum scaffolds. We got out at the top level, and I stopped in my tracks.

"Good Lord," I said to Richie. "Standing right here, I can see half the motorcycles I've ever owned—or ever wanted to. What a collection."

And the bikes were nicely mixed, scattered around on elevated stands and well separated so you could stroll around and look at them.

"We've tried to get away from the 'nice collection of front brake drums' you see walking down a row in some museums," Jeff said. "And we've made a conscious effort not to group them by marques. We've found that if you put all the Harleys, BMWs, or Ducatis in one spot, the owners of those bikes tend to gravitate toward that corner, without seeing the rest of the museum. When you mix them up, people are constantly surprised, and they look at everything."

Good plan. Though as the Will Rogers of Motorcycling (I never met a brand of bike I didn't like), the effect was more of unfolding delight than forced enlightenment. I stumbled across a nice example of my old Harley XLCR Cafe Racer and stood transfixed, then turned and faced similar problems with a Honda CBX. It's a terrible burden, liking so many bikes.

But during the two or three hours we spent touring the museum, a strange metamorphosis took place in my thinking.

When we first got off the elevator and I beheld so many of my favorite old motorcycles, my first instinct was to think I need to collect more bikes and hang on to them. I must have another late-1960s Bonneville like that one . . . and another CB550 like that one over there. . . .

But as the hour hand moved around the clock, I began to feel somewhat overwhelmed by it all, a victim of what a psychologist once called "option paralysis." So many bikes, so little time. I found myself doing a slow segue from unrequited desire to a mood of contented simplicity and restraint in only a few hours. From restless agitation to a strange sense of peacefulness.

As we said good-bye to Jeff and walked back toward the Cadillac, I suddenly remembered something my friend George Allez had said to me years ago.

I told him I needed money and was thinking of selling my beautifully restored Ducati Mach 1—which was not running at that moment because it had a fried voltage regulator—but couldn't bring myself to let it go because "it looks so good, sitting in my garage."

George just smiled and said, "It'll look just as good sitting in someone else's garage."

And maybe that's the real function of a place like the Barber: it's the world's most perfect someone else's garage.

26

Things Change

IT WAS AN IMPRESSIVE SIGHT. FIFTY BIKES OR MORE rumbling down the avenue from the funeral home to the cemetery. Lots of Harleys, but also a few sportbikes, the odd Guzzi, and a few BMWs. I was on my KTM 950. The only one in the group, I think. It usually is.

As you might have guessed, it was the funeral of a motorcyclist. A guy named Kenny Bahl, gone at age 75 from cancer. Kenny was a body shop owner and well-known motorcycle collector in the Madison, Wisconsin, area. You saw him at every swap meet, auction, and bike show, and he was always friendly, upbeat, and hot on the trail of some unusual old bike.

I'd say hi to Kenny, and he'd tilt his head like an alert bird and say, "By golly, Pete, there's a nice R75/5 down at the end of that row. I've already got a good one, but somebody ought to buy that thing."

I met Kenny about 35 years ago when I saw an ad in the paper for a Velocette Thruxton and quickly rode my '67 Bonneville over for a look. Kenny got there first and bought the bike, which was an immaculate, low-mileage beauty in black and gold. I hated to miss out on the Velo, but Kenny was such a nice guy I really didn't mind losing it to him. I couldn't really afford it, anyway.

A year later, I wanted to ride out to Watkins Glen with my buddy John Jaeger—who had a new BMW R90S—and realized my aged Bonneville would not be up to the task. So I decided to sell it and buy something newer.

I put an ad in the paper and Kenny showed up. "I'll trade you a really nice 1975 Honda CB750 for that Triumph," he said. Done deal; everyone happy.

After that, every time I put an ad in the paper to sell an unusual motorcycle, Kenny showed up. He ended up owning the Bonneville plus my Honda 150 Dream and a square-case Ducati 900SS.

When I finally visited his home, I discovered he had an entire rec room filled with rows of great or interesting motorcycles. And there, in the middle, was that lovely Thruxton.

Kenny was a good friend of our local Harley dealer, Al Decker. The two of them used to ride to Alaska and Daytona together nearly every year—rain, snow, sleet, or hail—usually on Harleys.

Decker was a gruff, no-nonsense guy of the old Harley dealer school, when shops had oil-stained wood floors and men didn't have tattoos unless they'd been in the Navy or Marine Corps and could fight their way out of a Shanghai gin joint.

If Al liked you, he was very loyal and helpful. If he didn't, he might not even sell you a bike. I once saw him turn on his heel and walk away from a pushy guy who was trying to negotiate a deal. He was known, if you got on his wrong side, to be "difficult."

For some reason, he was always friendly to me, even when I was an indigent, long-haired youth in the 1970s. Maybe because I knew Kenny. On Saturday mornings, we'd sit around Decker Harley-Davidson, drink coffee, and talk, with Al's huge Hound-of-the-Baskervilles-sized dog at our feet.

Al sold me three different FLHs over the years. Even during the red-hot Evo era of long Harley waiting lists, he refused to mark bikes up over MSRP. His local, regular customers came first. All others could take a hike if they didn't like it.

His shop was small and cramped, and Milwaukee, of course, wanted him to build a big, new, well-lighted emporium.

Al just shook his head. "Back in the days when you could barely give a Harley away, I sold every bike they dropped off on my doorstep. Now they want me to spend my money on a big, new building. I think it's time to retire."

And that's what he did. After he sold the business, a huge new Harley store was built out by the Interstate. Beautiful place, but not quite the same.

Al died a few weeks ago, too. The day before Kenny passed away. He was 88.

Right up the road from Al Decker's shop on Highway 51 was another favorite hangout of mine, Barr Kawasaki. Another small, old-fashioned motorcycle shop.

Bob Barr sold not only Kawasakis, but Ducatis and KTMs, so of course I had to go there about once a week to lead myself into temptation. Over the years, Bob sold me a ZX-11, three Ducatis, three KTMs, and an old Honda CB550.

All without one moment of pressure, hype, or sales pitch. If you got serious about buying a bike, Bob would go into his office, do some calculations, come back out, and hand you a scrap of paper with a price on it. It was always so fair and reasonable you just nodded and said, "Okay!"

Bob stood behind his bikes, too. He was a good man to deal with—as was his son, Steve—and I always enjoyed the low-key nature of their shop.

Last month, I went into Barr's and all the Ducatis were gone. Bob said he'd had a dispute with the company and told them to take their bikes away. Short time later, all the Kawasakis disappeared. Same story.

I won't pretend to know what business machinations were behind all this, but a few weeks later Barr closed his shop. Now the building stands empty.

So it's been a weird summer, a sort of sea-change in the scene here.

Barr Kawasaki and Decker Harley-Davidson were a mile apart on Highway 51, and Kenny Bahl lived less than a mile from both of them. A little triangle of motorcycle activity and good times, all gone.

I cruised through the neighborhood on a ride this weekend and peered in the window of Barr's old shop. Looks bigger now, all cleaned out. But you can still see sidestand divots in the checkered-flag tile floor where Ducati 916s once sat. And my KTM 950 Adventure.

Down the road, Decker's old shop is booming again. It houses a nice motorcycle parts place called Madison Motorsports and a good repair shop called Motorcycle Solutions. They just put some sticky new tires on my Honda VFR. Nice people, lots of activity.

So things change and the finite energy stored in the universe moves on and takes new shapes. But nothing—and no one—can ever really be replaced.

27

Late Interception

I'VE BEEN CALLED A LOT OF THINGS IN MY life, but avant-garde isn't one of them. Other people usually get there first.

For instance, all my friends were Neil Young and Allman Brothers fans for about two years before I suddenly realized these guys were musical geniuses and ran out and bought all their albums. And the world was essentially overrun with four-cylinder motorcycles before I finally took a test ride on a Honda CB750 in 1976. Anyone could see that light, narrow British vertical-Twins were better in every way.

Also, I still don't have a cell phone, but I may have to cave in on this one.

I was at the bookstore yesterday and wanted to call home and tell Barb I'd be a little late for dinner (as usual) because I was loading up on costly British motorcycle magazines, and I discovered the store had actually removed its pay phone from the wall.

"Pay phone?" the young clerk said, blinking in confusion. "No, we don't have a pay phone."

Her tone implied I might have better luck finding a live mastodon stuck in a tar pit.

Anyway, I'm usually a little bit behind the curve. Ideas and concepts develop slowly in my brain, kind of like beautiful crystals forming deep underground, or a termite infestation in the structural beams of your house. These things take time.

And so it was with the Honda VFR800 Interceptor.

We're talking last generation here, the 1998–2001. (I haven't quite warmed up to the current VTEC models; you'll have to give me time.)

But a mere nine years ago, when the last-generation Interceptors came out, I was visiting California from my rustic, rural Wisconsin home, and Editor Edwards was kind enough to lend me a new VFR800 testbike for the weekend.

I did what I always do, which is rip over the Ortega Highway at dawn in search of coffee at the Lookout Café and Mexican food in Lake Elsinore.

By the time I returned the bike to our office, I was fairly smitten with the red Honda.

It didn't have quite the midrange wallop of my favorite big-bore Twins, but it had surprisingly good torque for an 800 and was plenty fast. Good sounds, too, from cam gears and tailpipe alike.

At low rpm the V-Four sounded like a small-block Chevy, and on the upper end it howled like an Indy car. The off-beat shuffle at idle was interesting, too.

But what I mainly liked about the bike was its completeness. Nice turn-in, compliant yet taut suspension, comfortable seat, perfectly positioned handlebars, nice overall size. Not too big, not too small. Typical Honda controls, as if everything had been lined with teflon and velvet. Civilized, yet not to the point of blandness. The bike still had a racebike edge beneath that smooth bodywork.

I parked the bike at CW and walked away looking over my shoulder, making a mental note to resume the relationship at some point in the future.

Well, that future arrived last spring.

I was facing the summer with a mere two motorcycles in my "collection," if you don't count a Bridgestone 50 that doesn't run yet, despite my best efforts to think about working on it. I had just my Suzuki DR650 and KTM 950 Adventure.

Yes, I was—as Paul Roberts, the drummer in our garage band, put it—"Skating on thin bikes."

The DR had big knobbies on it for trail riding, so the KTM had become my main road bike. A good one, too. I could travel on it, or blast the backroads reasonably well with my sportbike buddies. It was fast, flickable, and charismatic. But . . .

But you corner differently on a big adventure-tourer with tall, skinny dual-sport tires. Enter straight, flick it in, and power out. You tend not to get a knee out, lean hard on that front tire, and ooze through an apex while dialing the power on, as you do on a sportbike. I missed the alternate riding style that comes with a big fat set of gummy street tires.

So this spring my brain shuffled through its paltry set of index cards and extracted that memory of riding the VFR in California—along with the 30 or 40 positive road tests and "Best of Class" awards the Interceptor has generated over the years. I decided I needed another sportbike, and the VFR was a likely finalist.

Lo and behold, one showed up in the classifieds of our local paper. A 2001 with 16,000 miles on the clock. Immaculate, the ad said. It was, and the owner lived just six miles from our house, so I bought it—for a reasonable price.

The bike has a Two Brothers canister on it, pleasantly growly but not too loud, as well as a Corbin seat (original included). Since buying it, I've replaced the chain and sprockets, had a tune-up and valve adjust done, and installed a set of Pirelli Diablos on the recommendation of a friend who rides faster than I do and doesn't crash. (I call this "passive/aggressive tire testing.")

So far, it's been a great summer with the Interceptor. Sunday-morning rides, weekend trips, two-up getaways into the hinterlands (Barb likes the back seat).

I'd go anywhere on this thing, and it's good to have a sportbike again, even if it's not at the sharply pointed racer-replica end of the stick.

Back when the Interceptor was first being tested in the magazines, a common editorial comment was "If I had to have just one streetbike, this would be it."

So could the VFR become my only bike?

I suppose so.

But on alternate days the KTM makes a perfect stablemate, a more raw-boned and eccentric yin to the Honda's civilized yang. The VFR is so good, it almost requires a second bike for pure contrast—something more evil and unfiltered, with larger individual bangs.

An older classic might work in this role as well. Norton Commando . . . BSA 441 Victor . . . Shovelhead Harley . . . bevel Ducati . . . the possibilities are endless.

Too endless, maybe. That's why Mr. Honda was always smiling and got so wealthy.

28

Return of the Black Beauty

A S THE MOUNTAINS OF COLORADO DISAPPEARED IN THE REARVIEW mirror of my Ford van, I noted with keen scientific interest (at about a third-grade level) that my image of the Rockies was remarkably undistorted, considering how many layers of glass and plastic were interposed between us.

I had rays of light passing through the rear windows of the van and the plexiglass windscreen of a 1981 Ducati 900SS, then bouncing off the van's rearview mirror through a pair of cheap clip-on sunglasses and my own bifocals, which are powerful enough to start a campfire if I'm ever marooned on a desert island. Five layers of stuff.

Yet the visual picture of a local thunderstorm moving in over Fort Collins was crystal clear, complete with lightning bolts sizzling out of the dark clouds and hitting God-knows-what, like the random finger of fate.

"Good screen," I muttered to myself. "Almost optically correct."

Then, of course, I swiveled the mirror downward so I could look at the bike itself. Majestic mountains are all very well, but a bike in the back of your truck is indeed a thing of beauty. The round Ducati headlight peered between the seats as if to see where we were going.

And where we were going was home. Back to Wisconsin, after seven years away.

Long-time readers of this magazine who are old enough to recall the days before grown men walked around with little telephones stuck on one ear may remember my writing about this bike.

It's a black-and-gold bevel-drive 900SS, titled in 1981 but probably built in 1980, among the last of the pure Taglioni-designed 900s. Gold FPS alloy wheels, square-case motor, café fairing, Conti "mufflers," 40mm Dell'Orto carbs, clip-ons. Bought sight unseen, a decade ago.

In December of 1997, I saw an ad for the Ducati in *Walneck's Classic Cycle Trader* and called the owner, a pleasant gentleman named Gerald Wild, who lived near Philadelphia. He mailed me some pictures (pre e-mail) and the bike looked good, so I mailed him $8,500 and he loaded the bike in a Liberty moving van.

It arrived the day after Christmas, and we unloaded it in the snow. Beautiful, clean bike, exactly as represented. I rode it all over the backroads of Wisconsin for two years, then suddenly sold it to buy . . . what?

Ah, yes. A modern Ducati 996, so I could do track days with my friends, who had similarly modern weapons of speed. Good times, no regrets.

The 900SS was purchased by one Mike Mosiman, of Fort Collins, Colorado. He drove his pickup to Wisconsin to get the bike, and we've been friends ever since.

Mike rode the black beauty for about a year, then sold it to buy . . . what?

I can't remember, and neither can he. Probably something more practical.

You see, no one needs a bevel-drive 900SS. It's a charismatic steed of narrow focus, ideal for racing and Sunday-morning rides of high intensity, but a useful daily commuter it's not.

Nor is it generally a calming influence on one's riding style. Mike got three big speeding tickets in one month.

So he sold the 900SS to his buddy Tom Barbour, an inveterate collector of bevel-drive Ducatis, old Jaguars, and vintage electric guitars.

When I was in Fort Collins a few years ago riding dirt bikes, we naturally went over to Tom's house to ogle bikes and cars, and ended up playing guitars until the wee hours of the morning. My old black Ducati was sitting in the corner of his garage, looking a little dusty. Tom confessed he wasn't riding it much anymore.

"If you ever decide to sell that bike," I said, "I'll buy it back from you." (I should just have this phrase printed on a business card with my phone number.)

Well, this past summer Tom decided to simplify his life and reduce his vehicle count to a less distracting level.

Incredibly, he offered to sell the 900SS back to me at his 2001 purchase price, even though these bikes have appreciated. A mighty test of karma, indeed.

"I'll keep it for good this time," I assured him. "It's not going anywhere—unless I get some extremely bad medical news or the bank takes the house."

So two weeks ago, I drove my Ford van to Fort Collins. Tom and his mechanic pal Norm Miller had aired the tires, put fresh fuel in the tank, and polished the paint and chrome. It looked stunning, untouched by time.

That afternoon, Mike got his new Triumph Tiger out and we took a long ride up the Poudre River canyon into the mountains. The brand-new six-year-old tires were a little hard and dry, but otherwise the bike felt great.

And it sounded good, too, those big 40mm Dell'Ortos hissing like rattlesnakes (yes, I know rattlesnakes don't actually hiss) and the twin Contis booming like a series of explosions from inside a talcum powder mine. This is a bike that can almost make you delirious from sensory overload. Why did I ever sell it?

Ah, yes, the 996.

Well, this time I'd make sure I kept some perfectly wonderful modern bike to represent the present era, and the old 900SS to celebrate the past. No either/or action this time around.

The 900SS is still a great ride, but it almost doesn't have to be. If we ran out of oil tomorrow, this is the one bike I'd keep as an artifact of the era, a reminder of what it was all about.

Everyone, I suppose, has an all-time favorite bike, and this has become mine. It represents, to me, the collision of perfect aesthetics with an ideal time in history, a small window when simplicity of line was in easy balance with clear and purposeful technical thinking.

Since I got the 900SS home, I keep making up excuses to go out to the garage and look at it. ("Barb, I think I left my wristwatch out by the parts cleaner. . . .") I can sit there for an hour, moving my chair around to view the bike from different angles.

Some people watch TV; I watch Ducati.

And, unlike TV, there's always something good on. Always will be. You just hit the light switch.

29

The Road to Harleysville

A VERY DANGEROUS THING HAPPENED TO ME LAST MONTH: I sold my 1953 Cadillac Fleetwood to a friend in California. His parents had one exactly like it when he was a kid, and he had to have the old Caddy as a keepsake and reminder of the era. So off it went to California.

When the car was gone, of course, I had two big problems on my hands:

1) Too much money in the bank for a person of my intelligence;

2) Enough empty garage space to park the U.S.S. Lexington.

I don't really need an aircraft carrier, so my next inclination was to get something smaller, such as another motorcycle. Or two.

Seems I've finally reached the age (I hesitantly admit) when I'm seriously in the mood for a small number of "keepers," favorite bikes that will stay in my garage pretty much for the duration.

The first bike on my short list of keepers was the bevel-drive 900SS Ducati I bought back from my friend Tom Barbour last month. Next on the hit list, if you will, is a Harley XLCR Cafe Racer like the one I foolishly sold seven years ago.

Most of my sportbike friends understand the Ducati re-purchase perfectly, but are mystified by my attraction to the Cafe Racer. My defense of the bike always includes words like "charismatic" and "instant, bottomless torque," but the fact is there's no good rationale. It's like trying to explain Guinness to someone who thinks beer should be translucent; you've simply gotta like the stuff.

So on a canoe trip down the Brule River in northern Wisconsin last month, I mentioned to my friend Jeff Craig that I was looking for a nice XLCR, and he said, "Oh, a neighbor of mine has one for sale that I recall is pretty clean."

Unfortunately, Jeff lives just north of Philadelphia and I live in Wisconsin, so his neighbor was not exactly freeway close. But he sent me some pictures and the bike looked okay, so last weekend I impulsively threw a ramp in the back of my blue Ford van and blasted out to the East Coast for a look.

Even if the bike wasn't exactly what I had in mind, I'd get to visit Jeff and his wife, Nancy, cruise through the Appalachian fall color, and see historic

Bucks County, where Washington crossed the Delaware and where—more significantly—Jeff has four Velocettes and three Triumphs in his garage. Not to mention a steam launch, several classic wood canoes, a Yamaha SRX600, and a Miss NGK poster.

After a day and a half of relentless driving, I exited the turnpike, drove through a town called Harleysville (yes), and a few miles down the road turned into the correct driveway. I'd zeroed my odometer before leaving home, and I glanced down as the van rolled to a stop. The odometer clicked over from 999.9 to 1,000.0 miles, on the dot. I am not making this up.

I always appreciate pointless coincidence, and driving through Harleysville to buy a 1000cc Harley exactly 1,000 miles from home seemed like a good omen.

Unfortunately, the bike was a little more thoroughly broken-in than what I was looking for. Leaking forks, mushy brakes, nicks in the paint, and more miles on the odo than expected. It was in need of much TLC to be as nice as my old one. And my old XLCR is the gold standard, the elusive Holy Grail I carry around in my head.

I hemmed and hawed for a while and actually considered buying the Harley, but decided I just didn't want to face another project. I have a Lotus Elan and Bridgestone 50 exploded in my garage right now, and was afraid a third explosion might just reduce me to total option paralysis.

Also, I have finally learned from my last few bike restorations that you just can't get there from here. Which is to say, it always costs more to restore a tired bike than it does to just go out and buy the nicest low-mileage example on earth. Plus you get to spend two years in your garage, running a bead blaster, breathing fumes, and spinning wrenches.

Not that there's anything wrong with that, if redeeming old bikes is your passion. In fact, I probably have two or three more restorations left in me—I always look forward to bringing these lost old souls back to life—but what I'm trying to avoid at this stage of my life is accidental restorations.

I knew if I replaced the leaking fork seals, I'd have to polish those corroded fork legs. And while the forks were off, I'd have to get that gas tank repainted . . . and Jet-Hot the faded black exhaust system . . . and then the engine would come out. . . .

Noble work, all. But I was looking for a nice, clean XLCR, not another chance to atone for my sins.

Nevertheless, I took the bike for a ride before I made up my mind. It ran well, and I was instantly reminded why I like these things so much. Swinging down those winding Bucks County roads, past old stone farms, colonial inns, single-lane timber bridges, and pubs with names like The Stag and Hounds, the XLCR was right in its element—thundering, torquey, and mechanically direct as a hammer.

"I must have one of these bikes," I muttered inside my helmet, "but I shall not weaken and buy this one."

Spent the rest of the weekend with the Craigs, dining and drinking well, riding Jeff's SRX and new Triumph Scrambler, visiting local bike and car shops, and looking at vintage planes at nearby Van Sant Airport. Lovely country, this part of Pennsylvania.

I drove straight through coming home. A thousand miles in 18 hours. I should have been tired, but I was fired up on a combination of coffee and desire to find an XLCR. Maybe the nicest example on earth. Or at least one of them.

And now, after being home for two days, I see on the Internet there's a pretty clean-looking, low-mileage example for sale in suburban Chicago.

I might run down there this weekend, but I should probably change the oil in my van first. And maybe catch up on my sleep. This Holy Grail business really runs up the miles.

30

The Carb Cleaner Chronicles

ACCORDING TO MY ILLUMINATED CLOCK, IT WAS 3:23 A.M. when I suddenly sat bolt upright in bed. A primal alarm bell had gone off in my head (which is nothing but a vast warehouse of primal stuff) telling me that something was wrong.

"Wazzamatter?" Barb inquired, without enunciating properly.

"I smell something. . . ." I said. "A furnace or chemical smell or something. . . ."

I sniffed the air and then realized it was just my hands. Carb cleaner and old gasoline.

Ah, yes. After working in the garage that evening, I'd showered and cleaned my fingernails with a painfully stiff brush, but it still wasn't enough to eradicate that weird combination of odors, a blend that conjures up images of a Superfund cleanup site, or the rich soil beneath an ancient automobile wrecking yard after a rainstorm. In the springtime.

It's a terrible thing when your own hands wake you out of a sound sleep, but there it is. I've been doing a lot of carburetor cleaning lately. It's almost an epidemic, by normal standards.

It started with my black 1981 Ducati 900SS, the bike I bought back from my friend Tom Barbour in Colorado (see "Ducatis & Cigarettes," page 291).

When I picked it up two months ago, it ran pretty well in the high mountains near Fort Collins. But when I hauled it downhill to our home in Wisconsin, where the air is dense and all the children are above normal, the engine started missing at around 6,000 rpm. Tom had ridden this bike only occasionally in recent years, so I suspected carb gumming in some form. Time to pull my handy Snap-On roller stool up next to the bike and remove those great big Dell'Orto 40mm carbs.

This is a pretty easy job on the Ducati, as the carbs stick out from the heads like alien eyeballs on stalks. Only BMW airheads make it easier.

On a Beemer, you could probably repair your carbs while riding down the road, if you were only more dexterous with your toes. But, alas, many

BMW owners have evolved away from that primitive state. And so have their bikes, which are fuel-injected and now repairable only by scientists or smart people.

Anyway, I got the Ducati carbs off and carefully disassembled them over a pair of aluminum cake pans. I have to be extremely methodical and talk to myself like a child when I take carbs apart so I don't lose parts or mix them up. I say things like, "Okay, now I am taking this little O-ring from the throttle-stop screw and placing it in the upper right-hand corner of the cake pan, so it will not dissolve in the carb cleaner and I will remember where it is two hours from now."

I also count the exact number of turns out on each adjustment needle and write it down, so I have some starting point when it's time to fire up the bike. As a mechanic, it's important never to overestimate your own intelligence or memory. Humility is an asset—and I have much to be humble about, as Churchill once said about someone else.

Gratifyingly, I found some strange green sludge surrounding the needles at the bottom of both main jets. Many particles of carburetor grit are so small they fall out while you're disassembling the thing, so you never get the satisfaction of saying, "Ah-HAH!" Which is half the fun.

So the Dell'Ortos found themselves sinking beneath the brownish waves in my can of carburetor cleaner like a pair of small U-boats. An hour later they surfaced, all clean. I washed them off in our kitchen sink (which now smells curiously like an ancient junkyard after a spring rain) and put everything back together.

The bike started right up. When it was warm enough, I disconnected the spark plugs one at a time and adjusted the air-mixture screws and idle speed and synched the throttles. I went for a test ride, wearing my green shop coveralls and old tennis shoes (which you never see in Ducati brochures.) Amazingly, the bike ran perfectly. Success.

I took the Ducati for a long afternoon ride, then came home and decided to give my DR650 Suzuki a little exercise, as it has knobbies on it and doesn't get much street use any more. My dirt rides are "widely spaced," so it sits a lot. The Suzuki, of course, would not start.

It would fire once or twice, spit back a few times, and then die. Choke, no choke; it didn't matter. I'd seen this before. The DR has a pilot jet with very small drillings and seems especially susceptible to carb blockage whenever it sits for more than about three weeks. I've had the carburetor completely off the bike three times in the past two years.

I've never actually seen any debris in the carburetor, but this is a ritual I have to go through to appease the carburetor gods, like a witch doctor shaking a rattle-gourd at a volcano. You gotta do what works.

And I did. Cleaned the DR carb, squeezed it back between the cursed rubber intake manifold and air cleaner, and fired the bike up. It runs fine now.

But of course my hands woke me up in the middle of the night, as mentioned. I got up and put on some of Barb's lightly scented hand cream, but it didn't work. Hopeless, like using English Leather on your horse.

So rather than waste the moment, I decided to go out in the morning and rebuild the clogged carburetor on my 1973 Jacobsen snowblower, which had also failed to start this week.

I did the job and now it runs.

The next day, I made a complex trade deal to get back my old 1977 Harley XLCR Cafe Racer. Which has been sitting in an unheated garage for seven years. I figured once you've got the carb cleaner out and are radiating stink rays in all directions like a beacon of liver damage, you might as well keep going. My hands should be back to normal by summer.

It may take that long. We went to the movies last night (*Across the Universe*), and I actually noticed the couple seated ahead of us sniffing the air and looking at each other, as if puzzled by something.

I was tempted to lean forward and say, "You oughtta hear that Ducati run."

31

High Mass

THERE WERE SUSPICIOUS TIRE TRACKS IN THE SNOW LEADING up to my workshop last Saturday when I returned home after a hard day of snowblower shopping.

Yes, our old Jacobsen unit finally bit the dust last week, so I spent the day driving around to farm-implement stores, looking for a replacement. Ended up with a new Ariens (made right here in Wisconsin, where people know about snow—not to mention the Packers, cheese, beer, and ice fishing). It has an 8-horse Tecumseh engine, and I've been telling friends I just bought a classic big Single, which takes some of the sting out of spending money on something that goes 1.7 mph.

Anyway, I came home from shopping and immediately noticed those big, aggressive tire tread marks going right up the driveway to my workshop. I parked my van, walked inside, and what to my wondering eyes should appear but a huge, flat cardboard box about the length of my workbench, all wrapped in steel bands.

"Handy Motorcycle Lift" it said in bright red letters on the carton.

Barb appeared from nowhere and said, "Happy birthday. Your present arrived early. The truck driver and I just unloaded it, and it's heavy!"

A dream come true for me. A real motorcycle lift, like the kind you see in professional motorcycle shops where dignified people stand upright and work calmly and methodically on bikes instead of writhing around on a cold concrete floor, looking for drain plugs. Pneumatic cylinder to run the scissor jack beneath it; front wheel chock to hold the bike steady; removable plate under the rear wheel so you can drop it out without fender-tweaking.

I've been working on motorcycles all my life (well, since I was 15), and have never owned a real lift. If I have to raise a bike, I usually put a flat oak board across my hydraulic automotive floor jack and raise the motorcycle very . . . very . . . carefully, while hanging onto the handlebars and watching for disastrous tipping tendencies. Precarious indeed.

A few weeks ago, I put two new Metzelers on my vintage Ducati 900SS and had both wheels off the bike while I ran them over to my friend Al Gothard's shop for a session on his tire machine. So here's this beautiful old black Ducati with no wheels, teetering on a floor jack, nearly two feet off the ground. I attached tie-down straps from the bike to an overhead beam in my garage, just to help reduce the level of paranoia, but it was still an iffy deal.

The wheels and new tires went back on the bike the moment I returned from Al's shop. I couldn't have slept that night with the bike on a jack. But then I can't leave a car engine dangling on a chain, either. It causes nightmares in which I'm visited by the ghost of Sir Isaac Newton, who shakes his head sadly and leaves me a printed copy of his universal law of gravitation, only it's in Latin and I can't read it.

Real motorcycle floor jacks, of course, are a much more stable solution to this problem, but for some reason I've never gotten around to buying one. Even these, however, can be tippy if you don't have a good flat frame or engine surface under the bike. An added problem with floor jacks is contained in the very name: they're near the floor.

Which is exactly where your eyes and hands are not, unless you're on all fours, crouching, or seated low to the ground and cross-legged, like a Hindu wise man. And as a fallen-away agnostic with limited wisdom and bad knees, this doesn't work well for me. As I found out some years ago.

I was restoring my 1967 Triumph TR-6C and spent one entire morning crouched next to the engine while I tightened mounting bolts, hooked up cables, wires, fuel lines, etc. When I stood up, my right leg didn't work. Numb as a post. And it stayed that way.

My doctor said I'd killed or damaged some nerves by cutting off the blood supply; I might get some of them back, but maybe not. I had to wear a plastic foot brace for weeks before things got better, and Barb still says she can hear my right foot dragging slightly when we take a walk. Even now, you can stick a pin into the side of my leg just above the ankle and I can't feel a thing, though I have asked my friends to stop doing this, especially while I'm speaking at public events.

So crouching is not good, but neither is kneeling. I have three pairs of coveralls with the right knee worn out, and half my blue jeans, too, rendering them useless as "airline travel jeans," at least in business class. I hate it when some woman with a laptop computer keeps glancing at my bad knee.

Both crouching and kneeling are hard on the back as well, so I spend much of my motorcycle maintenance time lying on the floor on my side, like someone trying to coax a cat out from under the bed.

Which is not all that dignified when you're almost 60. Also, it gives your coveralls that dusty, caked-on, greasy look you normally get while pulling an old engine out of a pickup under a tree, and it leaves you wondering if you shouldn't have aspired to something higher in life. Like finishing medical school, or learning Latin.

So it was with great joy that I severed the metal bands and removed the cardboard box around my new Handy Lift last weekend. It was so heavy, I had to use my engine hoist to flop it over, but I got the thing assembled and upright in no time, hooked up to the air hose from my compressor. Using my Honda VFR as a guinea pig, I rolled it onto the lift, firmly clamped the front wheel, strapped it down, and raised the bike high into the air.

I opened a Capital Amber and walked around for 15 or 20 minutes, just regarding the Honda from a whole new set of perspectives. It looked quite grand and imposing in this elevated state, like a golden calf in some biblical tale of forbidden idolatry.

The underside of the fairing was dirtier than I expected, but that can be fixed quite easily and casually now, without kneeling or other evidence of humble supplication to my small collection of sacred objects.

32

The Curious Case
of the Black Venom

"**A**RE YOU DRIVING OUT TO CALIFORNIA TO PICK UP that Velocette?" my friend Mike asked over the phone.

"No," I said. "That would take at least a week, plus all the mountain passes between Wisconsin and California are closed with heavy snow right now. And one of them is named after the Donner Party. I had the bike shipped by truck. It should be here in about a week."

"Oh man, you broke your vow!" Mike said.

"Which vow was that?" I asked. "You mean the one about not buying another bike with magneto ignition?"

"No."

"The one about Lucas electrics?"

"No, not that one."

"Ah, you're thinking of the vow about no more old British bikes. . . ."

"Nope."

"You mean that one I made in Mexico, about not making important decisions when I've been drinking mescal with no label on the bottle?"

"No! You swore you'd never buy another vehicle sight unseen!"

"Oh yeah, that one . . ."

I'd made this declaration a few years ago, shortly after buying a '53 Cadillac on eBay. I won't say the seller was dishonest, but he omitted many details that might have caused me to call in an air strike on the car instead of buying it.

"This deal's different," I told Mike. "The owner is a retired gentleman who used to work for Rolls-Royce in England. His name is Derek Belvoir, and we have mutual friends who speak highly of him. The bike looks good in pictures, too, and the price seems fair."

"Uh huh . . ."

"Also," I added by way of self-assurance, "the bike was restored by a Velocette enthusiast named Ellie Taylor, who used to make prescription goggles. Years ago, I wrote a column mentioning my interest in Velocettes, and Ellie wrote me a nice letter. He said if I ever got serious about looking for a Venom or Thruxton, he'd help me find one. And now, 20 years later, I'm buying the Venom he owned when he wrote that letter. It's a small, strange world. . . ."

A week later a big box van came slithering up our icy driveway and two guys got out and opened the back of the truck in five-below-zero degree weather. They unhooked four tie-down straps from a wood pallet and rolled a black-and-gold 1961 Velocette Venom out onto the hydraulic rear lift. They lowered it to the ground and then drove away.

The bike sat alone in the cold winter sunlight, looking great. I carefully rolled it down the shoveled snow path and into the welcome shelter of my heated workshop. My neighbor Chris Beebe (Norton Commando, Ariel Square Four, Honda GB500 owner) came over to have a look.

"Can you imagine what this bike has been thinking?" he asked. "It spends its life in sunny California, then gets loaded onto a truck and spends a week in the dark with the temperature getting colder and colder and frost forming on the inside of the truck. Then the door opens and it's here in the frozen north, getting unloaded in your snow-covered driveway. . . ."

I didn't know whether to commit suicide, move to Florida, or just feel bad for the bike, so I walked over and kicked the thermostat up another two degrees.

When Chris left, I did a light cleanup on the bike and then sat back with a can of Guinness (no tapper in my workshop, alas) to look at the Velocette.

My first British Single, ever, after a lifetime of admiration from afar. And up close as well.

I've always loved the architecture of these beautifully finished 500s from Hall Green—classics, to my mind, right in there with the BSA Gold Star or the AJS 7R. Among these, the Velocette is somehow the most "British," as if the music of Sir Edward Elgar or the novels of Thomas Hardy had been transformed into metal. If Holmes and Watson had lived long enough, they would have owned Velocettes, the motorcycle counterpart of the Webley revolver. Like Morgan cars, Velocettes held on to their conservative styling long after the world around them moved on, making no changes for change's sake.

I have no personal experience with these bikes, but friends who've owned them say they're surprisingly stout, maybe the most durable of the old Singles. A Venom did set a 24-hour endurance record at Montlhéry in 1961, averaging just over 100 mph. Another one, in high performance Thruxton tune, won the Isle of Man Production TT as late as 1967.

So why a Velocette Single at this stage of my life? (The bike arrived a few days after my 60th birthday.)

Timing and opportunity, I guess. I've been keeping an eye open for a decent 500 Velo ever since I missed out on a beautiful Thruxton in the mid-1970s. Had a photo of it taped above my desk for years. Then, last fall, I drove back to visit my friends Jeff and Nancy Craig in Pennsylvania, and Jeff has four Velos in his garage. This got the gears turning again.

When I got home I called our own resident CW Velocette nut, Mark Hoyer, and told him the hunt was officially on.

"I'm buying a KSS from a man named Derek Belvoir in Grass Valley, California," Mark said. "He's also got a Venom for sale. I'll give you his e-mail address."

Derek e-mailed me photos of the bike, and I was stunned. It was exactly the combination I would have put together, had I built the bike for myself. Thruxton tank, rearsets, clubman exhaust pipe, twin gauges, flat early-1960s seat, alloy rims, low sport bars . . . I was instantly smitten.

Still am. I've started the bike up twice in my garage, and it sounds great. While waiting for spring, I've been polishing the bike and listening to Elgar's "Serenade for Strings" on our big garage-band PA system, which hardly knows how to handle such refinement.

Nice music, but not as good as the geese I heard honking overhead this morning, headed north. I can't wait to ride this thing and see if all those old vows were really meant to be broken. Simultaneously, by just one machine of considerable beauty and extreme Britishness.

33

Radio Flyer

THE PHONE RANG LAST SATURDAY EVENING, AND IT WAS my friend Rick Olson.

"You want to ride up to Pine Bluff for the start of the Slimey Crud Café Racer Run with me tomorrow morning? I'm taking my new Can-Am Spyder."

I stared vacantly at a nearby wall, trying to picture my almost comically vintage 1961 Velocette Venom running down the road with Rick's bright yellow Spyder three-wheeler. Talk about the odd couple.

If he rode behind me, he'd look like an F-22 adjusting his thrust nozzles to get a target fix on a Sopwith Camel.

If I rode behind him, I'd look like Father Time chasing a large yellow hovercraft.

But aesthetics were not the crux of it all. We had serenity and metallurgy to consider.

"I've vowed to ride to Pine Bluff alone this year," I told Rick. "The Velocette is really happy cruising along at 55 or 60 mph, and whenever I try riding with modern stuff, I start hammering it too hard. I think I'd just like to relax and ride at my own pace."

"I understand completely," Rick said. "I'll see you up there."

Certain motorcycles, I've noticed over the years, should really be ridden solo, or only in the company of others exactly like themselves.

Back in the mid-1980s, I bought a new 883 Sportster and made a project out of it—FXE tank, low bars, rearsets, black paint, vintage tank emblems, 2-into-1 exhaust system, and so on. I guess I was trying to build a modern XLCR Cafe Racer. In any case, it was a nice bike to ride and I spent a lot of pleasant summer afternoons plying the backroads with it. By myself.

Then I foolishly took it on an all-day ride with a group of fast guys mounted on Ducatis, Cagiva Gran Canyons, BMW Oilheads, Bimotas, etc.

All of a sudden, my Sportster, which had been so enjoyable and serene rumbling solo along those country lanes, turned surly on me. I was absolutely thrashing it to keep up with the group. Gears clanged, forks dived, and the engine bellowed harshly to redline. The formerly pleasant midrange torque was not enough. The bike felt asthmatic and overmatched.

I sold the Harley not too much later, I think because that ride had taken some of the bloom off owning it. This was probably a mistake on my part. The Sportster was simply intended for a different, though perfectly pleasant, type of riding. Same with the Velocette. Riding with a gang of new sport-bikes—or Rick's Spyder—would be a similar mismatch, like taking the Queen Mother out for a date at the roller rink. Nothing good could come of it.

So I got up on Sunday morning, put on my Barbour jacket, and went out to the garage to kick-start the Velo. It started on about the ninth kick—at least three kicks shy of my total exhaustion/unbridled profanity threshold—and I was happily on my way. It ran great, thudding along the back lanes under cathedral arches of green budding trees, flicking easily through the turns along creeks and rivers.

Every vintage bike suggests its own historical place and time to me, and on a Velocette it is always 1940, somewhere in England, right in the middle of that unusually warm, clear summer before the Battle of Britain.

Yes, I know Velocettes were manufactured until 1970 and that my bike was made in 1961, but the look and sound of these things take you back to their design roots in a much earlier part of that century. They're stuck in time.

Some of this historic vibe may just be a distant echo from the Velocette factory itself, which was situated in Hall Green, a suburb of Birmingham. There's a very good chance my bike was built by people who were actually there in 1940, scanning the skies for Messerschmitts and Heinkels.

Anyway, after a 30-mile trip through pre-war England, I arrived at Pine Bluff, Wisconsin, in 2008, and there were an estimated 1,200 bikes parked in the little town. After much coffee and bike gazing, I mounted up for the 35-mile trip to Leland. I kicked the Venom many times, adhering carefully to the known ritual, but it would not fire. About six kicks past my ankle damage/profanity threshold, I accepted a quick push from some guys and it bump-started immediately.

A big cheer went up from the usual mixture of well-wishers and those who have never kick-started a big Single in their lives but enjoy the *schadenfreude* of watching some other fool try his luck.

Had a great afternoon looking at bikes in Leland, then headed home when the shadows began to lengthen. This time the Velo started miraculously on about the fourth kick, and I was on my way. My buddy Randy Wade decided to follow me on his Honda VFR800 Interceptor.

It was a nice ride, but with a VFR in the mirrors I found myself inadver-tently cruising at 65 or 70 mph, as if to show off what an ageless, competent bike I had. The clutch began to slip slightly on long hills, and the engine smelled a bit hot and oily at stop signs.

Randy peeled off for Madison, and I continued the last 30 miles alone. My speed soon crept back down into the 55-60-mph range, and the big 500 Single fell into its serene sweet spot, clicking along easily and smoothly at 4,000 rpm. I could hear birds now, instead of just the wind around my faceshield.

By the time I turned onto Old Stage Road, I was firmly back in the summer of 1940 again, without a modern car or bike in sight to tell me otherwise. I had a sudden flashback to an old *Twilight Zone* episode in which a man buys an antique radio and discovers it plays nothing but programs from the past—Glenn Miller tunes, Roosevelt's Fireside Chats, that sort of thing. Pure science-fiction nonsense, of course, but an interesting concept nonetheless.

As I neared home, the lilacs were blooming in the farmyards along the lane, and the clear blue skies were filled with contrails from aircraft.

Spitfires and Hurricanes, probably.

34

Imperial Gallons

*W*HAT WITH THE PERFECT SUMMER EVENINGS WE'VE BEEN HAVING recently, I've been going for a lot of after-dinner rides in the endless twilight we get here in the Wisconsin north country.

The only place I've ever seen with an even longer dusk is England, where being at 50-55 degrees north latitude allows you to walk home from the pub in perfectly good navigating light until about 11:00 p.m. If you can.

Here on the 43rd parallel, things are only slightly dimmer, and those summer evenings go a long way toward making up for winter, when it gets dark just after lunch.

The bike I nearly always pick for these twilight rides is my surprisingly trusty 1961 Velocette Venom, which seems to have been built for meandering down narrow country lanes. It chatters smoothly along at perfect landscape-observation speed, and the valve clatter seems to confuse and immobilize the deer.

Anyway, last week one of those narrow lanes took me into the little town of Evansville, where I stopped at the BP station (real gasoline, no ethanol) to fill up.

Doing a rough calculation, I came up with about 65 mpg on my last tank. Commendable mileage, yes, but I must admit the bike also leaks a quart of oil about every 200 miles—most of it on my garage floor—somewhat deflating my illusions of environmental virtue.

While I was putting on my gloves to flee the gas station before anyone slipped on my latest oil deposit (initiating a nasty lawsuit), a slightly over-heated old gent at the next pump finished filling his Suburban. He slammed the fuel nozzle back into its slot and came over with his lower lip thrust out, an expression I would describe as "Winston Churchill doing his famous bulldog imitation." He pointed a finger at my old Velocette.

"You're going to be seeing a lot more of those on the road!" he growled.

I turned and stared at my bike for a moment, trying to envision such an unlikely development. Row upon row of Velocettes coming toward me . . . It was like an acid dream from a Beatles cartoon.

"What?" I said, "Velocette Venoms? They didn't make very many. . . ."

He narrowed his eyes and looked at me as if I were speaking pig Latin.

"Motorcycles!" he exploded. "I'm talking about motorcycles! You're going to be seeing a lot more of them, I can tell you that!" He got into his SUV and roared away.

On the ride home, I started to ponder what the man had said

This is about the fourth gas crisis I've lived through, starting with the Arab oil embargo in 1973, and during each one people predicted a boom in motorcycle sales. But it never materialized.

Those of us who already had bikes felt more justified in our natural habits and, perhaps, rode a little more often. Meanwhile, that vast horde of timid souls who fear motorcycles remained fearful and stayed away in droves.

But maybe this time it will be different. Gas is genuinely expensive now, many sectors of the economy are doing poorly, and disposable income is down. Paying $100 to go a few hundred miles in a 6,000-pound brick suddenly seems . . . odd. We are tired of excess.

For all that, this fuel spike doesn't feel as grim to me as the 1973 crisis did. The mood is different, and I get the weird feeling that many people—despite their grousing—are actually having fun thinking of ways to outsmart the oil industry. And motorcycles and scooters are a fun solution.

Fine, you say, but does this mood translate into any real increase in sales?

The universal answer, when I called the usual suspects at the shops where I've hung out over the years, was "Absolutely!"

An old friend in California who runs a Honda/Yamaha/Kawasaki shop said, "It's for real this time. People are actually buying motorcycles to get better mileage, instead of just talking about it."

I asked what he was selling most of and he said, "The scooters are gone, and I sold out my allotment of 250 Ninjas a long time ago. Big sportbikes are doing okay, but they're moving a little slower than the small stuff."

A Triumph dealer in Iowa told me that everything's selling pretty well, especially the Bonnevilles, but says, "I'm often asked why the average motorcycle isn't getting better mileage than a hybrid or a regular economy car. I think that's a fair question."

It is a fair question. But until now, of course, it didn't matter to most people. If you could have 149 horsepower and still get 40 mpg, what difference did it make? That was as good or better than some stodgy little car, and a small price to pay for high performance and good times. Still is, even now.

But there may be a new market emerging, a demand for adult-sized bikes that specifically get mileage worth bragging about, while also keeping up with modern commuter traffic. Honda produced a whole range of bikes like this— with stunning mileage—in the 1960s. So did the Europeans, for that matter, and the Brits. We know how to do this stuff. Have forever.

So if I were designing a new bike for myself right now, it might turn out surprisingly like a modern version of the old Velocette I'm riding, a bike originally designed as real transportation in post-war England, when fuel was costly and money hard to come by.

It would be an adult-sized 500cc Single with handsome engine architecture and a dry weight of no more than 375 pounds. It would have a flat, comfortable dual-seat, quality chrome, exquisite finish, a great exhaust note, and owner-adjustable valves, and handle well enough to do track days—if anyone felt like it. It would be an object of pride, rather than just dismal utility.

Best of all, it would get better mileage than a 2,890-pound Toyota Prius. Which, of the six bikes I have in my garage, only the Velocette now does.

The only thing it wouldn't do is leak a large puddle of oil when parked. Good mileage is nice, but I hate leaving carbon footprints all over my workshop.

35

The Great Midwestern Fly-Over Tour

BOUT 23 YEARS AGO, WHEN I WAS WORKING AT *Road & Track*, the good editor strode into my highly organized office, eventually spotted me behind a pile of unanswered mail, and asked if I could fly up to the Napa Valley and do a story on a 1953 Bentley Continental R. This rare car, he said, belonged to a guy named Gil Nickel. Who owned the prestigious Far Niente winery.

I must admit that I tried to duck out of this assignment because I secretly feared the owner might be a stuffy old wine snob with an ascot, a crested blazer, and half-framed glasses hanging around his neck on a little chain. I'd seen guys like this in the movies.

As usual, I should have checked my preconceptions at the door.

Gil Nickel turned out to be as unpretentious as they come, a good ol' boy from Oklahoma who was also an avid motorcyclist. Not to mention private pilot, former rocket scientist, and racer of old British sports cars. Except for my low I.Q. and inability to plot missile trajectories accurately, we had much in common and hit it off instantly.

Gil told me that, back in the late 1960s, he and his brother had taken a couple of BMW R69Ss all the way from their home in Oklahoma to the Panama Canal. Furthermore, he'd just bought a new BMW K1 and was planning a trip through the Canadian Rockies with a bunch of his buddies who called themselves the NVTS (Napa Valley Touring Society). Would Barb and I like to come along?

Well, yes we would.

We rode a Buell borrowed from the Calgary dealer and spent a week zapping ourselves through the mountain with Gil, his future wife, Beth, and about a dozen of their wild and crazy friends, most of whom were connected with the wine business. Over the next two decades, we had reunion tours of the Ozarks, Mexico's Copper Canyon, the Colorado Rockies, the Alps, the Cascades, and northern California.

Gil's good friends quickly became ours as well. Mostly couples about our age, they liked to ride fast and party in the evening, bringing many cases of their own wine along in a chase wagon. There were about five great vineyards represented in this group, so on many evenings our brain cells were tricked into forgetting how serious life can be, and much laughter was heard. Probably from several blocks away.

As a side benefit, I quit drinking Thunderbird and Night Train exclusively and began to experiment with wines that cost more than a dollar.

On one of these trips, however, we noticed that Gil was not drinking much. Normally the life of the party, he seemed pensive and withdrawn, often regarding the rest of us with a quiet, thoughtful smile. "I think maybe he's gotten some bad medical news," Barb said. Sadly, she guessed right.

A few years later, Gil died of cancer.

We held a memorial ride in northern California the following summer. At dinner one night, we toasted Gil's memory, and someone wondered aloud where our next group tour might be.

"How about Wisconsin," I suggested in a low, nearly inaudible voice.

I wasn't really sure how this would go over. The Rockies, Ozarks, Cascades, Alps, and . . . Stoughton, Wisconsin?

Those of us who love her know Wisconsin as a green and beautiful land of ridges, hills, deep valleys, red barns, one-lane bridges, rocky harbors on the Great Lakes, towering north woods, high Mississippi bluffs, classic American small towns, and an endless network of winding roads that run through the countryside like a nicely paved nervous system.

Meanwhile, those who have never been here picture one large cornfield with a straight road running through it.

Nevertheless, the NVTS (which looks suspiciously like "Nuts" done in Roman letters) seemed open-minded and ready to ride. A few weeks ago, people started arriving at our place. Some shipped their bikes and flew in; others rode all the way from the West Coast. We had 17 people, 9 bikes, and 3 rental cars for those with health or bike-shipping problems. Seven of the bikes were BMWs, Barb and I rode our Honda VFR800, and Randy Lewis (the former IndyCar driver, now of Lewis Cellars) and his wife, Debbie, rode their Ducati ST4S.

One of the BMW guys jokingly chided me for taking the only Japanese bike on this tour, to which I replied, "Hey, Randy and I just won't ride on any brand that hasn't won a world championship. . . ."

We left on a Tuesday morning and hit the road for six days. Where did we go? Well, from Stoughton to Galena, Illinois—a scenic river town with many antique shops—and then up through the western hill country along the Mississippi to Trempealeau, Wisconsin. From there we sped into the north woods to Solon Springs, to visit the "little cabin in the woods" girlhood home of Beth Nickel.

Another long 415-mile day took us to Sister Bay on the Door Peninsula, which I like to call "Wisconsin's Cape Cod." It's the narrow thumb that pikes northeast into upper Lake Michigan. Then it was back to our house for a huge bratwurst fest and a workshop party blasted by my ineffably loud garage band, the infamous Defenders.

In the morning, after our friends left for the airport or turned their bikes toward Napa, there were many wine and beer bottles left to recycle. And a few great vintages left behind, as yet unopened.

It is said that a forest fire starts with a single match. Well, this whole 20-year tradition of good times started with a single guy who thought his friends should all ride together. Gil was the missing airplane in the formation, but the Wisconsin fly-over was all because of him.

And I think everyone had a good ride, even without the Rockies or the Alps. We kept hearing our guests remark how green and beautiful and hilly the country was, "and so many great roads—with no traffic on them!"

For anyone thinking of moving here, however, I would like to say that our state is one large cornfield with a straight road running through it.

36

Bonneville, the
Pre-Collector Edition

WHAT WITH TRIUMPH CELEBRATING THE 50TH ANNIVERSARY OF THE legendary Bonneville for 2009, I did what any crafty investor would do and ran right over to my Triumph shop three weeks ago and bought a 2008 Bonneville T100. Yes, the meaningless 49th-anniversary model!

Meanwhile, the new 2009 fuel-injected bikes were flooding in, and the shop's owner, Lyall Sharer, decided to scoop up the one new orange-and-pale-blue 50th-anniversary collector's edition and keep it for himself. As well he should.

Anyway, I saw my own particular purchase coming a long time ago, locked in as surely as fate.

About five months ago, I was paging through a Triumph accessory catalog and stumbled on a photo of a new T100 that was painted almost exactly like my favorite early Bonneville, the "Astral Red" 1970 model. Deep claret tank, with silver-aluminum "ram's horn" stripes curling across the tank, set off with gold pinstripes.

I tossed the catalog aside, leaped over our two sleeping dogs, and dialed up Sharer Cycle Center. I asked salesman John Musillami if this was actually an available color combination or just one of those enticing "Europe-only" photographs.

"We've got one right here," he said. "Just came in."

So of course I jumped on my XLCR Cafe Racer and chuffed right over there on the winding backroads.

Lyall's place is out in the country, near Verona, Wisconsin, in about as charming a setting as you can have for a motorcycle shop—at least in my demented outlook, where all the best scenery resembles something out of rural England. The shop sits on a scenic ridge, and Lyall's family runs a riding stable, so you also have white fences and a big red barn with a Union Jack painted on the side. When you're looking at bikes, you half expect the London Mail Coach to show up in the farmyard. Or maybe Susannah York.

So I throttled back the Harley to keep from spooking the steeds, picked my way through the horse apples, and pulled up in front of the shop. And there in the showroom, sure enough, was the claret-and-silver Bonneville. My brain clicked with that typical Lee-Enfield .303 bolt-action finality, and I said to John, "I must have one of these."

"But not right now," I added.

This has been quite a financial summer for us. Trees fall down, cars fail, roofs leak, cats need—I am not kidding—CAT scans. And then we had the Revenge of the Appliances. Don't let anyone tell you the Maytag man has nothing to do. Or the guy who sold us that kitchen vent hood with the howling, eccentric fan. . . . All it does is spew dead insect parts into my latest batch of Carroll Shelby's Original Texas Chili.

Protein, yes, but is it the right protein?

Anyway, there was a slight delay while I "liquidated other resources" and simultaneously discovered a wonderful new bank resource called "an instant line of credit." You guessed it: I personally precipitated the current credit meltdown.

So I eventually bought the third Bonneville of my surprisingly long lifetime, and it took almost three days to accumulate the 600 break-in miles for my requisite first oil change (straight synthetic) and dealer check-up. Before I took it to the shop, I installed a pair of Norman Hyde mufflers, adding some

much-needed throatiness to the bike. Also, they're angled slightly upward, eliminating some of that dreaded "bent-pipe" look. A carb re-jet and opening of the airbox was needed, and now the bike runs and sounds great.

In my first three weeks of ownership, I've put 1,600 miles on the Triumph, and I haven't actually gone anywhere. I've just been exploring backroads, running errands, visiting friends (more often than really makes them comfortable), and riding into the city for our Slimey Crud Motorcycle Gang meetings. I can't stay off the thing, and it's eaten into about half the time I normally spend on my trusty (seriously) Velocette Venom.

Speaking of the Cruds, there are now four new-generation Triumph Twins in the group, a Scrambler, and three Bonnevilles, so the curb in front of the Blue Moon is starting to look like a Hinckley product display.

It's hard not to like the new Bonneville. It's a genuinely comfortable bike with intuitive steering and handling. Flat seat, nice bars, effortless to ride. It also has garage appeal. It looks kind of like that 1970 Bonneville (though not as pure and purposeful, but what does?) and it has real brakes. Also, it doesn't have two sets of independent contact points mounted on a greasy movable plate, as my 1967 did. Most of all, the Triumph is fun. It brings back some magical combination of size, performance, and agility that got many of us into this sport in the first place.

For a really long trip, I might look to a larger Twin of a more thudding and laid-back nature—with hard luggage—and the Bonnie is far from being a killer sportbike of limitless top speed. But it works so well for everything else that I sometimes have a hard time remembering what other bikes are supposed to do for me that this one doesn't.

The other thing the Bonneville is not, of course, is a Scrambler. I almost bought one of these instead of the T100. Similar to the Bonneville in construction, the Scrambler is a slightly different animal. More suspension travel, a little roomier riding position for tall dudes such as myself, quicker (but less imperturbable) steering, and a 270-degree crank that lowers the torque curve and sounds neat but makes a little less power. Also very nice-looking, I think.

Lyall has one of these on the showroom floor. A leftover 2008 in tangerine and silver-aluminum. I keep stopping by to look at it.

A reckless person could have two 2008 Triumph Twins, I suppose, but that would be wrong, as Nixon once said.

Still, Nixon went ahead and did the wrong thing anyway.

He wasn't exactly my favorite president, but you have to give the guy credit for listening to his inner demons.

37

Art and the Motorcycle Museum

OVELIST KURT VONNEGUT ONCE WROTE THAT HIS SISTER, WHO WAS A professional artist, never understood how anyone could spend hours in an art museum, sitting on a bench and staring quietly at a famous painting. She claimed she could race through a museum on roller skates, give each painting a quick look, say, "Got it!" and then skate on to the next room. She thought a great painting either hit you with that magical flash of insight or it didn't.

I think we can all see the problem here: she was skating through a museum full of paintings rather than motorcycles.

I know this because I just spent a couple of back-to-back weekends visiting two famous motorcycle museums, and I never had the slightest desire for a pair of roller skates.

What I needed was a large collection of strategically placed La-Z-Boys. The kind with drink holders built into the arms. But then I can spend three hours just staring at the right side of a BSA Gold Star, so I may not be the typical art critic.

First, I went to the AMA Hall of Fame Museum in Pickerington, Ohio. I was invited to their concours to pick a favorite bike for a *Cycle World* trophy (1974 Penton 175 Jackpiner owned by Kent Knudson) and also to give moral support to our publisher, Larry Little ("Atta boy, Larry!"), who was MC at the Hall of Fame induction dinner.

Inductees this year were former Harley CEO Vaughn Beals, who helped bring H-D back from the brink during the 1980s; Rod Coates, who won the Daytona 100-miler on a Triumph 500 in 1950 and became Triumph's East Coast service manager during the glory years of 1951–1970; and Larry "Supermouth" Huffman, the entertaining and fast-talking "Voice of Motocross." Racing legends inducted were flat-tracker Terry Poovey, 500cc Motocross World Champion Rolf Tibblin, and off-road ace Scot Harden, two-time winner of the Baja 1000—and many other races.

Hearing about the career paths of these energetic guys is both inspiring and a little depressing, as it can make you feel like your own life has been, essentially, one long nap.

Nevertheless, I did summon the energy to go through the museum for several hours. It's an interesting mix of legendary racing machines, motorcycles donated by celebrities, Arlen Ness customs, and just plain neat bikes.

My personal favorite was Bill Baird's 1968 Triumph T100C, on which he won his last of seven national enduro championships for Triumph.

I stood in front of this bike for about 15 minutes, skillfully intercepting waiters with trays of hors d'oeuvres, sipping merlot from a plastic wineglass, and just looking at the thing. This bike is a touchstone for everything I found compelling about the world of motorcycling in my school and army years. I hung around the Triumph as if soaking in some kind of force field.

The following weekend, I drove 800 miles with my friends Pat Donnelly and Lew Terpstra, down to the Barber Museum near Birmingham, Alabama, for the Fall Vintage Festival. Luckily, it was raining when we got there on Friday, so we had an excuse to spend the entire day in the museum.

Much has already been written about the Barber Museum and racetrack complex, so I will just say it's the Eighth Wonder of the World. And maybe the Ninth and Tenth, as well. It seems impossible that anyone put this much time, money, and good taste into such an excellent idea.

In the evening, the museum put on a nice dinner "under the stars" on the upper floor, and the honored guests were former *Cycle* editors Cook Neilson and Phil Schilling, whose Ducati 750SS won the 1977 Daytona Superbike race with Cook in the saddle.

At a time when I was just getting into roadracing myself, these two were the guys, the personification of everything intriguing and cool about bikes, racing, and motorcycle journalism. They did important stuff, then wrote about it—beautifully.

At the dinner, they both read favorite stories they'd written. Schilling read a piece on the Moto Guzzi V-8 racebike, and Neilson read a story he wrote for *Cycle World* a few years ago, describing the reunion with their Ducati racebike, "Old Blue," at Daytona. Their words washed over the audience and created a mesmerized hush that was equal parts appreciation of their work and pure pleasure at seeing these two old friends together again.

And just when we thought the evening was over, the Barber staff rolled out a just-completed replica of "Old Blue," which they dubbed "Deja Blue." The original is ensconced in a very private collection, so the museum had Rich Lambrecht build an exact copy. Neilson took the bike out on the track later that weekend and did several laps for the crowd.

When Lew and Pat and I left the museum after dinner that evening, it took us a long time to go down the huge spiral staircase to the ground floor, past those many tiers of perfectly lighted motorcycles. We kept stopping, leaning on the railings, and just looking at bikes, silently.

No roller skates needed here. Paintings are all very well, but they're flat and you can't ride them anywhere. Also, they don't evoke the same kinds of memories.

A Rembrandt cannot transport you through a cold autumn night to visit a distant girlfriend who looks better than any painting.

Hardly any soldier is motivated to get through a year of combat duty by a Picasso brochure taped to the inside of his foot locker.

When you come home, you can't ride a Monet to a campground where firelight glitters off its frame while you sit on a log and sip tequila from a tin cup with your friends.

And when an art museum closes for the night, lights are usually turned off one room at a time, while the lights on your 1968 Triumph 500 all go out at once, saving valuable time that can be used to enjoy the starry night. Or even the dark, pouring rain.

38

Bridgestone Summer

NOT EVERYONE IS ABLE TO THROW HIS BACK OUT merely by sneezing, but I managed this difficult feat about a week ago. Since then, I've been shuffling around like one of those zombies from *Night of the Living Dead*. But—luckily for all concerned—I have no appetite for human flesh and have been getting by quite nicely on my usual diet, which is based on the premise that ancho peppers and dark beer are the basic building blocks of life.

In other words, productive garage work has pretty much come to a halt. Last night, however, I did manage to Boris Karloff my way out to the workshop and was pleased to see I was still walking fast enough to trip the motion detector light in the driveway. Never mind that I had to swing my arms around like a sailor waving off a bad carrier landing. Once inside the workshop, I turned on the heat, sat down on a shop stool and soon found myself basking in the radiant beams of guilt from several unfinished projects.

Most radiant of all, of course, was my Bridgestone 7, a sporty little red 50cc two-stroke almost exactly like the one I bought new in 1964. I wrote about this bike a while back but should probably reiterate:

About two years ago, in a rare weak moment of nostalgia, I made the mistake of telling my friend Rob Himmelmann that I'd like to have another one of these machines "someday." About 15 minutes later, he called me from a motorcycle shop in Wisconsin Rapids and said he'd found one. No title, non-running, but almost complete. How can you resist a combination like that? One Ford van trip and $200 later, I had me a Bridgestone 7.

And I've still got it.

When I first brought the Bridgestone home, I went through a flurry of work to get it running. The inside of the gas tank was a seething mass of rusty scale and brown smut, so I ran two doses of chemical tank cleaner through it, with only moderate results. Experts in dilapidation and decay have told me the next step is to rattle a mixture of small stones and tank cleaner around for a couple of hours, like someone shaking a toxic martini. This I will have to try, just as soon as I can locate the very worst clothes in my closet. Which shouldn't be too hard.

It also needs a new phenolic carburetor mount, one upper motor mount, and "a little electrical work." I installed a new battery, but nothing lights up when the key is turned on. I don't know where the stray voltage is going. Maybe fish are leaping out of a nearby pond. Probably just a ground problem—or many ground problems.

In any case, none of this promises to be very difficult. All I have to do is get to work and get it done. Which I may yet do this winter, vertebrae permitting.

In the meantime, the Bridgestone is still doing an admirable job in its main role, which is to act as a kind of three-dimensional photograph from the album of life. And, like an old photograph, it projects a sensory sweep much wider than the non-mind-reading bystander might suspect.

When I bought my original Bridgestone 7 in 1964—straight out of the display window of Lee's Hardware in Elroy, Wisconsin—I had to get a small bank loan, and my dad laid down strict conditions before signing off: the money I was making in our family printing office ($1/hr.) would go exclusively into my dreaded College Fund. I would pay off the Bridgestone using money earned elsewhere, working evenings and weekends.

So I found two other jobs. One was mowing the local Catholic cemetery, and the other was working as a line-boy at the nearby Wonewoc Airport. The latter job suited me perfectly. I was a tri-polar motorcycle/car/airplane nut (picture Saint Patrick's famous Holy Trinity allegory, using the shamrock), and I had just taken a winter ground school and passed my FAA written pilot's exam. My dream was to become a professional pilot—fighters first, of course, and then the airlines.

With this new job, I'd be able to ride my Bridgestone to the airport on the weekends, work around airplanes, and possibly trade a little of my labor for a short flying lesson now and then. During the long summer evenings, I'd ride to the cemetery and mow until dark.

And that's exactly what I did. The Catholic cemetery was dutifully mown, and my original pilot log—which I am still using—shows that I had three flying lessons of 15-, 30-, and 20-minute duration in 1964, the first flown in an Aeronca Chief, the last two in a 7AC Aeronca Champ.

Then my dad made me quit flying to save more money for college and pay off the Bridgestone. He didn't believe in the full Trinity, apparently. By the time I went back to high school that fall, the bike was indeed paid off.

So that Bridgestone 7 sitting in my garage now may look like a cheap Japanese two-stroke and smell like stale gas to the average onlooker, but to me it still looks like a reasonably bright future and smells like fresh summer grass clippings, premix smoke, av-gas, airplane fabric, and nitrate dope.

Not to mention the aroma of the carefully hidden Camels I used to smoke while leaning on a tombstone at the cemetery, watching the sun go down after a hard day of printing or working on airplanes and mowing.

Strangely enough, I just finished a check ride last month in an airplane called a Citabria, which is nothing but a higher-performance, aerobatic version of the Champ in which I took some of my first lessons. I'm renting the plane now, and flying it about one hour a week.

I've been trying to save for a Citabria of my own this year, but haven't made much progress in this brave new economy of ours. There's no college fund anymore, but reality keeps intruding in fascinating new forms—car repairs, roof trouble, vet bills, retirement "investment" plans, etc. The less said about that last expense, the better.

Maybe I'll have to get a bank loan for the airplane and find a couple of part-time jobs to make the payments. Then I could save on gas by riding my Bridgestone 7 to the airport when I go flying next summer.

In some lives, progress is so faint as to be indistinguishable from regression.

39

The Captive Enfield

IT'S A QUIET WINTER DAY TODAY WITH SNOW DRIFTING down in big dreamy flakes, like the ones we made with scissors and folded construction paper in Miss Podruch's third-grade class and then plastered to the classroom wall with our names written on them. ("Why would anybody name a defective snowflake Pete?")

Anyway, the snow is piling up, so of course I did what anyone would do on a day like this and retired to the garage with a cup of coffee to look at my stationary bikes and ponder Man's fate in the encroaching Ice Age.

And one of the stationary bikes I've been staring at a lot lately is an Indian-made Royal Enfield Bullet 500—the one that was shipped to me for a riding impression late last fall.

I got in one good ride before the first winter storm hit, wrote about it for our March issue, and now the bike is sitting in the middle of my workshop, awaiting shipment back to its rightful owners. With the snowdrifts in our driveway, I'd wager it's not going anywhere soon.

The Bullet takes up a little extra space in my already cluttered workshop, but I don't mind. I enjoy having it around, partly because it's just a naturally good-looking bike and partly because the sight of it brings back fond—nay, almost pungent—memories of traveling in India.

I went to India with my friend Chris Beebe back in 1986, on the invitation of a tall Sikh gentleman named Kirit Singh. During the 1970s, Kirit, Chris, and I were all car mechanics at a place called Foreign Car Specialists in Madison, Wisconsin. Chris owned the business, and Kirit had a workbench right next to mine. He specialized in Fiats, and I specialized in MGs and Triumphs. All of which—you will note—are gone now from our shores.

After learning his trade in the United States, Kirit eventually returned to India and opened a large repair shop in New Delhi called (I kid you not) Foreign Car Specialists East. We stayed in touch, and Kirit invited Chris and me to visit India and take a car trip.

"We could drive across northern India into Nepal and see Katmandu and Mount Everest," he suggested. And that's exactly what we did.

When Chris and I arrived in New Delhi, we soon realized that—other than huge Tata trucks and small three-wheeler cabs—there were only two kinds of private cars and motorcycles on the roads of India, all of them Indian-made copies of old British (and Czech) vehicles designed in the 1950s. The cars were the Hindustan Ambassador (a copy of the Morris Oxford sedan) and an Indian version of the Triumph Herald.

The two motorcycles available were a 250cc two-stroke Jawa lookalike called the Yezdi and the thumping four-stroke Royal Enfield Bullet, available in 350 and 500cc models. There were almost no "foreign" cars or bikes.

We were told that Indian Prime Minister Jawaharlal Nehru had legislated against importing foreign vehicles in order to provide jobs for Indian workers and to throw off the yoke of colonial dependence. The model range was limited in order to save resources and to keep life affordable and simple. Their vehicles were frozen in time.

This certainly did make life simple—especially for mechanics. Kirit's shop had only two kinds of cars to repair, all with interchangeable parts from one decade to the next. Need a new cylinder head for your Hindustan Ambassador? No problem. We've got about 50 of them, ready to go.

Likewise, every little village in India seemed to have an Enfield and a Yezdi shop, all of them stacked to the ceilings with spare fenders, forks, wheels, tires, engine parts, cables, etc. If your Bullet broke down between, say, Gorakhpur and Lucknow, it was no big deal. Just push or tow it into the next village and get it fixed. All parts were in stock, and everybody knew how to work on the bikes.

But we soon discovered that, beyond the anointed four models of cars and bikes, India's narrow rural roads were crowded with other things. Elephants, baboons, oxcarts, camel caravans, bicycles, mendicants, monks, children chasing hoops, and many, many pedestrians.

And when those huge Tata trucks came roaring down the road, they didn't move over for anyone. Our Ambassador had to hit the ditch constantly, tucking in with the animals, farm carts and pedestrians. Sometimes there was nowhere to go. It was nerve-wracking to drive a car in India. Chris and I quickly reached the same conclusion on our first day: cars are too wide here; bikes are ideal.

After three weeks on the road, we somehow made it back to New Delhi alive, but felt that we had used up all our luck. We vowed that, if we ever took another trip here, it would be on Royal Enfield Bullets. They're exactly the right vehicles for the country roads, and those repair shops in every town are not only reassuring but almost inviting.

So as I sit and look at the new, improved Bullet in my wintry garage, 23 years later, it brings back memories of warm weather, excellent Indian food (which I still crave at regular intervals), the mind-boggling exoticism of the overlapping cultures, ancient temples, stately remnants of the British Raj, good company, and the open-ended notion of an ideal trip still not taken.

And then there's the beauty and simplicity of the machine itself.

I must have a little Nehru in me. Things that can be repaired simply—and locally—seem to have more and more appeal in our currently weird economy. I've already vowed that all future car and bike restorations (if I'm dumb enough to start any) will be done on vehicles where I can do nearly everything myself.

The Bullet in my garage, of course, isn't a project and doesn't need any work. It's a brand-new bike, ready to go—an improved and upgraded factory-fresh non-restoration of a classic, if you will.

There's much to be said for a "vintage" bike that lets your bead-blaster and micrometers gather a little dust. Harley and Triumph have had good luck with this concept. At least in my case.

40

The Empty Bookshelf

LAST MONTH, THE PUBLIC LIBRARY IN MY HOMETOWN OF Elroy, Wisconsin, invited me to speak at a Saturday afternoon "Local Authors Day." My friend Pat Donnelly asked me how many people I thought would be there, and I said, "Well, if Mary Waarvik, the librarian, doesn't show up, I'm going to be very disappointed."

Luckily she did, along with about 45 other people, many of them old high school and family friends. A sympathetic audience, in other words, and I'm pleased to report that I wasn't physically attacked for talking way too long, after pretty much describing my entire life and career. Except for the part where I set Milne's field on fire while smoking "used" cigarettes, scrounged off the sidewalk on Main Street while pretending to tie my shoe.

Some things you have to leave out or people get bored.

It was kind of strange, standing at this lectern in the library, because I could glance through a window behind the audience and look right up the hill at 309 Academy Street, the house where I grew up. Clearly visible, as well, was my second-floor bedroom window. This beatific vision, of course, prompted an anecdote.

I recalled that my dad once said all my actions when I was a kid followed a predictable pattern. "You'd go to the Elroy Theater," he said, "watch a movie about paratroopers, and then go straight down to the Elroy Library and bring home every book they had on the subject. Then you'd make a parachute out of an old bed sheet and jump off our roof and sprain your ankle."

My dad was exaggerating, of course. I didn't jump off the roof—I jumped out of my second-story bedroom window—and I didn't sprain my ankle. I hurt my back, and it still hurts today.

He was right, however, about all those inspirational movies and books. Architecture also may have been a factor.

Our library was one of the most elegant buildings in town, a classic brick edifice built with a grant from the Carnegie steel fortune. Here in this little midwestern town was a building that could just as easily have been sitting on campus at Cambridge University. Leaded glass windows . . . beautiful, dark woodwork . . . the smell of leather binding. . . . Like the reading room of the Royal Geographical Society, it was a great jumping-off point for possible adventures to the Congo or Timbuktu.

Or just jumping out of your bedroom window with a sheet for a parachute.

Yes, the library had inspirational books on deepest Africa or the 101st Airborne, all right. But what it did not have was a single book about motorcycles.

They had probably 10 books about dinosaurs—which you never see any more—but no mention of motorcycles, which could sometimes be observed passing by on the street.

If you went to see *Lawrence of Arabia* or *The Great Escape* or even *The Wild One* and emerged from the Saturday matinee wishing to read about Brough Superiors or Triumphs or Harleys, you were out of luck. There were only magazines—such as *Cycle World* or *Cycle*—available at the local drug store. Asking the librarian for a book about Harley-Davidsons was about like requesting a copy of *Cheerleaders in Heat*. She'd probably make a quick call to your parents.

But this was before what you might call "The Age of Epicureanism." Most people in the 1950s and 1960s had neither the money nor the inclination to collect things—or to chronicle their industrial history. As a result, there wasn't much market for a book on, say, Triumph Twins. Why would you spend money on a book about old Triumphs when you were desperately saving every dime for a new one? Old crap was just old crap, and new stuff was almost always better.

For the truly intrepid, however, there were actually some good motorcycle books in print, and most of them came out of England, where people were apparently more disposed to nostalgia for outdated Sunbeams and Ariels. But these had to be specially ordered from ads in bike magazines.

A quick check of my January, 1965, issue of *Cycle World* (which I just happen to have right here in my files, purchased from Lawrence's Drug Store, about a block from the Elroy Library) reveals on page 61 a full-page ad from Motor Racing Books in Englewood, California. There are 52 titles available, nearly all of them British imports.

One of them, *John Surtees' Motor-Cycling Book*, I actually have on my bookshelves, only because a kindly reader named Patrick Haley sent it to me a few years ago. I remember wanting this book at the time, but couldn't afford the extravagant $4 cover price because I was saving for a Honda Super 90.

So I got through high school—and my college and army years—with absolutely no motorcycle books. Zero. Just piles of magazines, which had road tests and ads for new stuff—all a man needed.

The first motorcycle book I ever bought, in 1973, was *Racing Motor Cycles* by Mick Woolett, an excellent read made even more excellent by a photo of Don Emde's stunningly cute sister standing with him in victory lane at Daytona (page 83). There were some nice pictures of motorcycles, too.

And now I must have at least 100 motorcycle books on my shelves. More than I need, really. Some I look at all the time, while others are basically redundant.

So when I went up to Elroy to speak last month, I put together a small collection of representative motorcycle books—Ducati, Triumph, Harley histories, etc. —and donated them to the library.

I figure if some kid comes out of the Elroy Theater (which I am pleased to see is still in business) after a motorcycle movie, he or she should be able to walk down the street and find a little inspiration to ride. Or travel or fix up an old bike or maybe just have some background history to read.

So, there you go, my selfless good deed for the year. But I'm not donating any of my paratrooper books. Too dangerous when they fall into the wrong hands.

41

Climate Control

"**WE'LL HAVE TO TAKE THOSE TOES OFF RIGHT ABOUT** here," Dr. Richard Hill told me last week as he made a hatchet-like chopping motion with his hand.

I looked at him for a silent moment, and then he grinned. "Just kidding," he said, "but you did manage to get frostbite on three of your toes. They should be fine in a few weeks, but try not to freeze your feet again from now on."

Dr. Hill and I grew up together in the same small town, and somewhere I've got a photo of him attending my seventh birthday party, at which I am inexplicably wearing an army uniform (my sister says I look like a member of the Hitler Youth), so he never hesitates to kid around and give me a hard time.

In any case, I was relieved to learn that I wouldn't be joining the ranks of Everest and K2 veterans by losing any toes. Sadly, nothing as romantic as mountain climbing had transpired. I got frostbite simply from a bad combination of activities. First, I stood on the cold slab floor of my workshop while adjusting the chain on my Triumph 900 Scrambler, and then (feet already numb) went out to snow-blow the driveway with a wind-chill of 46 degrees below zero.

I took this frostbite episode as a message from God that I need to 1) find myself a pair of RAF-style sheepskin boots, and then 2) move to a warmer climate.

So I've spent several evenings this week looking at websites for warmer boots and real estate or just staring at maps.

That and checking air-park communities in Trade-a-Plane. Florida, Georgia, the Carolinas, and Texas are full of them. Arizona and New Mexico, too.

I have this dream that the ideal residence would be a home with a large hangar/garage on an airstrip. That way, I could go flying without paying hangar rent, have plenty of garage space for bike and car projects, and also hang out with people who are sympathetic to interesting machinery rather than, say, golf or stultifying bovine tranquility.

I've found that people who live in air parks don't consider the exhaust note of a Ducati 900SS or a Continental 220 radial to be "noise." Nor are they likely to object to the sound of a table saw, a Bridgeport lathe, or a two-stage air compressor—or the smell and sizzle of arc welding.

Also, hangars are always full of interesting cars and motorcycles, so even if you lose your medical and can't fly, it's still a great environment.

So I've been looking at real estate and maps—as I do every year about this time, when Wisconsin goes all Siberian on us. It's an annual tradition but this year I've ratcheted up the seriousness. Maybe it's the toes, which are aching slightly even now, pulsing like an emergency warning light.

The problem, when you look at a map of the United States, is that there is something wrong with every part of the country. All states are a compromise, and no place is exactly perfect. We are not yet dead and ascended to Heaven, it seems.

Here are a few examples:

California—You can ride all year, but there's too much traffic in many of the (formerly) best places. If you live in the Los Angeles or Bay areas, it also takes forever to get out of town—and even longer to get back home on Sunday night. Also, real estate is high. Even with the current mortgage meltdown, Californians have not been able to face the fact that $700,000 is still too much for a two-bedroom double-wide on an alley next to a propane storage facility. Still, you can ride all year, and there are some idyllic spots, if you can somehow survive without glitzy stores.

Florida—Wonderful winters, really hot in the summer; only about 14 real curves in the entire state—and half of those are at Daytona. Lots of shrunken old people piloting apparently driverless large yellow sedans with white vinyl tops. Alligators eat your Chihuahua. Hurricanes cut your power while all the hamburger in your freezer goes bad. Huge cockroaches pose as "Palmetto bugs." Fire ants! Great property prices, though (another foreclosure hotbed), and a nearby ocean. Good orange juice and grapefruit. Short drives to Daytona and Sebring. The Keys are nice for a laid-back cruising ride.

The Southeast (Virginia, the Carolinas, Georgia) —Not too much wrong here, if you get a little mountain elevation, away from the hot coastal plain. Great roads, but if you take them far enough back into the hills, you can find rednecks who have more banjo strings than teeth. On the other hand, we have the same rednecks here in Wisconsin, and they can't even play banjo. I don't know what they do with their time. Complain about the weather, I guess. And freeze their toes. The Piedmont region of Virginia is quite beautiful and—I must admit—beckons strongly. Still has some winter, however, with the occasional ice storm. Humid summers.

The Southwest—Oven-hot summers but nice winters. You have to like the desert—which I do—otherwise it's quite brown and beige. Big gaps between rich and poor in many areas. Danger of "Kokopelli" and turquoise overdose. Brain-damaging levels of mystical Hopi flute music in bookstores.

Texas—Big. I like Texas a lot and have many friends there, but there's always danger of real weather sliding down off the Great Plains like a broken shingle. Still, it doesn't happen every day. . . . Food for thought.

The Northwest—Rain, but I'm told it's a relatively warm rain. You have to wonder about the temperature, though, in a place where people are so fixated on high-end coffee . . . .

Back to Wisconsin—Amazing network of roads through green hill country; great racetracks, nice depth of overlapping European cultures; lakes, woods, good road houses, supper clubs, and small-town cafés.

And five blasted months of winter.

Spring will come soon, though, and then I'll fall in love with this place all over again and develop Winter Amnesia. Next November I'll find myself trapped again.

If I don't escape this year, look for an even more strongly worded version of this column next winter.

42

Upturns and Downturns

ON MY CAR RADIO THE OTHER NIGHT, THERE WAS a psychologist giving advice on how married couples should handle the stress of the current economic downturn.

He said (and I paraphrase here, not having had a tape recorder on me):

"I would advise you to think back on what life was like when you were young and first married—the apartments, the budget meals, the cheap jug wine, the old cars—and ask yourself if it was really so bad. Was it the worst time in your life? Probably not. It may even have been the best. Sometimes it's not so bad to take yourself back there to a time of less stress and simpler pleasures."

Hmmm . . .

Easy to say, I thought to myself, if you don't have three kids in school and a mortgage—as so many in our own hard-hit county now do. Like telling people on the Titanic to savor their excellent new swimming opportunities.

Simplicity is a luxury not everyone can afford. Still, the man's point was worth pondering. Especially for some of us—like Barb and me—who are presently downsizing and scaling back a bit, as she's retiring this summer.

I shut off the radio and tried to reflect on the pros and cons of our own more frugal past. Would we want to go back there?

After I got out of the army in the early 1970s, I finished college and graduated with a shiny new journalism degree in December of 1972. Minutes after I got my diploma, someone phoned Wall Street and told them to flip on the Recession Switch.

There were no jobs. And I mean none.

The economy was in the dumpster, and newspapers were folding all over the place. Every time I applied for a writing job, the editor would roll open a file drawer and say, "Here are some job applications from people who used to work for the *Chicago Sun Times*. Should we hire them or you?"

Suitably browbeaten, I looked for other work. I had applications rejected for driving a garbage truck, driving a laundry truck, selling cameras at a camera shop, and stenciling road signs for the highway department. Finally our landlord, a good guy named Jim Corcoran, hired me to install rain gutters for his sheetmetal company.

I did that for about two years but finally quit one day after my extension ladder blew over in the wind—with me on it. I saved myself by whipping out my claw hammer and digging it into the sill of a third-story window, like a mountain climber with an ice axe.

Finding myself miraculously still alive, I took a job as an apprentice foreign car mechanic (starting wage, $2 per hour) and did that for seven years.

I enjoyed this career a lot, but during those early years of the 1970s I wasn't exactly buying yachts and caviar. Or 750SS Ducatis. Luckily, Barb had a job as a physical therapist at a nearby hospital and we got by.

We rented the upstairs of a nice old house in a shady, tree-lined neighborhood, where we had big spaghetti dinners and threw parties at which people drank gallons of Hearty Burgundy and Boone's Farm Apple Wine and listened to the Allman Brothers loud on the stereo. For further cheap entertainment, we went to $1 movies on campus, regularly turning our sofa upside down for loose change to get the money. For transportation, we owned a slightly rusty 1968 Volkswagen Beetle.

And a brand-new, dark green 1973 Honda CB350.

Which Barb bought for me as a birthday present in the frozen darkness of February, when I was feeling about as low as I've ever been.

She'd been secretly setting money aside in her credit union at work to come up with the $869 required. I wrote a column about this bike some years ago, so I won't dwell on it again.

But we had a place to live, good friends, a running car, enough to eat and drink—and a motorcycle.

Furthermore, I owned a Bell 500 TX helmet (still sitting here on my shelf), a black Buco roadracing jacket (still hanging in the closet behind me), and a pair of Red Wing work boots (long gone) that I wore on my job. We also owned a tent and an Optimus camp stove.

When we moved, virtually everything we owned—except the CB350 and the Volkswagen—fit into a friend's Chevy van.

Bad times?

No, they were not.

Sometimes, these days, I fly out to California to work on a *Cycle World* story. When I'm there, I generally stay with my sister, Barbara, in the nearby community of Irvine. I try to travel light, with one big duffel bag that contains my helmet, a leather jacket, and a pair of boots, as well as the few clothes I actually wear on a daily basis at home. Blue jeans, a few shirts, a sweatshirt.

All the necessities. And when I'm there, I usually borrow a testbike from CW to ride, so that's taken care of, too.

After a few days at my sister's house, I sometimes look at my riding gear, the contents of my suitcase, and the motorcycle out in the driveway and say to myself, "What, exactly, is all that other stuff I have at home?"

My mind goes blank, and I can't even picture what it is or why I need it.

At these moments, I realize that many of us—especially people in my generation—have come to believe that we need a great many possessions to be happy. But I think the guy on the radio was right; it isn't so.

When you get your mind straight, all you really need is friends, family, and the basics.

And, of course, one good bike.

Or just one old, troublesome bike. Any bike, really. Big, small, new, old—it doesn't matter.

One of the compensations of being a dedicated motorcyclist is that you could live quite happily in a small camper on the back of an old pickup truck—as long as you had a bike.

Maybe more happily.

In fact, sometimes when you look at all the complicated paraphernalia you've gathered around yourself, it might even be the dream.

43

This Is Your Brain on Motorcycles

AFTER SPENDING A SUNNY AFTERNOON OUT IN OUR YARD yesterday—raking up the leaves I should have raked last fall—I was too tired to make anything but popcorn for dinner, so I made a big batch and kicked back to read for the evening.

Casting about for something deeper and more intellectually stimulating than the usual pile of old motorcycle traders that dominate my "reading," I sifted down and discovered an actual book—yes, a thing with hardly any pictures—that my sister, Barbara, gave me last Christmas. It was called *This Is Your Brain on Music: The Science of a Human Obsession* by Daniel J. Levitin.

Only right that she should have given me this book. My sister ruined my life in 1956, when I was eight years old, by letting me listen to her 45-rpm copy of "Hound Dog" by Elvis Presley.

I played it on a record player that looked like a small suitcase and listened to it about 8,000 times, mesmerized by the beat and sound, trying to imagine where in the world this atmospheric magic could have come from. Certainly not my small hometown in Wisconsin, where bands with names like The Jolly Drunken Swiss Boys were playing at the Legion Hall.

Thus began a lifetime addiction to rock-n-roll, blues, etc. —or any music without tubas in it . . . .

So naturally I dug into Levitin's book with anticipation, spurred on by one of the thematic bullet points printed on the back cover: "Why we emotionally attach to the music we listen to as teenagers."

Hmmm . . . interesting subject. Maybe if Levitin could explain why I still crank up the radio for the Stones or Mitch Ryder, he could also unravel the mysterious attraction to bikes from my own formative years—if you call this "formed."

It can't be an accident, after all, that I now own two modern Triumph Twins that (almost) look like they could have been made while I was in high school, or that I still get all weak in the knees when I go to a swap meet and stand next to a Honda 305 Scrambler, a Harley Panhead, or a Bultaco Metralla. Or that I currently have the hots for another Road King, which is nothing but a modern iteration of the first motorcycle I ever rode upon.

Was I mentally ill, or was this normal? Perhaps the book would tell me.

So, I picked it up and started to read. I won't attempt to summarize the whole volume, because I could barely understand it, but the gist of it seems to be this: Our brains are rapidly developing during our teen years, filling with new information and forming thousands of new circuits, like a spontaneously self-generating wiring harness in a BSA 441 Victor, or—in the case of our more intelligent friends—a car with too many seatbelt buzzers and Check Engine lights. This process slows down sometime in our 20s, and we are stuck with a relatively hard-wired set of ideas and preferences. Levitin refers to this framework of personal tastes as your "schema."

Okay, this makes sense. But it doesn't explain everything.

For instance, I grew up in the 1950s and 1960s, and hit the 1970s in my early 20s, and I admit to being heavily influenced by the sights and sounds of that era. Yet I've never really felt "stuck" there. I like 1960s motorcycles, Triumphs especially, but I'm grateful I don't have to depend on them for transportation these days. And there have been lots of favorites since then.

The Ducati 916, for example, a bike to which I was instantly attracted when it came out in 1994. That thing no more resembled my first Honda 160 or Bonneville than the Space Shuttle looks like a Piper Cub. Yet I took one look at the 916 when it was introduced and said, "Oh yes, someday it shall be mine." By the time I got my money together, it had become a 996, but never mind that. It looked the same.

And then there's the KTM 950 Adventure. A less likely and more daring set of shapes has seldom appeared on two wheels—there seems to be no styling precedent at all—yet I took an instant liking to the bike and even bought a second one after a friend crashed my first.

I once described my black 950 as looking like a chess knight carved from ebony. I suppose this could have come from watching too many "Paladin" episodes on TV when I was 12. But, regardless of these brain-damaging psychological roots, the shape still looks timeless to me.

Flipping back to the other end of the time-space continuum, we also have to ponder the eternal appeal of the Harley Knuckleheads of the 1930s, or the beauty of the Henderson Fours of the 1910s and 1920s. These are machines made long before I was a gleam in anyone's eye, yet I'd love to own either bike—in a just world, where I was fabulously wealthy.

So I think Levitin was partly right. We obviously do connect with sights and sounds from our own developing years. And yet nearly all of us can easily escape that nostalgic box when the right object appears. Some designs are so good that they easily break through the artificial time barrier constructed by our youthful brains.

Years ago, I was sitting around with a bunch of guys having a deep, garage-quality discussion on car and motorcycle design, and someone inevitably concluded, "Well, I guess beauty is in the eye of the beholder."

There was a long silence, and then my buddy John Jaeger said, "No, it isn't."

We all looked at him, and he said, "That might be true with people, but I don't think it is with machines. I don't think an AMC Pacer ever looked as good as an E-type Jag, and a Ducati Indiana will always be less beautiful than a 750 Super Sport. There are real standards in this world. Some things are just better than others."

I'd have to say I agree with John, for the most part. When good stuff comes along, it's just plain good. Doesn't matter when we grew up.

Although it's quite clear that Triumphs looked especially excellent when I was in high school. . . .

44

Riding the Roof

WHEN IN THE COURSE OF HUMAN EVENTS IT BECOMES necessary to attend a family reunion, you can thank your lucky stars if it's hosted by a couple of avid motorcyclists who just happen to live on a mountainside overlooking Estes Park, Colorado.

I speak here of Barb's cousin, Gary Rumsey, and his charming wife, Bonnie, who live right in the heart of Rocky Mountain National Park.

I'm not saying you should absolutely not attend a family reunion held in, say, Normal, Illinois, hosted by a cousin who collects Hummel figurines, but you're much less likely to shoot yourself or suddenly cultivate a heroin habit while hanging out with fellow riders in the mountains of Colorado.

Yes, there we were, at about 7,200-foot elevation, standing on the deck of the Rumsey's mountain home, surrounded by a cirque of snowcapped peaks that looked like a backdrop for *The Sound of Music*, only with more cowboy boots and fewer examples of lederhosen. Stunning scenery, clear air, and smooth, twisting roads leading off in every direction.

Later, we retired to the living room to look at early family photos that were (I know you won't believe this) truly fascinating. The family is old American pioneer stock that farmed in Kansas and survived the terrible Dust Bowl years and then moved to Colorado after World War II. You see photos of Barb's dad on the farm with his three brothers, all dressed in their Sunday best. Hats, nice ties, and suits.

Behind them are the dusty plains, farm machinery, and gray, wind-blasted barns, but the brothers all look like Clark Gable or Tyrone Power in downtown Manhattan. Dignity and class in the hardest of hard times. The no-excuses generation.

So, the old family pictures were good to see, but my own favorite historic document of the evening was a map rather than a photo. After the slideshow, Gary took me aside and unfurled a large map of the United States, with all his lifetime motorcycle trips highlighted in black pen. Gary's been riding and touring all his adult life (he currently has a BMW R1150RT in the garage), so his route map looks like the wiring diagram for my Lotus Elan, only less prone to fire. He's been almost everywhere.

"I've often thought of doing this," I said, looking at the map. "Maybe I will when I get home—if I can still remember where I've been."

If I were to make such a map, of course, a lot of those highlighted routes would lead to Colorado.

You can always start a lively debate about the best state in the Union for riding motorcycles, but I suspect Colorado would make it into the top three for anyone who's ever been there. When you have a state "sometimes called the Roof of North America because between 50 and 60 peaks reach 14,000 feet or more above sea level" (according to my ancient *World Book Encyclopedia*), the riding pretty much has to be good.

I've been there so often I've gradually developed a mental road map of favorite places. The Black Canyon of the Gunnison, the Million Dollar Highway from Durango to Ouray, Highway 67 up to Cripple Creek and Victor . . . well, the list goes on and on.

And those are just the paved roads. . . .

Paved or dirt, there are almost no bad roads in Colorado, once you get west of the Front Range. I have favorite old Western towns, too: Craig, Montrose . . . . And our favorite Mexican restaurant used to be a place called the Stockmen's Café in Montrose, where we always stopped on our many backpacking and motorcycle trips in Colorado. Unfortunately, it was closed last time we passed through but scheduled to reopen. I hope it did. Once you ride in Colorado, you just keep going back.

But we didn't have to on this trip.

We said good-bye to the extended family and drove down the Big Thompson River canyon (in a Honda Odyssey, with Barb's sister Pam and brother-in-law Richard Ripp) to visit our friends Mike and Bonnie Mosiman in Fort Collins. Mike has an ever-rotating collection of motorcycles in his garage, so of course we immediately put on riding gear and went right back up into the mountains, this time along the Cache la Poudre River canyon.

I rode his Triumph 900 Scrambler (with its euphonious Norman Hyde exhaust) and Mike took his new BMW F800GS. Two other suspicious characters rode with us—Scott Barber on his BMW R1200S and Dave Scott on his beautifully restored R60/5. Dave is another survivor of our off-road trek through Mexico's Copper Canyon two years ago, during which Mike tried to murder us by taking a "scenic shortcut" through the mountains to Batopilas, as recommended by a drunken German in a cantina. Nevertheless, we are all still alive and have almost forgiven Mike. Though if I were him I wouldn't quit sleeping with that gun under my pillow just yet.

Anyway, we had a great ride up the Poudre before an evil, glowering thunderstorm turned us away at Cameron Pass. The downhill trip was like a dream of flying, with white rapids crashing through the rock gorge on the way down.

That night, we all had margaritas and enchiladas at the Rio Grande Mexican Restaurant in Fort Collins. We were joined by Tom Barbour, the musician/Ducati buff who was good enough to sell me back my original old black-and-gold bevel-drive 900SS last year.

Nice town, Fort Collins. Not too big, not too small. Good friends, great roads. Also excellent margaritas.

The next morning we headed east, back toward Wisconsin, and hit the plains of eastern Wyoming. The snowcapped peaks receded in our rearview mirror and then disappeared entirely, like Oz vanishing over the curvature of the earth.

Funny, I reflected, how many places start to feel like home when you ride there often enough. If you have friends with motorcycles—and they all have maps like cousin Gary's—this country makes a great neighborhood.

45

Planning a Great Big Road Trip

WELL, THE PLANNING HAS BEEN GOING ON FOR MONTHS now. Three of us—my local riding buddy Lew Terpstra, Mike Mosiman from Colorado, and I—are plotting a late-autumn bike trip.

From here in Wisconsin to the Smokies and then up along the Blue Ridge into Virginia, back along the Ohio River, home through Indiana and Illinois. Big trip. We're giving ourselves nine days on the road.

Which means that every evening for these past few weeks, I've been sitting in my reading chair, looking at maps.

Not just looking but mesmerized. I confess to being a map addict and can sit perfectly still and stare at a road atlas for hours. It's the kind of arrested-breathing intensity you normally see in soldiers reading letters from girlfriends back home, looking for signs and meaning, trying to divine the future from a turn of phrase or the language used.

With maps, of course, it's a language of curves and junctions along parallel mountain ridges, with lines of blue, red, and gray. You look at them and try to imagine how the trip will go, whether you'll somehow miss the best bike road in Tennessee and accidentally take a highway lined with shopping centers and stoplights. It takes some study to do it right.

And we are all studying. I talk to Lew and Mike often on the phone, and we've all been making suggestions over the past few months on how to make this A Really Good Trip. Some of our friends have also offered advice, and I thought it might be worth writing down a few of these tips.

So here goes: the accumulated travel wisdom of some of the century's great minds—not to mention Lew's, Mike's, and mine—and a virtual treasure trove of advice based on past blunders, tragic miscalculation, and wistful regret.

1. Find a Date and Protect It—We picked our travel dates about a month ago, and since then we've each had approximately 900 offers to do something more responsible, socially correct, or morally compelling on exactly those

dates, but somehow we've all managed to just say no. Adopt this mantra and repeat it to yourself: "A year from now, you won't remember why you stayed home, but you never forget a motorcycle trip."

2. Skip All Yellow Zones—A Yellow Zone is any American city so large, sprawling, and populated that it's depicted on the map in a large yellow blot, usually found at the convergence of several interstates, with a ring road around it. I also think of these as "Ruined Zones." There is nothing there for you, so treat each one as a repellent magnetic pole. The only exception is New Orleans.

3. Choose the Smallest Possible Roads—It's okay to use a road atlas or official state map to lay out your general direction of travel, but the best roads are often missing from these maps. Think of your own neighborhood and where you like to ride. Do you ever take that busy state highway full of truck traffic and motorhomes? No you don't. So why get stuck on some equally crowded artery 600 miles from home in, say, West Virginia?

Get a supply of *DeLorme Gazetteers* and seek out the small stuff. Regional bicycle maps are even better. If bicyclists like the road, you probably will, too. Generally, all people on two wheels are looking for the same brand of deliverance.

4. Use the "Never a Dull Moment" Principle—If you must ride through, say, Illinois, try to follow a river or ride through small towns with neat old main streets. Upshift, downshift, and amuse yourself with roadside scenery, however humble. Note the dead '53 Chevy pickup on the front lawn and the Yamaha DT-1 for sale in the driveway; look at that weird old farmhouse. . . . There's nothing worse on a motorcycle trip than looking at your watch and saying, "Gee, if I can hold on to these handlebars for just three more hours, I'll be in Toledo." A good trip is one where evening sneaks up on you and the passage of time seems downright lamentable.

5. Stop for the Night at Towns in Bold Type—My *Road & Track* colleague Bert Swift pointed out on a recent road trip that the best places to stop for the night (unless you know of a good campground or mountain lodge) are medium-sized towns depicted on the map in bold type. These usually have fuel, a couple of real restaurants, a small choice in motels, and at least one bar featuring the local tap beer you so richly deserve.

If the typeface on the map is too small, you'll be eating Cheetos for dinner and sleeping in a ditch. And if it's too large, you'll be dragging your saddlebags to the seventh floor of a hotel named Euro-Tel Pointe Executive Residence Suites, with your bike parked about a mile away.

6. Stay Flexible—Avoid a rigid schedule and ignore all these rules if something interesting and unexpected comes along. If someone says, "Hey, you boys oughtta stay here for our Annual Pig Roast and Miss Kentucky Bourbon Beauty Pageant," don't tell the guy you have hotel reservations in Cleveland. Go with the flow. Sure, you'll end up sleeping on a pool table, but think of the stories. . . .

7. Don't Plan Too Large a Loop—If you do, you won't be able to follow any of the guidelines above. I find 300 miles per day just about right, 400 slightly tedious, and 500-plus fit for nothing but dull roads and bragging rights. And no one else really cares how far you can ride. Trust me.

8. Don't Blow Off the Last Day—Every day on the road should be a good one. Don't get homing instinct on the last day and do 600 miles of interstate so you can check your e-mail messages. They'll keep. Everything will. And when you're dead, life will roll on exactly as it does now, like a tubeless tire with a self-sealing puncture. Your co-workers don't even know you're gone, and your family is ambivalent.

Relax and do what my friend Tom Daley does on that last day: stop at a bar 20 miles from home, eat peanuts and SlimJims, talk over the trip, and unwind for an hour or two.

If you haven't punished yourself too badly, you might even talk over a future trip.

46

Grace Days of the Fall

LAST FRIDAY, DURING THE FINAL HOUR OF OUR NINE-DAY tour, my riding buddy Lew split off for his home with a honk and a wave on Highway 151, while I swung east on Highway 39.

Stopping on a hilltop in Mineral Point, Wisconsin, I dug my rarely used cell phone out of a saddlebag and called home. Barb didn't answer, so I left a message saying, "It's about five in the afternoon, and I'll be home in an hour."

Then, following my own heartfelt advice to others, I tried something I had never done before. I slowed down and just cruised for that last hour, enjoying the scenery.

The sprawling Wisconsin hills and farmland were golden with the colors of early autumn, and the sign on a small-town bank said it was 75 degrees.

At 6:01, I pulled into our driveway, and Barb walked out of the house and handed me a Brandy Manhattan (it's a Wisconsin thing) as I climbed off the bike. Our friends Jim and Patty flooded out of the house, drinks in hand.

They were all getting ready to leave for dinner, so I washed my face, threw my riding boots in a corner with a dull thud, changed out of my dusty road clothes, and joined them.

Before leaving, I pushed my bug-spattered Road King into the garage and noted that the trip odometer said I'd gone 2,452 miles since leaving home.

"Perfect trip," I mumbled to myself.

Strangely, almost eerily perfect.

I say that because on most tours there's at least one thing wrong. Your valvetrain is making a funny noise; the Weather Channel predicts freezing rain; the new helmet you foolishly bought at the last minute is giving you a terrible headache; whatever. Something's wrong.

But not this time.

Maybe it was just because we'd outflanked the weather for the first time in history—pulled a reverse play and faked it out of its shoes, as my football coach used to say.

You see, my friends Mike and Lew and I had spent all summer planning a big trip to the Smoky Mountains and the Blue Ridge. Then Mike came riding in to join us from Fort Collins, Colorado, after three hard days on the road, and told us he had to get back a few days sooner than expected. Also, the weather forecast for the Southeast was beyond bad: torrential rains, unseasonably cool temperatures, possible flash flooding along the Appalachians.

"Why," I suggested cautiously, "don't we ride west, where the weather is warm and sunny, instead of east? That way, Mike can get home on time and we don't have to spend nine days in rainsuits."

Mike and Lew didn't bat an eye. "Sounds great," they said.

So we left the next morning, and the weather didn't have time to react. The newspaper showed high pressure and a big, smiling sun over the entire Great Plains. Bruised purple clouds and slanting rain over the East.

You can say all you want about the Zen-like joys of riding in the rain, but I'll take 75 degrees and sunny anytime. Riding into a dark storm front has about the same effect on my spirits as an upcoming IRS audit. I'll get through it, but—given a choice—I'd rather avoid it.

So we hit the road with deep blue skies overhead. Time seemed to be standing still in the Midwest, as if balanced between two seasons and stuck in neutral. We had summer warmth, but with a fresh autumn clarity to the air. Leather-jacket-with-T-shirt weather.

Was this heaven?

Maybe that young woman driving with her cell phone in hand last week had actually killed me, and I didn't know it yet. It was a suspiciously near miss. . . .

We rode northwest through Wisconsin's hill country and spent the night in Trempealeau, a little village on the Mississippi, then headed into Minnesota on Highway 16, along the twisty Root River Valley. Dropped down for a night on Spirit Lake in Iowa, then stopped in Lew's hometown of Sioux Center for lunch and a town tour.

If Lew were Bruce Springsteen, this would be his own personal setting for "The River" and "Racing in the Street." Little roads. Twists and turns from Iowa into Nebraska. One great small town after another. Fiery maples, football practice, yellow school buses, old brick banks that look like Bonnie and Clyde should have robbed them. And—in Everly, Iowa—did.

A night in Norfolk and another in Ogallala. One rainstorm—for character-building contrast—and then steady clearing as we cruised into Fort Collins.

Dinner and margaritas at the Rio Grande, a day ride into the Rockies, a new tire for Lew's Triumph Bonneville, and then it was time to head home.

But how? Lew and I had both been across Nebraska and Kansas about 25 times, so an untried route was called for. With map study, we found it: Highway 2 through the lonely and beautiful Sand Hills of Nebraska, then 91 and a maze of small county roads all the way to Iowa.

We spent the night in Mullen, Nebraska, literally the only town in Hooker County, and then made it across the Missouri River through the wind-sculpted Loess Hills to Denison, Iowa.

Favorite road sign of trip, on entering Lake City, Iowa:

Welcome to Lake City

Everything but a Lake

We made it home the next day, all on backroads again, riding just a little farther than our avowed 300-mile-per-day laid-back limit.

A minor failure, but the evening light was so good with the sun behind us we didn't want to stop riding. And we got home without seeing a drop of rain or a dark cloud for three days.

Blue skies, no wind, unlimited visibility.

I unpacked and washed my bike yesterday. Today it's raining like crazy, and this morning I threw my back out again for the first time in months. Meanwhile, in the Southeast, heavy rains and floods are washing away entire trailer parks.

Mike called and said it's 53 degrees and raining in Fort Collins today. Terror suspects were arrested in Denver. Suddenly it feels like National Back-to-Reality Week.

But, once or twice in a lifetime, you get lucky. The weather gods forget where you've gone, your bike runs perfectly, your helmet fits fine, and time stands still, mysteriously stuck in neutral on the best week of the year.

47

When the Winds of Changes Shift

WELL, THIS HAS BEEN QUITE A WEEK IN MOTORCYCLING. I'm starting to feel like someone standing on a golf course in a lightning storm.

First, I learned that our last remaining Ducati shop in Wisconsin is closing at the end of this month, a place called Corse Superbikes in Saukville, near Milwaukee. It's a beautiful facility, built nine years ago by a businessman/bike enthusiast named Virgil Kreder. The place also handled MV Agusta, Aprilia, KTM, and Suzuki, and it was headquarters for the Ducati Superbike team for three years.

Ever since it opened, Corse has been one of those destination shops where you plan your day off around a visit, to test yourself with dangerous temptations (I've caved in at least three times), buy some parts, or just talk to the guys—who are about as nice a group of people as you will find in motorcycling.

My buddies Lew and Jeff and I went over there this week on a cold autumn day, trying to tread that delicate ground between extending sympathy and looking for close-out bargains. ("Sorry to hear about the death of your husband, ma'am. Does he still have that Manx in the garage?") None of us, however, really needed anything too desperately, so it was mostly a goodwill trip rather than a typical visitation of vultures.

I'm going to miss these guys, and the shop. A lot of us are. And now we have half a dozen more highly qualified individuals looking for other work, no Ducati dealership in the state, and another unoccupied building.

On the way home from Saukville, we made our mandatory stop at Mischler's Harley-Davidson/Buell/BMW dealership in Beaver Dam, Wisconsin, partly so I could check out that small corner of the showroom where Buells are found.

Ever since I rode our first Buell Ulysses testbike on a trip through Virginia a few years back, I've had it in mind to buy one eventually. I found the bike to be comfortable, fine handling, and practical, with a unique combination of slightly untamed Harley charisma and scientific logic.

And I've long been a fan of Erik Buell's engineering ideas. His perimeter brakes—which shorten the load path to the tires and result in much lighter wheels—along with low cg and mass centralization (short, low-slung exhaust system, oil in swingarm, fuel in frame, etc.) all make good sense to me, and you can feel the result in the bike's dynamics. I also like a motorcycle with midrange torque—lots of it—and Buells have it. Fun bikes to ride.

Guess I should have acted on these opinions earlier. Late again.

I brought a 2010 Buell brochure home and studied it religiously in the evening (do I need the Ulysses XB12XT with full luggage or the taller and more off-roadish X?), then finally turned in.

The next morning, my friend Jim called to say that Buell had just closed its doors. Out of business.

Once again, I know Erik and many of the engineers who work at Buell—a smart, enthusiastic bunch with great talent and commitment to what they build.

I don't have a dime in that company, but its closing hit me very hard. Guess I should have bought that Ulysses instead of talking about it. I probably still will, but that won't do the factory at East Troy any good now.

The next morning, our editor of 21 years, David Edwards, called and said he'd been suddenly replaced at the helm.

Now, I'm too far removed from the daily running of the magazine to know what prompted this decision, but David is a good friend and longtime riding buddy, and has been a generous and understanding editor. (You'd have to be, to put up with me.) He kept me on the payroll for six months when I was too ill to get up and work more than about two days a week. And we've had great road trips together in places as far flung as the Alps, Canada, and New Zealand—where we dared each other into bungee jumping off a bridge into the Shotover River Gorge. Lots of good roads and good times. And great issues of the magazine.

David said Executive Editor Mark Hoyer was taking over as editor. No hard feelings there; David was already hoping Mark would be next in line when he eventually left. Mark is also a good friend of mine—and a fellow British-bike fanatic—so I was glad he got the job, too. And I don't just say that because he signs my checks. I say it because he needs to help me find a decent Commando.

In any case, these are strange and interesting times—a little too interesting, for some. I know things change, and objects in the universe realign themselves. Sometimes readjustments are overdue, and other times they're hard to fathom.

But the only consistent pattern I can see in any of it—whether at Corse Superbikes, Buell, or on the staff of this magazine—is that all the people mentioned here are crazy about motorcycles. Think about them all the time, look at them, ride them, collect and repair them, talk about them with our friends. Pore over glossy brochures or pick them up in trucks and bring them home in parts.

We were just born to it, or it came upon us like a gift or a sudden conversion like the bolt of lightning that hit Saul of Damascus, and there aren't that many of us, really. All these closings and setbacks aren't just business news; they're personal.

Motorcycling is basically a happy business. No one has to own a motorcycle in this country—cars are often cheaper and more practical—but we buy them because they make us happy. And we ride and hang out with other riders for the same reason. Bikes and motorcycle trips add color and texture to life, in the same way that rock-n-roll brought new life to gray old Liverpool when the Beatles came along. Like that music, they stand out in sharp contrast against everything predictable and ordinary. Those of us who know this have to stick together.

How do we do that?

I don't know. Maybe go buy a bike. Or install a new chain. Put some chain lube on it. Change your handlebars, take a ride, get a new rear tire, or go to a swap meet and buy a Bultaco T-shirt.

It's dark out there. We've gotta keep the lights on in this little house of ours.

48

The Bridgestone Awakens

NOT MANY PEOPLE WERE OUT RIDING LAST NIGHT.
Why?

Well, it was 35 degrees here in Wisconsin, with a light rain falling, and it was also midnight. In late November. But I had to ride.

More importantly still, I had to open the garage doors and let all the two-stroke smoke out before I suffocated.

Last night, you see, I finally got my 50cc 1964 Bridgestone 7 Sportster running, after four intensive days of fiddling.

Turned on the fuel tap, pushed the choke lever down, hit the starter button, and it fired instantly with a smooth and surprisingly quiet two-stroke purr.

Amazing. Years and years of sleep, and an engine just starts running. Settles down to a nice even idle and revs like a turbine. When was the last time that little cylinder had fired?

I don't know the ownership history of this bike, or when it last ran. I bought it three years ago for $200 from a shop called Country Sports in Wisconsin Rapids, and I have no idea who traded it in or how long it had languished in the back of a barn before that. It had no battery, dead electrics, a tank lining of pure rust, and a petcock filled with rock-hard silt. Also, the little carburetor was dangling loose on its worn-out intake manifold collar.

What else? The right footpeg was broken off—probably another victim of some high school kid who saw *The Great Escape* (as I did) at an impressionable age, tried to jump over something, and got a groin-wallop for his trouble. The original red paint was faded and the taillight broken. John Montgomery, the dealer who took the bike in on trade, had found a brand-new OEM taillight assembly and also had the tattered seat reupholstered (quite expertly, I must say) with beautiful, new red vinyl.

But clearly, the bike had not run in many years. It has 2,891 miles on the odometer, and in my mind's eye I can see some kid riding the hell out of it through the mid-1960s, then running into terminal carb or footpeg problems and sticking the bike in a corner. Or maybe escalating (as I did) to a big Honda Super 90 and CB160, then shipping off for Vietnam. It's entirely possible the Bridgestone hadn't run since, say, 1969. Forty years before I fired it up last night.

I sold my own Bridgestone 50 in 1966, right before I went off to college, because a) I needed the money for school and b) there was no place to park it except in a big, snow-swept parking lot near my dorm, and you couldn't ride on campus anyway. Sold it to a kid in a nearby town (Mauston, I think), and it got hauled away by his parents, never to be seen again.

Maybe.

I've often wondered if the Bridgestone now in my possession is, in fact, my original bike. It's the right year and color, and John Montgomery's shop is only about 50 miles from my hometown. I still have the original 1964 registration card from my Bridgestone in a scrapbook of high-school memorabilia, and the vehicle ID number on that card—E02311—is the same as the engine number on the bike I have now.

But there's also a chassis plate with a different serial number on it, so maybe all Bridgestone 50s have engine number E02311 and the dealer just recorded the wrong VIN onto the title.

Hard to say, but this Bridgestone might very well be my first motorcycle. Perhaps I should just believe it is and leave it at that.

Anyway, it took a little work to get this baby running. I filled the tank with old nuts and bolts and a caustic acid de-rusting chemical (twice) and shook it like a huge samba gourd to work the flaky stuff loose, then let it soak overnight. Bought a small 12-volt gel battery, hooked it up, and . . . nothing worked. Cleaned the main fuse and ground connection and—voila!—the lights came on like a Christmas tree and the starter cranked the engine over. No spark, though. A quick points filing and cleaning (through a hole in the flywheel), and the spark magically returned. Added gas (20:1 premix with some outboard oil I had on hand), hit the starter, and the engine was running.

My ride last night was a short one, because of that missing right footpeg. I discovered you can ride only so long with your foot dangling out there in space (try it sometime). My friend Jim says it's like crouching in a car and driving without a seat. Extreme Yoga.

The bike ran smoothly, though I had to re-learn the three-speed rotary gearbox, in which you start in neutral and shift downward until you hit third. Push downward once more and you're in neutral again. Ad infinitum. The *Groundhog Day* of gearboxes. I'd almost forgotten . . . .

When I got back to the garage, wet, happy, and well-chilled, the petcock and carb needle and seat were both weeping fuel (new ones needed), so I drained the tank to keep my shop from blowing up during the night and then kicked back for a beer.

What a delightful little machine. Willing, quick, and eerily smooth.

Before I bought my first one (which this may actually be), I took many detours on my way home from school so I could stare at it in the window of

Lee's Hardware in Elroy, Wisconsin. I was 15, and I thought, if I just had that bike, I could go anywhere on earth.

And people did in those days, traveled the globe on 50s, 90s, and small scooters. A cartoonist named Stan Mott went around the world in a go-kart, and my favorite book in high school, Peter S. Beagle's *I See by My Outfit*, was about two guys who rode a pair of Heinkels across the United States.

The improbability of it all made it almost more fun than having a big bike. Maximum mobility through minimalism, with a bike that cost $279, brand-new.

Strangely, that's almost exactly—to the dollar—what I've got in this one. Again.

These small bikes are a pretty good deal. I've had a great time this week, bringing the old Bridgestone back from the dead, and I honestly can't remember when I've been so happy to hear an engine start and run. Or to ponder an exhaust note.

It's the exact soundtrack music from an excellent old movie about the freedom to go almost anywhere.

49

The Call of the Black Commando

IT ISN'T VERY OFTEN THAT A TIRE-BALANCE PROBLEM ON a modern Triumph leads to the purchase of an old Norton, but in the universe I inhabit there's no such thing as coincidence. There's only inescapable Fate, whose machinations are no more complicated than an ordinary box trap held up with a stick.

A few weeks ago, you see, I rode my Triumph 900 Scrambler over to Sharer Cycle Center, and while mechanic Louis Brings balanced my vibratory tire, I wandered around the back of the shop, looking at various project bikes on workstands.

Among them was a 1974 Norton 850 Commando with the swingarm and rear wheel missing.

"This looks like a pretty clean Norton," I said to Louis.

"It belongs to a customer who stored the bike for several years, so I had to clean the tank, install new Amal carbs, change the fluids, and, let's see . . . adjust all the chains and the Isolastic engine mounts. Now it runs great. Only 6,700 miles on the odometer."

"Why is the swingarm off?"

"I'm installing new bushings. The bike is all stock, except it has a sixteen-inch Harley rim laced onto the rear hub."

I winced slightly.

Back in the 1970s and 1980s, it was common for Norton owners to install wider, smaller-diameter wheels to run more modern rubber, but I always liked the tall, elegant look of the old 19-inch Dunlop rims best.

I walked around the Norton and noted that the exhaust system was pretty banged up, and someone had repainted the black tank with red and silver trim, rather than classic gold. "Too bad they didn't go with a stock paint scheme," I said.

"Well," Louis said, "the owner's just fixing the bike up so he can sell it. I think he's asking five grand."

I inhaled sharply, and all my senses suddenly became incredibly keen, like a werewolf's, and I could smell the cheap vinyl imitation-leather cover on my checkbook from 25 miles away.

"Hmmm," I said. "You'll have to give me the guy's number. . . ."

I'd owned several Commandos in the distant past, and all were magnificent bikes, but they also had their share of typical old-British-bike problems. I'd sworn off them when my last one required four roadside repairs on one trip. Minor stuff, mostly, but still irksome.

But time heals all wounds—or blesses us with Alzheimer's—and at last year's *Cycle World* Show in Chicago, I wandered over to visit the Chicago Norton Owners Club (as usual) to admire their row of restored bikes. Turned out, John Revilla, the club president, had just completed a stunning restoration on a black 850 Commando, and he had it on display.

I stared at the bike for a while, then turned to my friend Jim and said, "Well, that's it: I'm getting another Commando. And not one word out of you, buddy."

Jim—a reformed Norton owner himself—rolled his eyes.

So the hunt began. Last summer, I looked at two Commandos that came up for sale in our area, but both were pretty rough—typical $3,500 bikes that needed $8,000 of restoration work to be worth $6,000.

And now this much nicer one at Sharer's. For $5,000. Was it worth it?

I added up what it needed: 1) correct paint, 2) exhaust system, 3) rear rim and spokes, 4) tires, and 5) new kick-start lever and turnsignal stalks (bad chrome on both). I figured I'd have to spend at least $1,500 just to make the Norton look really good again.

But this bike was exactly what I was looking for—a winter project without a lot of heavy lifting. I'd just come off the fairly grueling three-year restoration of a totally shot old British car (1964 Lotus Elan) and was in no great hurry to inspect the dodgy innards of another transmission. A winter of light cosmetic restoration on a mechanically sound bike would do just fine, thank you.

So I called the owner and asked if he'd reduce his price a bit to accommodate my Grand Plan, and he did. He was a pleasant guy and said I was welcome to test ride the bike before deciding. So I headed back to Sharer's the next morning, helmet in hand.

The Commando started first kick and idled perfectly. I climbed on and reviewed my Olde English shift pattern: one up and three down, on the right side. It'd been a while. Nice clutch, effortless gearbox, genuinely fast acceleration, tons of torque, and dead-smooth cruising above 2,700 rpm. Better brakes than I remembered, and the tightest, best handling chassis I'd yet experienced on a Norton. A lovely bike, and quick.

Commandos, when they go down the road, don't feel like anything else. They're light, yet they have a damped solidness to them, as if everything might be tightly packed with cotton. Some old Jags give you the same sensation. And that sound. . . . Barb's all-time favorite.

At her insistence, I bought the bike the next day. After I handed over the check at Sharer's, I took off for a ride through the hills. The weather was in its last few days of Indian summer, and I rode all weekend. On Monday, we got cold rain, followed by snow.

Now the Norton is on the workstand in my garage, snowed in for the duration. I spent yesterday polishing the cases with Simichrome (the most rewarding job, per minute, in all motorcycling) but haven't taken anything apart yet. I need to look at the thing for a few days in its complete form, just to soak it in.

It's a strange thing to say, but when I have a Norton in my garage, I actually feel more relaxed and content with the world, almost as if some part of my soul is fully at rest.

There are a few select things, I believe, that every individual is intended to have in this life, almost as a matter of course. Objects that seem to have been designed for someone with your exact genetic wiring, and you know it instinctively when you see them. For me, there are a few guitars like this, and a small handful of motorcycles. Besides the Norton, a black Les Paul Custom comes to mind . . . with three pickups. . . .

Crass materialism?

Perhaps, but I like to think of it in more spiritual terms, as a classic example of Predestination. But with more chrome and no funeral.

50

Buell Closeout Sale

GRAY DAY, MIDWINTER, THE PHONE RINGS, AND IT'S MY friend Jeff Underwood.

"Rob Himmelman and I are driving to East Troy tomorrow to the Buell factory for the liquidation sale. You wanna go?"

I'd seen the ads on the Internet—"Everything Must Go!"—with color photos of huge, bright red and blue tool boxes, work benches, office equipment, air tools, etc. I didn't need anything; I'm all tooled up, so to speak, but it never hurts to look. And then there's the curiosity factor, the natural human tendency to immerse oneself in elegiac events as a reminder that nothing lasts—as if any reminder were needed these days. I'd visited Buell several times when the place was humming—picked up one of the first new Ulysses there for a trip to the Appalachians—so what would it be like now?

Jeff and Rob picked me up in the morning, and we took mostly backroads down to East Troy, which is about 60 miles from my home here in Wisconsin. The liquidation sale had been going on for almost a week, so we didn't expect too much. When we turned into the industrial park and pulled into the Buell lot, we didn't find too much, either.

The Buell signs had been pried off the outside factory walls, leaving dark outlines where they'd been, and the liquidators had a table set up near the door. "Take a look around, boys. Everything's for sale. If something's not marked, just ask us about it."

The tool chests and benches were gone, and the remains were rather random—big bins of office phones and headsets, tables full of computer hard-drive units, upholstered rolling office chairs for $65, heavy-duty motorcycle lifts with no wheel chocks ($500 each), a Ford 1-ton van with Buell Racing painted on the side ($7,800), boxes of short, pre-calibrated torque wrenches, bins of air ratchets, random tables of old combination wrenches ($3 each) that would cost slightly less at Sears.

Everything was quite expensive, but the liquidators were obviously depending on a certain level of typical farm-auction feeding frenzy to keep prices high until only unsellable items were left—a brink they were rapidly nearing.

What this kind of liquidation sale impresses upon you is the immense effort and expense of creating a small company that produces a complex product. All those telephones and pagers and headsets, desks and file cabinets, probably bought new at full price when things were really rolling. Etched in the cavernous silence of that big, empty factory building was the message "Human activity and creativity, good; lack of same, very bad." Factories have a pulse, and when the heartbeat stops, the muscles and ganglia lose all their meaning and value.

Nevertheless, we bought a few things, just because we were there. Rob bought a Swingline stapler for a few bucks, and I spent $10 on a set of three dealer-display panels showing Buells on the road and in action. I'll probably put one of them up in my workshop.

It shows a guy sitting on an orange Ulysses—like the one I rode—stopped on a dry, sunlit ridge out West, gazing out on a large butte or rock formation. Could be the Badlands or maybe Monument Valley. Nice picture to look at when you're driving back home through a late afternoon snowstorm.

When I got home, I set the display panel up along the wall on my desk and spent a lot of time gazing at it.

Then, as one who has come perilously close to buying a Buell Ulysses several times since the introduction of the bike in late 2005, I suddenly found myself going on a Buell-finder website to see how many of these bikes were left at dealerships in Wisconsin. I was particularly interested in the taller, theoretically more off-road-ish model, the XB12X, with its heavier-duty fork and greater steering sweep.

The Internet said there were four left in Wisconsin, so I started calling the dealers. Three of the bikes were "just sold" and the last one, a 2009 blue version, was still available at Racine Harley-Davidson. Barb and I drove over for a look (in yet another blinding snowstorm), she approved of the pillion accommodations, and I ended up buying the bike at a reasonably good, but not jaw-dropping, discount. I also bought their last set of hard bags. Unfortunately, we were in our Jeep, so there was no way to get the bike home.

So, last Saturday I drove my Ford van over to pick it up, and my friend Lew Terpstra went along to help. The Harley dealership was absolutely hopping, and I watched and drank coffee while three other buyers took delivery on new Harleys before I loaded my bike up. Good to see—economic hope and spring fever, combined with tax returns.

Strangely, our route to and from the dealership took us right through East Troy on Highway 20 and, as Lew had never seen the old Buell factory, we decided to stop. The liquidation sale was still in progress—if that's the right word—and prices had dropped considerably, but there was very little left. I sat in a nice office chair on wheels ($8) and said to Lew, "This is the most comfortable chair I ever sat in. I'm going to buy it for the garage."

"You'd better buy two at that price," Lew said. "I'll need a comfortable chair when we get back to your garage to admire the Ulysses." So I got two. Near the cashier's table, there was a stack of large gray plastic parts bins with "PROPERTY OF BUELL MOTORCYCLE" stenciled on them, marked $20 each. "Kind of expensive," I remarked to the cashier.

"Yes," he said, "but they say 'Buell' on them, and it's the souvenir-type stuff that everyone wants."

So of course I bought one, and I had a sudden flashback to a cynical remark that some pundit made when he heard that Elvis had died: "Good career move."

It really was a strange phenomenon. When it was announced that Buell was closing, anyone who was interested in the bikes (like me) sprang into action and bought one. The parts man at Racine Harley-Davidson told me that buyers immediately swooped down and bought all the Buell memorabilia—hats, jackets, tankbags, etc.—they had in stock. Buell accessories, with two years of shelf dust on them, sold out immediately. We humans are a strange bunch, spring-loaded for enthusiasm and waiting for a sign or omen. Or maybe just a lower price.

When Lew and I got home, we unloaded the Ulysses in my driveway, rolled it through the snow into my workshop, turned up the heat, sat in our new/used Buell office chairs to look at the motorcycle, and opened up a couple bottles of Snowshoe Ale from the nearby New Glarus Brewing Company. Local bike, local beer, all made by highly skilled neighbors and friends.

This is the way life should be, and I'd hoped it would stay that way—or become more so with the passage of time.

51

Reflections on a Road King

WITH A HOWLIN' WOLF CD TUCKED UNDER ONE ARM, I trudged through the snow to my workshop last night, carrying my Les Paul (all 9.4 pounds of it) in its case, so I could go out and practice guitar in our lavishly carpeted (indoor/outdoor) band corner. I was determined to learn the Hubert Sumlin riff from "Smokestack Lightnin'," even if I have no talent. In my world, persistence is everything.

I set my guitar case down, switched on the lights, and turned up the heat. While the place warmed up, I did what I always do to kill time: sit on a motorcycle.

Bike-sitting—as any motorcycle salesman will tell you—is a time-honored tradition during which we not only dream of past and future rides but reflect quietly upon our relative levels of doubt and desire.

And last night, as often happens, I found myself sitting on my '09 Road King, a two-tone version in Red Hot Sunglo, as they say, and Smokey Gold.

I've been sitting on this bike quite a bit lately, partly because I like to think about the great road trip I took to Colorado last summer, and partly because I need to re-check the wisdom of a recent handlebar swap. The stock Road King bars are a little wide and far forward for me, so I tried a set of Electra Glide Standard bars, which feel better on my lower back. The old ones made me feel like someone straining to catch a grip on his own handlebars before they sped off into the distance.

I bought this bike last summer, and it was an unusual deal, as traditional Harley purchases go. I've owned several FLHs over the years—a couple of Electra Glides and a pair of Road Kings of successive generations—and I always had to get on a waiting list. The wait was usually short, but I still had to order the bike and stand by.

This time, thanks to our booming economy, most midwestern Harley dealers had a few leftover 2009 models. With 2010s arriving, I was able to buy the bike right off the showroom floor—at an end-of-season discount, no less.

Beyond that price reduction, I figured 2009 was a pretty good time to buy because a) I still had a job for the moment, and b) the Road King was nicely upgraded last year. It got a stronger and stiffer frame (with commensurately better handling), more cornering clearance, and dual-compound tires for longer cruising life. It also carried over the slick six-speed transmission and 96-inch engine, which has spot-on fuel injection and finally makes enough power and torque to be genuinely fun—and to pass trucks in the mountains, two-up. Hallelujah.

Another nice change is the mufflers, which sound full and mellow but don't give you a headache—or invite an RPG attack from bystanders. This is the first time in decades I haven't felt compelled to ditch a stock set of mufflers and find something more charismatic. Big savings there.

Nevertheless, I still managed to blow some accessory money on the bike. Before it ever left the dealership, I added a luggage rack and passenger backrest, as well as heated grips. Still, the bike has been cheap to maintain—thanks largely to the magic of hydraulic lifters—and dead reliable. And I rode it a lot last summer.

That big, flat, traditional FLH windshield is the secret weapon—you can sit behind it with an open-face helmet and your jacket unzipped on summer days and warm nights, deflecting bugs like crazy and listening to the dulcet song of the roadside lark. Which you can actually hear, because you don't need earplugs.

There is much to like here, but is the Road King perfect?

Well, it's very good indeed for its intended purpose but certainly not a do-everything bike for a sporting rogue such as I. Though relatively trim among today's gargantuan baggers, it's still a large object, and I wouldn't mind at all if it dropped 100 pounds. But then I suppose it would lose some of the historically festive gee-gaws that make it a Road King. Also—for my tastes—they could move the floorboards back a few inches and raise the seat height so you could get your feet under you, where Nature put them. Other than that I have few complaints.

The only drawback to Road King ownership, really, is you have to put up with droll comments from some of your riding buddies who wouldn't own a Harley at gunpoint, put off as they are by all the lifestyle nonsense that goes on around the marque.

I get to hear a constant litany of "Don't you need more conchos?" or "Where's your do-rag with skulls on it?"

I often play along with the joke and attack these people with my brass knuckles.

Just kidding. All this harmless flak never fazes a person of my low sensitivity and awareness, nor does it affect the quality of the bike. I ride for my own pleasure, so the motivations of others are moot. They have their fun; I have mine.

In any case, this reaction to Harley ownership is interesting for its reflection on technical progress, if nothing else.

In the bad old days (a.k.a. the 1970s), in order to cough up the money for a Big Twin, you had to really want one, ignoring the slow acceleration, bad brakes, clunky transmissions, destructive vibration, vague handling, etc.

Well, they fixed all that. Of the FLHs I've ridden or owned since my distant youth, this one is dynamically and mechanically the best by a large margin. And it's no longer just "good for a Harley." It sets standards of engineering precision, finish, and simplicity of maintenance that a few other manufactures might do well to emulate.

This is quite a change.

When I first came to *Cycle World* in 1980, Harleys weren't always very well-engineered or well-built, so you had to conjure up highly imaginative reasons—mostly based on personal taste and style—for wanting to own one at all. Now they're finally good enough that you need similar reasons not to.

Regardless of age or quality, Harleys seem destined to operate well outside the world of cold logic—as do virtually all the bikes we like to sit on while waiting for the heat to kick in.

52

Small Change

IT MAY BE TRUE THAT THE FLUTTERING OF A butterfly wing in the Amazon changes the weather in Des Moines, but nothing has more consequential echoes than the changing of a single part on a motorcycle.

Swap your handlebars—as I did for a more traditional 1960s bend on my Triumph Scrambler last week—and the ramifications proliferate. The bar-end weights on the stock bike have their anchors either pressed or glued in (I can't get them out, at any rate), so now I need a new set of weights or else new grips to cover the unsightly holes on the ends of the bars.

No big deal, but I have to find the parts or order them, and the job's not quite done at this moment. Also, the new bars keep the brake master from rotating into exactly the right position for my right hand, so I've moved the bars just a little higher to compensate. And on the left side, I naturally drilled one wrong "experimental" hole in the handlebars before I got the left switch cluster peg to index properly on the bars. I'm sure no one will ever see it— unless the left grip snaps off in a corner and kills me.

Then, this weekend, I took the non-stock, rear 16-inch wheel off my "new" 1974 Norton Commando so I could take it the nearly 100 miles to T.C. Christenson's famous shop, Sunset Motors in Kenosha, Wisconsin (Home of the World's Fastest Norton, the "Hogslayer"), and swap it for a proper, original spindly 19-inch wheel.

This operation was just a little more complicated than the handlebar swap—one of those projects you like to start early on a Saturday morning, when your mind is fresh and you haven't started cursing yet.

So, coffee mug in hand, I walked down to the workshop, rolled the Commando onto my Handy-Lift, and raised it up to working level.

As mentioned in a previous column, I bought the 1974 Commando at the end of the 2009 riding season, and it ran great but had a few aesthetic issues that I'd hoped to straighten out. The bike's principal problem, in my eyes, was that wide Harley wheel someone had laced onto the rear hub.

Norton owners have been installing fatter rubber on Commandos for decades now, apparently in search of more traction for stoplight drag racing or just a wider selection of modern tire compounds for better grip in corners. Admittedly, the stock 19-inch rear wheel looks almost like a bicycle rim by modern standards—and the typical 4.10-size Dunlop K81 has the same basic tread footprint as a large ring of Polish sausage.

Nevertheless, this stock, narrow combination looks "right" to me and gives the Commando a proper tall and rangy look, like an MG-TC with its "four harps supporting a coffin" 19-inch wire wheels. In other words, I'm willing to give up some grip for good looks—which reminds me of an unfortunate date I had in high school, but that's another story.

So, up the Norton went onto the workstand, and I began the process of removing the rear wheel.

Normally, this is a pretty pain-free operation. Nortons have a clever rear-hub design in which the brake drum/sprocket unit stays in place when you remove the rear wheel; you just pull the axle out, drop a spacer that rolls somewhere under your workbench, and then lift the wheel away from the cush drive in the brake drum. Chain tension and brake adjustment remain undisturbed.

But, of course, if you put a fat Harley tire in there, all bets are off, and the whole job is like extracting an impacted molar—from a dental patient who eats nothing but chain lube, axle grease, and dirt. The rim won't squeeze past the brake drum, so the whole brake assembly has to be removed, along with the lower shock bolts. And even then, you have to deflate the tire and squeeze it together with some big welding-clamp Vise-Grips to get it out.

By the time I got that wheel yanked out of there, I felt like I'd lost a wrestling match at Alligator Village. Crossed Band-Aids appeared magically on my forehead, my coveralls were soaked in sweat, and I was forced to flop into my plaid lawn chair and drink an entire Guinness to get my electrolytes back in balance.

A further consequence of the wide wheel could be seen in the chromed chainguard. Someone had hacksawed off a big chunk of metal to clear the oversize tire. Then the chainguard had cracked in half from losing its rigidity, and someone had repaired it with a piece of tin and six sheetmetal screws. A fine piece of European craftsmanship—if Europe were populated entirely by 9-year-olds using bent screwdrivers and their dads' electric drills.

Looking at that wheel-less Norton, I couldn't help thinking what a terrible job this would have been if I'd had to repair a roadside flat without a lift or a jack and a wide assortment of tools. It couldn't have been much fun to put the wheel in there the first time, either, and I can almost hear the ghost of that previous owner saying, "Oh, man . . ." as he realized his cool new tire wasn't going to fit unless he ruined the chainguard.

It all fits in with my two basic garage mottos, which are "Nothing is easy" and "It's always something."

In any case, I got the old wheel out of there, ran it down to Sunset Motors, and exchanged it for an old-but-serviceable 19-inch wheel they found under a workbench. I had the wheel trued at our local Triumph shop, and they installed and balanced a new K81, along with new bearings for the wheel and brake hub.

I installed the new wheel last night, and it was a piece of cake. Dropped right in there. Looks good, too.

I'm always amazed at how seamlessly things fit together on a stock bike, and how quickly it all goes upside down when you change just one thing. It gives you renewed respect for engineers and what they're up against building a whole motorcycle where everything fits.

You almost never see a new bike with sheetmetal screws and a piece of tin holding the chainguard together. Or an "experimental" hole in the handlebars that some idiot sincerely hopes no one will ever see.

53

At Home on the Range

WELL, LAST WEEK WAS NOT A GOOD ONE FOR my fellow Slimey Crud and riding buddy Jeff Underwood. He spent the morning helping a neighbor cut wood, then drove his pickup back to his nice old farmhouse—which is tucked into a scenic hollow west of Madison, Wisconsin—and found the place on fire.

The fire department responded quickly, but it was too late to save the home, and Jeff ended up with a basement full of smoldering embers. Personal possessions, including a large record collection and extensive library, all gone. He thinks the fire started with a wood furnace that kicked out some coals onto the basement floor.

The only bright side to all this was that Jeff had all his motorcycles (older BMWs, a Ducati MH900e, a few dirt bikes, and his "main bike," a KTM 950 Adventure) stored in his workshop, which is in a nearby barn.

When Jeff's fellow Cruds heard the house had burned down but his bikes had been spared, they all breathed a sigh of relief, as if he'd said, "I wrecked my car but didn't damage the beer in the trunk." Not that we don't care about Jeff's home, but we all share a tacit understanding that houses are just a support system for riding motorcycles. A good place to warm up and do laundry between rides.

Easy to say, of course, if you haven't lost your home. Anyway, Jeff is now living in his pickup-mounted camper and wondering where, if, or how to rebuild. Luckily, he has good insurance and a surprising number of nice-looking women friends who seem intent on bringing him the finest meats and cheeses.

I called to see what I could do, and he said, "Bring me some good books to read, and let's take a ride this Thursday. It's supposed to be beautiful weather, and I need to get out and clear my head."

So last Thursday, six of us showed up at Jeff's former abode to ride the hilly backroads of Dane and Iowa Counties. It truly was a beautiful late spring morning, and before the ride, we all sat in lawn chairs on the concrete slab in front of his workshop/red barn and drank coffee and ate homemade cookies someone had dropped off.

The bikes that showed up were an interesting mix.

I had my Buell Ulysses, Jeff was poised to ride his KTM 950 Adventure, Jason Daniels showed up on his new BMW F800GS, Rob Himmelmann motored in on his BMW R1100GS, and another old friend of Jeff's named Craig Johnson thundered up on yet another KTM 950 Adventure. The only "normal" road bikes in the group were Matt Rosen's Triumph Sprint ST and Lew Terpstra's modern Bonneville.

Five big adventure-tourers out of the seven bikes, all sitting high and wide.

This is an interesting change. When I first joined the Cruds in 1990, nearly everyone in the gang rode a sportbike or a "standard"—Ducati 900SSs, airhead BMWs, Suzuki GS1100s, etc.

Slowly, those bikes have been supplanted by adventure-tourers—a class that barely existed 20 years ago. Several of us still have pure sportbikes or old British or Italian classics, but the motorcycle almost every member chooses to ride on a long trip—or on a twisty backroad with uncertain pavement—is a big, tall adventure-tourer.

The reasons are fairly self-evident. First, these bikes are roomy and comfortable, and most have hard luggage, so you can travel on them. Second, they have wide bars for good leverage. Third, there are a variety of dual-sport tires available, so you can tackle a moderate amount of gravel and dirt without turning back or falling on your elbow. You might say they represent the motorcycle version of Roosevelt's Four Freedoms. Only in this case it's Freedom from wrist pain, Freedom from clean pavement, Freedom from soft luggage, and the Freedom to sit up and look around.

A cynic here might add "Freedom from youthfulness," as most of us were a lot more comfortable on sportbikes when we were 20 or 30 than we are now.

Be that as it may, the Freedom from clean pavement thing was important on Jeff's ride. He led us on some very narrow and twisty back lanes whose tarmac had not yet been washed clean of winter's sand and gravel by the spring rains. Our swift passage stirred up large clouds of fine dust, and I quickly discovered that the Pirelli Scorpion Syncs on my Ulysses aren't exactly knobbies. The Ulysses is a wonderful torque-monster, so it spins that street-oriented rear quite readily on loose sand and dirt.

When Erik Buell first introduced the Ulysses, it came with a special Dunlop dual-sport tire that worked moderately well on gravel and dry dirt trails; but it soon became evident that most Ulysses owners were not going to be running Paris-Dakar with that 17-inch front wheel (or a muffler doubling as a skidplate), so Buell started putting pure street rubber on the Ulysses.

Good idea, most of the time, but the Buell still has an almost perfect dirt-bike riding position, despite the small wheel, and I wouldn't mind a little more soil capability. So my goal now is to wear the Scorpion Syncs out as soon as possible (a noble endeavor) and put something with more duality and knobs on there.

At noon, our little group stopped at a hilltop biker bar, a spot accurately called Pleasant Ridge, with a great view of the surrounding hills. We all ordered cheeseburgers and drank Cokes. (In another sign of maturity, people seldom drink beer anymore on our rides, but this may be more a Darwinian thing than a case of acquired wisdom.)

After lunch, we went back out to our bikes for the ride home.

For Jeff, of course, there was no home at the moment, just the camper. But he was also going back to his workshop and collection of bikes. As he himself said, "Things could be worse."

Indeed, they could. He didn't perish in the fire, and on that big KTM he can go anywhere in the world. Which is exactly what Jeff is inclined to do. This guy rides. In the meantime, we wish him luck on rebuilding his base camp.

If he ever gets back from Moab, Utah. Which is where he's trail riding at this moment.

54

The DR650 Appreciation Society

WELL, I GOT ABSOLUTELY MURDERED ON TAXES THIS YEAR. Following a financial planning guide that recommends "practicing for retirement" several years before you actually retire, I foolishly cut back on the sort of large, ruinous old car and motorcycle restoration projects that have always been the financial black hole of my earthly existence.

Unfortunately, the IRS saw all this thrift as a surge in personal wealth and politely asked me to send them enough money to pay for the cleanup of the BP oil spill in the Gulf. Like, next week. So I did what I always do when pressed for a big chunk of money in a hurry: I sold my Road King.

Put an ad in the paper and sold it the next day to a very nice fellow who lives only a few miles from our house. He had a 1995 Road King with high miles on it, and when he bought my bike he said, "Well, my old Harley lasted for 15 years and I'm 55 years old now, so if this one lasts 15 years I'll be 70. It might be my last bike."

This is a novel concept to someone who trades and restores motorcycles as often as I do. For me, it would be like Hugh Hefner saying, "This is my last date with a buxom young blonde woman."

Anyway, I ran the Road King money straight to the bank, and my tax bill was paid. Several friends expressed their condolences, but I have to confess that I wasn't all that grieved by the loss.

I'd contemplated selling the Harley this summer anyway, though I hadn't planned on turning the money over to the Feds. My new motto at this stage of life is "Ride more, own less," so the shedding of another insurance policy and registration renewal was not exactly at odds with my current mood. Also, my Buell Ulysses is such a good all-purpose motorcycle, I've hardly been riding anything else lately. It's almost an Only Bike.

Almost. I say that because, only a month or so after this tax debacle, my Colorado riding buddy Mike Mosiman called to invite me on a trail ride. He and his two brothers, Bob and David, meet every year at their grandparents' ranch in Wyoming—just west of the Black Hills—and spend several days dirt riding in the area.

Sounded like fun, but I haven't ridden a dual-sport or dirt bike since Mike, Bob, and Dave Scott and I spent a week off-roading in Mexico's Copper Canyon three years ago. As the following year drew to a close, I realized I hadn't done any trail riding all summer, so I sold my Suzuki DR650 to my friend Jim Wargula, who still rides it all the time and won't even discuss selling it back to me.

In other words, I'd need another dirt bike to ride on the ranch.

So I did what I always do when I need a versatile dual-sport bike: I bought another DR650.

This was a black '07 model with 3,500 miles, belonging to parts man Craig Grant at our local Honda/Suzuki/Yamaha/Kawasaki store. Craig bought it used as an inexpensive fuel miser for his 60-mile commute to work and realized, after about one round trip, that something a little larger—say, an SV650—would be a more relaxed and comfortable highway bike.

I agree completely, but the DR has always been a strangely ideal motorcycle for my own anticipated mix of highway, single-track, gravel, and backroads. It's a simple, durable air-cooled bike with good suspension, yet it's not excessively

tall. It's light enough for real off-roading but way better than most "purer" dirt bikes on the highway (if you have an aftermarket seat), and it'll cruise easily at 70 or 80 mph. Nice torque, low cost—whether new or used—and easy to maintain. And it still looks like a motorcycle. A basic, honest one.

We have at least eight of them in our Slimey Crud Motorcycle Gang. One of our guys, Aaron Fisher, rode his from Wisconsin to Alaska a few years ago. He got to the Arctic Circle and decided it would be fun to ride down the West Coast and see California. When he got to San Diego, it seemed like a good idea to dip into northern Baja. From there he meandered back to Wisconsin.

He rode up to the outdoor tables at our Crud meeting one summer evening, having literally just ridden back into town. He had a huge mound of camping equipment on the back, including a portable electric guitar and battery-operated amp. (Aaron is one of the best slide guitar players I've ever heard.) When he climbed off the dusty DR, we all stood up and applauded.

This, folks, is the adventure rider we'd all like to be, but—alas—are probably not. (See his whole story under "Snowrider" on www.advrider.com.)

Anyway, I've finally got another DR and couldn't be happier. I ordered the usual luggage rack, skidplate, and Barkbusters for it, and after I call Corbin for a seat the bike will be nearly complete. The only question now is tires.

I need knobbies for the ranch trip but hesitate to remove the stock dual-sport Bridgestone Trail Wings because they're so comfortable and quiet on the road. These past two weeks I've been riding to Crud meetings, running errands, and just going for evening rides on our local farm roads, and I'd almost forgotten what a fun streetbike it is. With chunky tires, you lose some of that serenity (and grip) on pavement and don't ride it as often. You can change tires or wheels, as needed, but that's a lot of work.

Maybe that's why one of our Cruds, Rob Himmelmann, has two of them—a crisp, clean street version and one with a big plastic tank and knobbies. Come to think of it, Rob's brother also has two. Maybe they both just want spares in case Suzuki ever stops making them. You can buy these bikes used, in good condition, in the $2,000–$4,000 range, so the investment is not beyond reason.

Which raises the question, should a guy who's "practicing for retirement" own more than one DR650?

Probably not. A better plan might be just to unlimber my tire irons and save up for next year's tax bill, as I am now completely out of Road Kings to sell.

55

The Big Blue Ambulance

HAVE YOU TOLD YOUR DIRT BIKE RIDING BUDDIES YOU'RE sixty-two years old?" my doctor asked last Wednesday as he studied the X-rays.

"No," I said, "I told them I'm forty-eight."

"Well, young man, you've got three broken ribs on your left side and three broken bones in your left foot. I can't believe you drove yourself all the way back to Wisconsin from Wyoming without checking into an emergency room."

"The guys I was with," I explained, "wanted me to go to the hospital, but the driver's seat in my Ford van was the only comfortable place to sit. I couldn't lie down and I couldn't stand up, so I figured I might as well strap myself into the van and drive home."

"Well, you probably aren't going to be riding a motorcycle again for two or three months."

This was not especially good news on the first true week of summer, exactly one day after the summer solstice, but you have to play the cards you're dealt. Or, in my case, the cards you've dealt yourself. All our wounds, as former *CW* Editor Allan Girdler once observed, are self-inflicted. I'd willfully broken at least three of my own basic laws of motorcycling.

First, after three perfect days of trail riding, I'd decided to go for "one last ride" with the guys late in the afternoon before putting my bike in the van for the trip home. It was that always dangerous "hour of the long shadows," as I call it in skiing, the fading time of day when you're mentally disengaged and just a bit tired.

Second, because it was just going to be a short, casual ride up a nearby trail, I didn't put on any body armor other than my helmet, motocross boots, and knee protectors. No chest, elbow, hip, or back protection. Yup—you guessed it—I was "not planning to crash."

My third mistake was just a basic technical error, usually made by rank beginners: out-riding my vision in the gathering darkness, I'd dropped both wheels into an unseen rain rut in the trail and then tried to roost out of it, rather than just stopping.

Sure as Newton, the bike instantly flicked itself sideways and spat me onto the ground like a badly aimed Roman catapult, then bounced off my ankle. I slid down the trail for several feet before a large boulder intercepted my rib cage.

Wind knocked clean out of me, I spent about a minute in the fetal position, gasping for air with a strange whooping sound, while closely inspecting the writhing grubs and worms that had been living peacefully under the boulder before I'd displaced it.

Truthfully, I thought I was a goner, just on the theory that you can't hit anything that hard with your chest and live. Luckily, I was wrong, and the guys soon had me on my feet, limping around, wheezing and grousing.

Damage to my DR650 was minimal—dented tank (my aftermarket plastic one had not arrived before the trip), snapped-off mirror, bent shift lever. I climbed carefully onto my bike, hit the start button, and she was running. Slowly, we all rode the easy two miles back to the ranch house, where I put a bag of ice from our beer cooler against my ribs.

Ranch house, you say? Beer cooler? Sounds nice.

And it was.

You see, my riding buddies, the brothers Mosiman (Mike, Bob, and Dave) and their cousin Mike, gather every year for some trail riding at the old Wyoming ranch that once belonged to their grandparents. The ranch is in a lovely valley on the western edge of the Black Hills, not far from the South Dakota border, so there are lots of good single- and double-track trails to explore. And this year, they were kind enough to invite me along, possibly for comic relief, as not one of them has crashed his brains out in many years. So, I loaded the DR into my blue Ford Econoline and headed west, through Minnesota and South Dakota, down through the Black Hills to Newcastle, Wyoming. There we met and headed out to the ranch for three days of the best riding imaginable. Cow trails, Jeep trails, old railroad beds, ghost towns, and the ruins of mines. The evening I crashed, we were returning from a forested plateau known to the Mosiman brothers as "the old Indian burial ground." When the boys were young, they and their mother used to find red and blue Indian beads among the pine needles. While we were there, poking around for artifacts, thunder rumbled and pitchfork lightning rustled nervously through the hills and cliffs above us.

Omens, perhaps?

Custer died for our sins, as the book title says. Or maybe he died for our right to ride dirt bikes in the Black Hills. As we got on our bikes to leave, Mike actually said, "I don't think the Indians want us here."

Half an hour later, I was on the ground, all busted up.

I slept fitfully that night, through a tremendous thunderstorm, complete with hail and high winds, but the morning was beautiful and clear. The guys gave up trying to talk me into heading for the ER in Newcastle—or allowing them to personally drive or fly me home—and reluctantly loaded my bike and luggage into the van.

Bob Mosiman, who lives in Illinois, followed me most of the way home with his SUV and bike trailer, in case I needed help. We stopped for the night in Sioux Falls, where he fueled the van for me, and then I cruised across Minnesota, crossed the Mississippi at LaCrosse, and headed home.

On the way to our house, I stopped at the Stoughton Hospital emergency room for a few X-rays. Barb met me there.

As I pulled into the hospital parking lot, I realized this was the third time I'd arrived home from a bike adventure in this same blue van, limping from my injuries and slightly the worse for wear. Daytona . . . Mexico . . . the Badlands . . . Maybe I needed a new/luckier truck.

Or better judgment.

Barb unpacked my riding gear this morning, and I noticed, while lying on the sofa and popping another Vicodin, that my chest protector was undamaged and just like new.

56

Beatnik Bikes

WELL, MOTORCYCLE-WISE, I'M BACK IN ACTION—IF LOOKING AT OLD bikes rather than riding them can be called "action." In a first big outing since my Wyoming dirt bike crash last month, I climbed somewhat stiffly yesterday into the back seat of a Pontiac Vibe (aluminum bike trailer attached) and rode all the way up into the wilds of northern Wisconsin with my friends Rob and Lew.

Rob was headed there to buy a 1983 BMW R80ST from an old buddy named Nick who is feeling his age and selling off a bunch of his old BMWs and Guzzis. Seems Nick has discovered that a Kawasaki 250 Ninja is a lot easier to move in and out of the garage than some of his old classic iron, and it's also fun to ride and doesn't need any work.

Hmm . . . Riding for fun, with no expensive repairs or suffering? How's a man to redeem his soul and gain the Kingdom of Heaven with a plan like that?

Anyway, we got to Nick's garage full of earthly delights, and, while Rob loaded his new/used R80ST onto the trailer, I found myself mesmerized by a black 1972 BMW R75/5 in nice original condition. Apparently, Nick is thinking of selling this bike, too.

On the way home, I posited to Rob and Lew the many theoretical advantages of owning a bike exactly like Nick's R75/5 if a person were to weaken and buy such a thing for no good reason.

Lew shook his head. "If you're going to get an old airhead BMW, you're a lot better off with a later slash-six. You get real instruments, better brakes, a five-speed transmission, and more power."

"True," I admitted, "but there's just something cool about those early 1970s slash-fives. They're a little mellower and smoother, and feel like they could motor down the road forever. They're more of a beatnik bike."

Rob and Lew both nodded. They knew instantly what I meant.

The "beatnik bike" concept is one I've carried around in my head ever since I was a kid, visiting my grandparents in San Francisco during the late 1950s.

San Francisco—and more specifically, the North Beach neighborhood—was one of the great gathering grounds of Beat poets and writers such as Jack Kerouac, Allen Ginsberg, Gregory Corso, Gary Snyder, Neal Cassady, Lawrence Ferlinghetti, etc.

As such, the city always nurtured a certain sense of eccentric cool among the motorcycles one saw there, and it hasn't changed much, even today. San Francisco simply has a different bike scene than anywhere else. There's more emphasis on off-beat utility and not so much on carbon-fiber clutch covers or titanium bits. You sense the presence of a subculture that would rather sidestep the marketing world than embrace it. Cheapness and honesty are recognized virtues—as long as they have an undertone of artistic flair. A serviceable bike you find in a shed and paint with a brush may have more cachet than a perfect restoration of a known classic. Wrong handlebars are encouraged.

The Beat writers didn't talk much about motorcycles, but the 1960s bike boom was partly a generational extension of the same free-roaming, try-everything spirit. In my own case, I read Kerouac's *On the Road* and *The Dharma Bums* at an impressionable age and immediately began hitchhiking all over the place. After being given a ride on the back of a Harley Panhead, however, I soon realized that motorcycles were the next obvious step. They were still hip, but you didn't have to stand in the rain for five hours with your thumb out on the industrial outskirts of Skokie while no one picked you up. You could go anywhere for very little money while still camping out and living the rugged life.

Bohemian types like James Dean picked up on this immediately and started making romantic motorcycle journeys across America, occasionally freezing half to death and getting rained on, just like Kerouac or Cassady with their freight trains and lonely highways. With a bike, you could die of exposure on your own schedule and not depend on others.

Anyway, Rob and Lew understood all this instinctively, having lived through it, and we soon began a lively discussion on what, exactly, constituted a beatnik bike. It's a class that's hard to define, but you know them when you see them. We all agreed that the following machines pretty much fit the bill: 1) Old BMW Singles and all of the /2 and /5 bikes; 2) Vespas and Lambrettas—even though they're scooters; 3) most Guzzis—particularly those with floorboards; 4) all British Singles and most 1960s Twins, as long as they have just one carburetor—Bonnevilles and Spitfires may be too flashy and obvious; 5) Suzuki Water Buffalos and Titan 500s; 6) Honda CB500s and 550s, especially those with vintage 4-into-1 headers.

After that, the choices became a little less certain.

Any Harleys? No new ones, certainly. Lew thought a Harley 45 might be a beatnik bike, but Rob and I thought it might be too old-fashioned and heavy on maintenance. Rob suggested a plain, Shovelhead-era Sportster, and I agreed, perhaps from the Bronson effect.

We all thought the great mass of Eastern European bikes—Jawa, CZ, MZ, DKW, etc. — might qualify. Also anything Spanish. Bultaco, Montesa.

Ducatis? Non-desmo models only. Lew thought most 1960s Hondas—especially the 450 Black Bomber—should be included. I suggested the 1975–1976 CB400F and was voted down.

So, naturally, we had to come up with a solid definition of what constitutes a beatnik bike and what doesn't.

We finally decided the acid test might be to park your bike in front of the City Lights bookstore on Columbus Avenue in North Beach. If a customer walks out with a copy of *Kaddish* or *The Dharma Bums* under one arm, stops to look at your bike, nods wisely, and quietly says, "Cool," then you've probably got yourself a beatnik bike.

I still think the 400F would do it. . . .

Assuming the customer is truly enlightened and beatific (which Kerouac always claimed was the source of the term "Beat") and not just some punk kid from Wisconsin visiting his grandma.

57

The Eternal Scooter Dilemma

A COUPLE OF WEEKS AGO, ONE OF BARB'S FAVORITE RELATIVES (and mine), Aunt Betty, died at the age of 93, so on a Saturday morning we got dressed up to go to the funeral in Middleton, Wisconsin. After rushing around to make sure we wouldn't be late, we somehow managed to arrive in Middleton nearly an hour early, before the church even opened.

"Well, how do we kill an hour in Middleton on a Saturday morning?" Barb asked as we drove aimlessly around.

I frowned in concentration, trying to remember if the town had any guitar shops or motorcycle dealerships, which it did not. Going to a bar wasn't really a good idea before a non-Irish funeral. . . .

"I've got it!" I said. "There's a Vespa dealership here, and I've always wanted to see what kind of place it is." So, off we went.

I should explain here that I've never owned a scooter, except for the 50cc Honda Spree I rescued from a scrap-metal dumpster a few years ago. I got it running and illegally rode it around a lot but couldn't pry a title out of our inscrutable state bureaucracy, so I donated the Spree to my friend Pat Donnelly to use as a pit bike.

Before that, however, I'd had a couple of pleasant encounters with scooterdom. I worked one summer on a railroad section crew, and my buddy Roger Riedel had a two-stroke Lambretta—a 150, I think—and we two tall galloots used to pile on that thing after work and ride from Columbus, Wisconsin, into the big city of Madison to see if there was any action at swinging bars. Which there never was—at least for two guys on a Lambretta. Go-go girls who looked like Nancy Sinatra were not impressed.

But I remember being impressed myself with the speed and comfort of that scooter. It cruised easily at highway speed and seemed at least as quick as the Honda CB160 I bought later—or maybe quicker. Such is the magic of a well-developed two-stroke.

After Barb and I were married and I got out of college, we celebrated my immediate unemployment and fistful of delayed G.I. Bill checks by touring

Europe for three months in a clapped-out $450 Simca we bought in Amsterdam from a shyster in a shiny suit and wraparound sunglasses. The kind of guy who grips a cigarette between his thumb and all four fingers and always looks around nervously, as if expecting police.

When we got to Rome, we naturally had to rent a Vespa to explore the city. After all, we'd seen Gregory Peck and Audrey Hepburn do just that in *Roman Holiday*, and we were also Fellini buffs who'd seen *8½* and *La Dolce Vita* one too many times. When in Rome, you must ride a scooter. We rode out to Tivoli and to Cinecittà, the movie city, as well as down the Appian Way, around the Colosseum and you name it. We had a great, stylish, carefree time, though I remember being initially unnerved by the reduced gyro stability with the small scooter wheels.

Anyway, I have largely fond memories of classic Italian scooters and have always admired their design and architecture. The old Lambrettas and Vespas belong—and are found—in most catalogs of great design, along with the Nikon F camera, the Olivetti portable typewriter, etc. They're timeless. The Lambrettas are gone now, but the new four-stroke Vespas have managed to hang on to that great classic look.

So, with that soft spot in mind, Barb and I pulled into the parking lot of Vespa of Madison on University Avenue, right next to a foreign-car repair shop called Dunn's Import. We walked into the Vespa shop and found a very cool vibe, with lots of scooters and the walls filled with framed vintage Vespa posters and huge pictures of, yes, Gregory Peck and Audrey Hepburn on their Vespa, as well as classic photos of Italian street life.

And who should the owner of the place turn out to be but Jeff Dunn, an acquaintance I hadn't seen in many years. Jeff and I were both foreign-car mechanics in the 1970s, working at different shops that were about six blocks apart. We were also both novice motorcycle roadracers in WERA's 400 Box Stock class. Jeff and I were among a handful of riders who showed up the very first day Blackhawk Farms Raceway in Illinois opened its gates to motorcycles. They did it on a practice-day trial basis, I suppose to see if we would kill ourselves or steal the bathroom fixtures. It was a great non-lethal, crime-free success, and bikes have been racing there ever since.

So, here was Jeff, 30-some years later, running Dunn's Import and a Vespa shop. We caught up on old times briefly, then Barb and I had to leave for the funeral. But I came back two days later, and Jeff fired up a couple of Vespas for me to ride, a leftover 2009 250 GTS and a new 300 GTS.

What can you say? They were both quick, electrically smooth, beautifully crafted, and effortlessly fun to ride. And they still have those 12-inch wheels, so they're never going to be quite as naturally stable as a motorcycle. But the Vespas still give you a great sense of mobility and freedom in town, sort of like your first small-bore motorcycle—except the larger models go 65-80 mph on the highway now and can cruise serenely with freeway traffic. You could easily tour on them.

I suppose I'm eventually going to have to get one of these things, just to put in my vote for a great design I've always admired. Also, I think I'm just about the only member of the Slimey Crud Motorcycle Gang right now without some kind of scooter in his small collection of bikes.

I've come very close to buying one several times in the past but have always balked when I realized I could buy yet another leaky, worn-out (but possibly restorable) Norton or Triumph for the same price.

Well, I've got an old Norton now—and that obligatory pool of oil on the garage floor—so maybe it's time to rent *La Dolce Vita* from Netflix again and consider my options.

58

A Short Ulyssean Summer

WELL, I DON'T THINK I'LL APPLY FOR A GUINNESS World Record for miles traveled by motorcycle this past summer. After breaking my ribs and foot in a dirt bike crash last June, I spent about two months in a La-Z-Boy, tilted back and watching the paint dry on our living room wall. Which I painted 20 years ago, so there wasn't much action.

Nevertheless, I arose from the chair one bright August morning and discovered that I could once more pull a boot onto my left foot, so I clumped out to my garage and began riding again. Climbed on my nearly new blue '09 Buell Ulysses and headed out into the great wide open.

Destination? Off to Mischler's Harley-Davidson in Beaver Dam, Wisconsin, to get my official post-break-in oil change and drive-belt adjustment done.

I rode those first few miles rather tentatively, making an effort not to hold the bike up with my left foot at stop signs—or low-side on a patch of sand in a corner. Never had the prospect of landing on my rib cage (again) seemed quite so unappealing.

I won't say I rode like a little old man, but picture Wilford Brimley taking his first-ever motorcycle ride on the way home from filming an ad for burial insurance. "Let's see, the clutch is the one on the left . . . ." After about 10 miles, I got back in the flow and began to wick it up a bit. Great to be back on a motorcycle.

The Ulysses (for those who missed last year's epic column) was the bike I'd bought—literally—in the middle of a blizzard last winter from Racine Harley-Davidson. I got it shortly after Buell folded, and it was, according to the "Buell Finder" factory website, the last new XB12X sitting on a showroom floor in Wisconsin. I guess this makes me the direct opposite of an "early adopter." Just in time to be too late, as Hank Williams would say.

Actually, I could have been the early adopter with this bike, as I was one of the first journalists in the United States to ride a Ulysses any distance, right after the original 2006 model's introduction. I picked up a Barricade Orange version from the East Troy factory—about 65 miles straight east of my house—and rode it on a long autumn Bluegrass music tour, down through the backroads of Virginia.

I took an immediate liking to the bike and found it comfortable and nimble, with great luggage, fantastic brakes, first-rate suspension, and the best seat in the industry.

Drawbacks? Well, the rear cylinder was cooled by a loud fan that stayed running for about a minute after you shut the bike off, and the Check Engine light came on when I was still about 400 miles from home. In West Virginia, on a Sunday. This turned out to be a faulty worm-drive screw that was supposed to open a flap in the muffler at high rpm—an early production problem that was quickly rectified.

Also, the engine, though dead-smooth on the highway, did its typical 1200 Sportster dance on its rubber mounts at idle. Frankly, this didn't bother me much, as ownership of Road Kings and Norton Commandos has turned me into the very poster child for vibratory Twins with rubber mounts. If you like the overall personality of a motorcycle enough, it's possible to see nearly any engineering fault as pure charisma. Something I felt the Ulysses had in abundance. And still has.

Nonetheless, I was just a little uneasy when I bought the Buell last winter. I'd liked the bike on a long autumn road trip—five years ago in cool weather—but how would it hold up now as a daily rider? Friends warned me that it might not be so good in the heat of summer. Which we had plenty of this year, followed by an unusually warm and beautiful Indian summer, all through October.

As it turns out, everything I liked about the Ulysses on my trip in 2005 I still like, and the bike's quirks have turned into non-issues for me. I've got just over 1,500 miles on the Buell now and have ridden it in 100-degree weather with no problem. Granted, if you're heading north and the wind is coming from the west, there's quite a bit of heat on your right leg, but then you just swing your knee temporarily away from the frame/gas tank (or turn east) and all is well.

The loud fan still irritates just a little bit and sometimes makes me wish I still smoked so I could walk over there, light up a Camel, and wait beneath a tree while the bike cools down, but that's a pretty minor problem. I suspect if Buell had stayed in business for another year, the engineers would have developed a "Whisper-Jet" fan or some such thing.

Mileage? The Buell brochure advertised an enticing 51/64 mpg for city and highway, but I've yet to exceed about 44 mpg, mostly gassing it around on backroads. Maybe I need to get out on the highway and cruise sedately at 55 mph, without those wide saddlebags. Or hire a shorter rider.

Anyway, the report from this truncated summer is a good one. The Ulysses has quietly become my Main Bike, the one I ride almost all the time, just as my old Kawasaki KZ1000 Mk. II was in the 1980s. I rode the KZ everywhere for eight years, and its usefulness allowed me to dabble in all kinds of arcane and less sensible projects—old Triumph 500s, clapped-out Yamaha

RD400s, early Honda Fours with faulty float levels, café racers with impossible handlebars, etc.

And that's what the Ulysses allows me to do now. I don't see myself replacing it any time in the foreseeable future because it does so many things well. It has real garage appeal for me—I like its strangely offbeat styling and ingenious mechanical architecture. And it fits me well and does everything I want to do on a modern bike—tour, carve corners, run errands, go fast, or just go slow and soak up the scenery while listening to that nice, loping Twin. And then there's the marvelous roll-on torque, my favorite trait in a motorcycle engine.

So, with reality taken care of, I can once more indulge wholeheartedly in what you might call the peripheral fringe of riding logic.

Just this week, I found myself looking at an orange 1975 Yamaha RD350 that needs a little work. It doesn't run right now, but it doesn't have to. I've got the Ulysses.

59

Bonneville Fever

ESTERDAY—AS I WRITE THIS—WAS BLACK FRIDAY, THAT INFAMOUS SHOPPING day after Thanksgiving when consumers line up in front of shopping malls and try to kill each other. This morning's paper reports that a fistfight broke out between two women at Toys"R"Us, and one woman was taken away in handcuffs. The Christmas season starts early around here.

How blessed we motorcyclists are. While all this mayhem was taking place, I was up early and out in my garage in a state of tranquil calm, standing at the parts cleaner and degreasing the chainguard on a rusty 1971 Triumph Bonneville. My garage radio was playing something by Brahms.

They said it was his "Rhapsody in E-flat Major," and I found myself wondering why classical composers didn't just name their tunes, like the Rolling Stones did with "Paint It Black." Then you'd have some idea what mood you're supposed to be in.

Anyway, my mood was good because I was working on an old British bike and didn't have a dime in it. The Triumph belonged to my friend Lew Terpstra.

Seems Lew flew out to the Bonneville Salt Flats this past fall for his first trip to the World Finals and came back much-inspired with stars in his eyes.

"Here's what I'm going to do," he told me about five minutes after his return. "I'm going to buy an old British Twin—maybe a Norton 650SS or a Triumph Bonneville—and fix it up and see if I can set a new land-speed record for the Production Pushrod 650 class on my seventieth birthday."

"A laudable goal," I observed, "but you're only sixty-eight."

"Yes, I need one year to go out there and see how the bike runs, and the next year to improve it and set a new record."

"What's the current class record?"

"It's one hundred and two mph, just set this year by a Triumph Bonneville."

"Gee," I said. "I'd have thought that someone would have built a faster Production-class Triumph by now. Those bikes were supposed to go one hundred and twenty right off the showroom floor—even if mine never did."

"Well, you've got high elevation," Lew said. "The Salt Flats are at about 4,700 feet, and the salt can also slow you down a little. In the Production class, you can modify the engine internals—cams, pistons, and so on—but the carbs and the mufflers have to be the original style. You can hog the carbs out, but the part numbers have to be correct for that year. You also have to keep the stock tank, seat, fenders, headlight, brakes, rim size, and handlebar mounts."

"Sounds like a fun project," I said. "Are you going to ride the bike?"

"Yes," Lew said. "I'm going to lose weight and get in shape—which my doctor has told me I should do, anyway. It'll be a good incentive."

Lew—I should mention here—is a big guy. He's about 6-foot-3 and looks like a defensive lineman for the Packers. If Lew showed up at your front door in a bear costume, you'd put the Winchester .30-30 away and get out the .460 Weatherby Magnum.

But I've found that there's nothing like the prospect of motorcycle racing to help you get in shape. Back when I was roadracing, I used to run six miles every morning, just so I could keep using the same old leathers. Lew told me he'd already joined a gym and started dieting.

He'd also started looking for a bike. His first choice was a Norton—just because so many people build Triumphs—but rarity and high collector prices turned out to be a problem for the 650SS, so he set his sights instead on a Triumph Bonneville.

And last week he called and asked if I'd like to go down to Morrie's Place, a famous British bike shop in Ringwood, Illinois, and look for a cheap old Triumph to build. We drove down there, and shop owner Ed Zender led us back through his parts shelves to the Dark Aisle of Lost Bikes, where we found a tired but complete 1971 Bonneville. Oil-in-the-frame model 650. Engine seized, some rust. Perfect. Lew bought it for $1,500.

He took the bike to Motorcycle Performance, a shop in Madison, Wisconsin, to have owner Bill Whisenant build the engine. Bill is highly regarded as a tuner and rider of fast Triumphs—and Ducatis, as well. He went 205.09 mph this fall on a turbocharged Ducati 999 partial streamliner—the first Ducati to go over 200 mph at Bonneville and the fastest Ducati in North America.

He also did much of the work on my friend Jim Haraughty's Team MS blown Triumph 650, which set a record last year and then broke it this year by 10 mph, at 132.290 mph. Jim had to fly home when his mother became ill, so Nick Moore rode the bike.

Anyway, Bill knows Triumphs and said he'd have the engine done in a couple of months. In the meantime, he wanted us to restore the rest of the bike so he could put the engine back in it.

So, last weekend, Lew and I hauled the engineless Triumph out to my workshop, where the blessings of a propane furnace and a Handy bike lift will allow us to work in luxurious comfort this winter. The Triumph needs new fork tubes, wheel bearings, tires, paint, wiring, and a general cleanup. Lew wants to powdercoat the frame so he can someday put it back on the street, and we should probably replace the rusty wheel rims. But Bill warned us not to go overboard on paint and plating until after the bike has been exposed to salt for a week. Good point.

Still, you have to have some pride in a project bike, so yesterday morning, I celebrated Black Friday by degreasing and bead-blasting the brake pedal, chainguard, and sidecovers. Lew, who was gone for the holidays, started working on it today. (He's out in my workshop right now, working feverishly, I suspect.)

This is really fun. My hands now smell like parts cleaner and my right ear is ringing from the roar of the air compressor next to my bead blaster, but it'll all be worth it if we can get to Bonneville. I've been there several times and gazed out upon the empty and silent Salt Flats, but never during Speed Week or for the fall World Finals. I'm new to all this.

And my hat is off to Lew. This is the best plan I've ever heard for celebrating a 70th birthday.

60

A Short History of Hitting My Head

*J*UST BEFORE WE TOOK OFF FOR FLORIDA LAST WEEK on a spring-break vacation, Barb's sister Pam and her husband, Richard, called from Fort Myers. "A good friend of ours named Scott Fischer is the local Harley dealer," said Pam, "and when he heard you were coming to visit us, he said he could lend you a Harley while you're here."

"Great!" I said, eyeing the small carry-on suitcase I'd just begun to pack. "I'll just bring a larger suitcase so we can take a couple of helmets along."

"Oh, you don't need a helmet in Florida," she said. "It's just like Wisconsin— we don't have a helmet law down here."

I held the phone and stared into space for a moment, scanning my memory for images of traffic in coastal Florida at the height of the winter tourist season. Lots of cars, many of them quite large and driven by elderly folks whose heads were not quite visible above their seatbacks, so that you were never really sure if the car ahead of you had a driver at the wheel or not. Often, it made no difference.

My parents lived in Florida for many years, and I used to joke (rather cruelly) that if you blew up a paper bag and popped it loudly, half the state population would die of a heart attack. Now that I'm a little closer to that age myself, it doesn't seem quite as funny, but I still stand by the scientific principle.

Anyway, Florida didn't seem like the best state in the Union in which to go helmetless, even if there was a certain warm-weather appeal to letting your freak flag fly and being free to do your own thing and ride your machine and not be hassled by the man, etc. I knew from previous trips that, while there were plenty of great places to ride in Florida, there would also be many pale yellow Lincoln Town Cars with white vinyl tops on their way to the Early Bird Senior Special at the Crab Shack, so you had to keep your wits about you. Also lots of half-lost visitors like me careening around.

"Well, I think I'll bring helmets anyway," I told Pam. "I just had my life saved by a helmet about six months ago, so I'm in kind of a helmet mood."

I may have been overstating the case, as I have no proof that the helmet in question—a dual-sport Arai XD—actually saved my life, but I'd guess it did. If nothing else, it certainly saved me from a good spell in rehab, trying to guess (wrongly) how many fingers the therapist is holding up now.

It was a dirt bike crash in Wyoming last year that broke my foot and a bunch of ribs. During the accident, my helmet also took a pretty good bounce off a rock, and the impact was hard enough to leave my ears ringing for a few minutes. The helmet just had a small scuff mark and paint chip, and I didn't even have a headache after the accident. Or maybe I did, but I was too busy grousing about my ribs and foot to notice. Anyway, I'm still here, after having my bell well and truly rung.

Actually, looking back at a lifetime of high adventure mixed with natural clumsiness, I would say helmets have spared me to ride another day at least three other times. One was a crash in the Barstow-to-Vegas Dual Sport ride, during which I flew over the handlebars of my XL500 and failed to attain lift, alighting amid some rocks on that portion of the helmet where my bare forehead would normally have been found. The other two were roadracing crashes—at Grattan and Riverside—where I lost the front end and low-sided, smacking my face into the pavement like somebody bobbing for blacktop, then slid for so long that I became bored and tried to stand up, falling again. In those last two cases, it was the chinbar on the helmet that took most of the impact.

You'd think those last two hits would have taught me a lesson, but—illogically—I still own a couple of open-face helmets and wear them quite a bit for street riding on those bright, sunny days when my superstition and foreboding levels are especially low. I read an interview a few years ago with one of my heroes, four-time 500cc World Champion John Surtees, and he said he still prefers to wear an open-face helmet when doing track sessions and exhibition races, mainly because he's always liked the openness of vision and hearing, the added peripheral awareness of his surroundings, that an open helmet provides.

I feel the same way. If I wear a full-face helmet, I adapt to it instantly and don't give it a second thought. But when I switch to an open helmet, I feel strangely liberated and more attuned to what's going on around me, like a guy who's just put the convertible top down on his car.

Wearing no helmet at all adds yet another dimension of freedom, of course, unless it's cold, windy, dusty, buggy, or rainy, at which time that lack of helmet becomes just another of life's many aggravations, like losing your gloves during a dogsled race. As so often happens here in the north.

Anyway, when it was time to pack for Florida last week, the helmet I chose was an open-face Shoei J-Wing with a dark-tinted, flip-up shield. Never mind my long and violent history of chin-smacking; it just seemed like the right thing for Florida.

And it was. I picked up a nearly new Road Glide from my new friends at Harley-Davidson of Fort Myers and was soon cruising down the wide boulevard that is Highway 41, headed toward Naples, with a short swing out toward Sanibel Island.

Palm trees along the highway reflected in the chromed gas cap on the Harley, and a light sea breeze wafted up the sleeves of my open Levi's jacket. Bright red bougainvillea bloomed in front of homes with iridescently green lawns. The Big Twin was percolating nicely, with a relaxed and muted burble.

Ah, Florida. And warm air and sunlight and bridges and blue water passing by. It was my first ride in three months, and I'd almost forgotten what those motorcycles in my garage were for. They were for exactly this.

"Good to be here," I said to myself. Then I thought about it for a moment and added that famous Keith Richards afterthought, "Good to be anywhere."

61

The Art of the Valve Adjust

WELL, WE FINALLY HAD OUR FIRST REALLY SWELTERING SPRING day (58 degrees!) yesterday, so I put the battery in my Suzuki DR650 and took that gratifying first ride of the season, a long meandering trip into a sunny countryside dotted with melting lumps of snow. What fun.

I came home toward evening and immediately released my Buell Ulysses battery from the grip of its Battery Tender tentacles and installed it in the bike. I'd planned to take another ride this morning, but the temperature dropped 20 degrees overnight, and it started hammering down cold rain at dawn. I went out to my workshop and looked at the Buell.

What to do on a rainy Sunday in spring? Go to the bookstore? No. Not in the mood. Did that too much this past winter. Plug in the Les Paul and practice guitar? Ditto.

I looked around the workshop, and my gaze fell on the DR650. An uneasy sense of guilt stirred somewhere deep within my minuscule conscience. The DR now has just over 4,400 miles on the odometer, and I'd bought it last year from its second owner when it had about 3,400 miles on the clock. I asked if anyone had ever checked or adjusted the valves and he said he didn't know. Note to self: check the valves eventually someday when you get time.

Then I proceeded to ride the DR another thousand miles last summer. The valves weren't noisy, but what if they were tightening up and the two exhaust valves were running a deep cherry red because they didn't have enough time to transfer heat?

Now, I'm not exactly compulsive about bike maintenance (ask anyone), but I can't fully relax while riding if I think the bike is hurting itself in some way. For instance, the sound of a tight drive chain makes me tense because I picture the bearings and seal at the countershaft sprocket grinding themselves into a pile of rubber dust and metal shavings. That's why I'm a slightly loose-chain guy. And a cool-running-exhaust-valve guy.

So, I rolled the bike onto my Handy lift and went to work. Took off the seat and gas tank to get at the valve caps on the head. My slim owner's manual didn't say a thing about how to adjust the valves, only that they should be inspected at 600 and 7,500 miles and adjusted, if necessary, by a qualified mechanic at your dealership.

Luckily, I just happen to have a factory DR650 shop manual and a Suzuki valve-adjust tool that holds the adjuster in place while you tighten the locknut. These were both given to me by my buddy Mike Mosiman after he sold his DR650 last year. Since then, he's bought another DR, so I've had my phone number changed in case he wants them back.

The shop manual gives very specific instructions: remove the spark plugs and alternator cover cap so you can turn the engine over with a socket, remove the timing light/inspection cap to find the TDC marker on the compression stroke, set your intakes at 0.003-0.005 inch and your exhausts to 0.007-0.009 inch.

My intake valves were still spot-on at a perfect 0.004, so I left them alone. Both exhaust valves had tightened up to 0.006 though, so I adjusted them to 0.008. Moderation in all things.

Like most valve-cap openings, the Suzuki's are a little tight, but I squeezed in there with my favorite Snap-on gap gauge and then did a final go/no-go check before putting everything back together. The DR fired right up and sounded fine. No funny loud clacking, no backfires; the bike was not engulfed in flame. Done.

It was kind of fun fiddling with the bike, and Suzuki's valve adjust procedure on this big Single is just straightforward enough to be satisfying on a rainy Sunday afternoon.

Still, during the job, I got to thinking. . . .

Sitting next to the Suzuki were my Buell and Ducati 900SS. The Buell has hydraulic lifters, so the valves never need adjusting, while the Ducati has the famous desmo system, where you either need to be a skilled and patient mechanic with a selection of valve shims or take it to a good shop to get the valves adjusted—at considerable expense.

When I was a foreign-car mechanic during the 1970s, I spent half my time adjusting valves—either setting tappets on ohv cars with rocker arms or going through the dog-and-pony show of removing cams and inserting little shims under inverted buckets on dohc engines, then (hopefully) retiming the cams without having the cam-chain tensioner or sprockets move and skip a tooth. Some, thankfully, had shims above the buckets. These days, most of this nonsense is gone—along with the adjustment of ignition points—and the art of the valve adjust is rarely practiced except on the most exotic cars. Or old classics. Hydraulic lifters are the rule.

A lot of bikes, however, still have those shim-under-bucket arrangements, while others use the more home-mechanic-friendly system of overhead cams working on adjustable fingers. Most adjustment intervals are now pretty extended, but it still has to be done.

It occurred to me that, in this age when sportbikes have been a slow sell for many dealers, the $300 or $500 valve adjust is just one more impediment to bike ownership, especially for young people who are facing difficult financing and high insurance costs.

I know that direct cam-on-bucket (and desmo) valve actuation is light, compact, and efficient, remaining precise at high rpm, but is it possible that today's hard-pressed motorcyclist might be able to live with, say, 100 instead of 110 horsepower? My Buell makes a claimed 103 hp—though, granted, it's a big ol' 1200cc engine. Still, it works fine and isn't too heavy. And that maintenance-free valvetrain is one of the reasons I bought the bike.

It's also worth noting that any time you don't have to open a perfectly good engine to the dirt and dust of the outside world—or to the wanderings of the human attention span (like mine)—it's a good thing.

Maybe the art of the valve adjust should be just that—an art, rather than an industry. A special craft we apply to exotic racebikes, lightweight dirt bikes, or those old British Twins we love.

Might be time for the valve adjust to join the adjustment of ignition points as a folk ritual for the hardcore racer or the hobbyist who, like me, still has a drawer full of gap gauges that need exercise.

62

Triumph of the Killer Bees

A FEW MONTHS AGO, I WAS TRYING TO ORGANIZE SOME small corner of my chaotic office by methodically cleaning out a few desk drawers because, well, you've got to start somewhere, and you can't always use a flamethrower. While dumping stuff all over the floor, I accidentally discovered a long-forgotten file of old black-and-white photos taken during the first few years I worked at *Cycle World*, in the early 1980s.

Yes, in the last century.

One photo, taken by our then-managing editor, Steve Kimball, was an unused picture from an old story assignment—and one of this magazine's greatest shining moments in the history of motorcycle competition. Taken in the parking lot behind our Newport Beach offices, the picture showed me sitting on a little Honda C70 Passport step-through with four champagne bottles nestled comfortably in the front basket.

I showed the picture to Barb, and she said, "What was going on there?"

"I must have been arriving for my first job interview," I joked.

So, of course, I had to send the photo in to Editor Hoyer as a possible Slipstream contender, with the caption, "January, 1980: Peter Egan arrives for his first job interview at the *Cycle World* offices." A few months later, the picture appeared on our back page.

Almost immediately, I started getting calls from friends who wanted to know what I was really doing, riding around—helmetless, with sunglasses and long hair—on a Honda Passport with all that champagne in the basket.

Frankly, I was a little hurt that none of these guys had read the story I wrote all those years ago (March, 1982) called "Invasion of the Killer Bees."

But then I remembered that a lot of my younger friends were still sitting in highchairs at that time, gumming soggy graham crackers or trying to pick up Cheerios with their fingers. They not only couldn't read in those days, but couldn't even chew, so I thought I'd better explain the whole scenario.

Seems that in 1981, Craig Vetter—inventor of the famous Vetter Windjammer fairing (which could be found on virtually every long-distance touring bike in the United States at that time)—decided it would be interesting to organize a motorcycle mileage contest, held on a mountainous closed course near his home in San Luis Obispo on the central coast of California. The rules were fairly simple: You had to ride any two- or three-wheeler on a 64-mile loop and finish the course in an ideal time of 1 hour and 40 minutes, with 10 minutes latitude on either side. An average speed of about 35 mph, in other words. Fuel tanks would be topped off, sealed with tamper-proof glue, and then refilled at the end of the course.

Sounded like an interesting challenge, so Kimball and I looked over the CW test fleet for a couple of appropriate bikes. We settled on the Honda C70 Passport, with its sohc 73cc Single, and another Honda, the zippy little MB5, a 50cc two-stroke repli-racer with a real telescopic fork and a front disc brake.

Alas, then-Editor Allan Girdler was not a fan of tiddlers and scooters and dismissed them as urban toys upon which it was impossible to really go anywhere. After Kimball and I whined and moped for about two days, Girdler finally relented and said we could enter the two bikes if we actually rode them to San Luis Obispo and back. A round trip of about 700 miles. Hmmm . . . Both bikes were illegal on the freeways, so we'd have to take what are called "surface streets" in California, as if freeways were some kind of cosmic phenomenon suspended in space.

So, we took the surface streets through L.A., stoplight by stoplight, and jigged and jogged over dusty backroads all the way to San Luis Obispo, arriving somewhat butt-sore after nine hours in the saddle. On the trip up there, the MB5 averaged 81 mpg and the Passport 102 mpg, running flat-out at 40-50 mph.

The crowded starting line for the contest the next morning was amazing. There were engineering-school entrants with aerodynamic fairings fashioned from coat-hanger wire and transparent plastic dry-cleaner bags, tiny two-stroke motors driving 10-speed bicycles through their derailleur systems, a diesel-powered three-wheeler, and a couple of very sophisticated streamliners, one sponsored by Vetter himself and one by American Honda.

We decided that Kimball should ride the Passport, as it had a much better chance of winning, and Steve—who'd lived in the San Luis Obispo area—had a photographic memory for the local county roads that was almost spooky. "Idiot savant," I suggested, was the clinical term. I rode the MB5 and tried to keep up with him—distantly. (Drafting was forbidden.)

Well, Kimball slashed through the course effortlessly, easy on the throttle and hardly using his brakes, while many of the more sophisticated (i.e., smarty-pants) entrants either suffered low-speed crashes on gravel-strewn corners or broke down from an excess of frail and exotic engineering ideas.

In the end, Steve won easily on his dead-stock $748 Honda Passport, and the organizers claimed he'd averaged 198 mpg, while the MB5 had done 139 mpg. Our own calculations had the Passport at about 135 mpg, but the judges insisted they were right. In any case, the C70 was so far ahead of the others it didn't matter.

Industry Trophy in hand (or front basket), we motored back to Newport Beach the next day. Another nine hours in the saddle, cruising the surface streets past some of L.A.'s finest transmission-repair and bail-bond shops. Despite being unarmed, we arrived safely back at the *Cycle World* office at dusk, brain-dead but triumphant.

The next day, there was a big party, not only for our victory, but—as I recall—for someone's birthday, as well. A collection was taken up, and I was sent to the corner liquor store, where I filled the Passport's basket with four bottles of the finest champagne $20 can buy. Barb drove me home, and the headache I had the next morning was hard to appreciate unless you've actually had a railroad spike driven into your skull just above the left eye.

So, I must admit that our Slipstream photo had nothing to do with my job interview here at the magazine. It was just another opportunity for Editor Girdler to look out the window and wonder if he'd made a terrible mistake.

63

Springfield Novice

WELL, I HAVE TO ADMIT THAT I PROBABLY WOULD have missed the Springfield Mile again for the 63rd year in a row if not for our intrepid associate editor, Mark Cernicky.

Seems he's had this classic flat-track race on his bucket list for a long time and, upon turning 40, decided it was now or never. So he signed up for the AMA Pro Singles class, stuck a 450 Honda in the back of the *CW* Chevy van, and drove solo from California to Illinois. It would be only his second-ever Mile flat-track race.

We couldn't have the poor homeless lad without a midwestern cheering section, so three of us—my friends Lew and Pat and I—decided to go.

We made the four-hour drive down from Wisconsin in my swanky new (used) Cadillac in a toad-strangler rainstorm, wipers flapping on the frenetic setting. It didn't look good for the Saturday race program.

After checking into a Red Roof Inn near the Interstate, we headed into town to find the State Fairgrounds. I'd been through Lincoln's hometown twice before on motorcycle trips but had never seen the Mile.

I'd also never seen an afternoon sky quite as black as the one that hovered over us as we drove into town; it looked like midnight, and the streetlights were flickering on. Luckily, it suddenly stopped raining long enough for a severe hailstorm, then started raining again. Nevertheless, we navigated by headlight and found the fairgrounds. All racing had been cancelled for the day, but we got out and explored the beautiful old stadium-like grandstands, which had a massive Indy-like roof overhead.

Covered grandstands: what a noble idea. Shade from the sun, protection from the rain. Every race venue should have them, but not many do.

We looked out at the glistening, rain-soaked 1-mile oval and the grayish hair quite literally stood up on the back of my neck. I turned to Lew and said, "This is a big track, and most of it is curve. These guys are going to be sideways almost all the time. And it's fast."

I whipped out my cell phone to give Cernicky a call and found him lounging in his room at the Howard Johnson's near the track, having given up wrenching on his bike out in the rainy parking lot. He told me, "I've been getting all kinds of assistance from a Harley dude who drinks quite a bit of beer but has been incredibly helpful. Everyone's been really nice here." I said we'd explore the town and pick him up later for dinner.

It really was Mark's entry that finally got me to set the date in stone and come here for the first time myself. Seemed some other Memorial Day gathering always got in the way, so, as you might guess, I'd endured a lifetime of hearing "You've never seen the Mile? And you call yourself a motorcyclist?" Etc., etc.

Being more of a roadracer than a steel-shoe guy, I'd attended only one other big flat-track race. That was in 1981, when CW Managing Editor Steve Kimball and I had just gotten our pilot's licenses, and we blithely flew his two-place Grumman from Orange County to San Jose. With our fancy photo passes, we stood right on the inside of Turn 1 and got to see Jay Springsteen and friends thunder past at 100-plus mph. Great racing, and I still have the windburn, grin, and hearing loss.

But if a person needed incentive to return to flat-track, this was the year. The great Chris Carr had announced his retirement—after 7 AMA Grand National Championship titles and 12 Springfield wins. This was the summer of his Farewell Tour.

That evening, we picked up Mark and went to an excellent old downtown restaurant called Maldaner's, and I asked about his trip from California. Mark told us he'd gotten so addle-brained from ceaseless driving that during the middle of the night he'd seen an exit sign for Springfield and, rejoicing, had pulled off the Interstate only to discover he was in Springfield, Missouri. Big disappointment.

The next day, we had breakfast at another fine local institution—a café called Jungle Jim's—and went to the track. Racing was delayed until mid-afternoon while the track dried, and the program was shortened. Each group—Pro Singles and Expert Twins—would get just three practice laps before their elimination heat races and main events.

Mark ran well and stayed with his practice group, neither losing nor gaining places. In the heat race, however, he lost the back end accelerating hard through Turn 3 and low-sided at high speed. He virtually bounced off the track and back onto his bike, rejoining the fray, but the session ended before he could get in another fast lap. So, after all that driving, he didn't qualify for the main. He'd be running the TT on Monday, however. With a very sore knee.

In the Expert Twin main event late that afternoon, the low-number plates surged to the front, and Brad Baker led much of the race on a Ducati (yes!), despite its harrowing headshake, mixing it up with Jared Mees, Sammy Halbert, number-one plateholder Jake Johnson, Kenny Coolbeth, and Carr. In the end, the Ducati faded to fifth and Mees won on an XR-750. Carr ended up seventh, passed on the last lap by Willie McCoy.

The race was terrific, but on the long drive home, I kept thinking back to one brief moment during the weekend.

I've found—in years of viewing all kinds of races—that most of the action fades from memory, but certain sublime moments stand out and imprint themselves permanently onto your mental circuit board. I had one of those moments in the third qualifying heat for the main.

Carr suddenly pulled out all the stops and passed three other riders on his last lap, moving smoothly through traffic and throwing his Harley XR into a huge slide for the final corner, winning by a wheel. The crowd stood up and cheered, and people grinned at each other and shook their heads. We'd just been given a little demonstration of the talent and sheer force of will that produced all those championships.

It's these small moments that make you forget the rainy drive, the hailstorm, the cost of tickets, and the long wait in the grandstands. It's really what you take home from the races. Everything else fades away.

I might have to go to the Peoria TT later this summer and see if any more of these moments are available. Never been there, and I call myself a motorcyclist.

64

Cascading with the R1100S

*I*N THE WORLD OF WRONG DECISIONS, I'VE DISCOVERED THAT choosing to fly rather than ride to your destination is almost always a mistake—unless you have, say, the Pacific Ocean in your path. But sometimes you just gotta fly.

And that was the case recently, when Barb and I joined some old northern California friends on a ride through the Cascades near Sunriver, Oregon.

We've been getting together with this crew nearly every summer for about 25 years now and riding somewhere together—northern Mexico, the Ozarks, Colorado, British Columbia, etc. The wallpaper slideshow on my computer screen is filled with photos of euphoric-looking (not to say glassy-eyed) people in riding gear sitting at tables in a wide variety of hotel restaurants that have mountain roads lurking just outside.

It's a fairly fast-riding group, although health problems (gout, mostly, and centerstand-related back injuries) have recently forced one or two to follow along in cars. Luckily, these cars nearly always have their trunks filled with cases of wine, as several of these guys are in the Napa Valley wine business. Barb and I look forward to this annual opportunity to sample wines that actually cost more, per gallon, than unleaded premium or bottled water.

This year, our destination was the Northwest, as several riders had recently bought condos or cabins at Sunriver, a vacation development surrounded by snowcapped peaks, mountain lakes, tall timber, and surreal landscapes with lava flows and extinct (?) volcanoes. Our friends Ren and Marilyn Harris invited us to stay at their cabin and take day rides into the mountains.

We'd originally planned to ride our Buell Ulysses out there but soon realized we didn't have the extra week of travel time to make it from Wisconsin and back.

Ren to the rescue: "Why don't you fly out, and I can bring our 'guest' R1100S up to the cabin on the trailer with my R1200GS."

No arm-twisting required. The R1100S remains one of my favorite sport-touring bikes, and I'd ridden this one before, on a visit to California. It's a black, low-mileage beauty that belonged to Ren and Marilyn's late son, Ren Jr., who died of cancer when he was still quite young. It sat, polished and alone, in front of their house during the memorial dinner we all attended some years ago.

But before we could ride, we had to get to Oregon and back. It turned out this involved a couple of United Express flights on which the bathrooms had not been recently cleaned, so the cabin smelled just like the little house behind my great Aunt Margaret's big farmhouse. Minus the quicklime. Also, I had a broken seatback.

Other than that—and the lack of peanuts—it was quite opulent.

Sometimes, though, the modern airport experience can actually be erased (without traditional shock therapy) by the ride on the other end.

Ren and Marilyn led us on a spectacular 200-mile loop. And Ren is not one to get stuck cheerfully behind a 35-mph motorhome and a line of timid drivers. Yes, we did some passing.

After one particularly exhilarating zoom past a couple of dawdlers, followed by a nice blast through a fast uphill curve, Barb leaned forward and shouted, "What model BMW is this?"

"An R1100S!" I shouted back. "It's just like that first yellow testbike we rode through Colorado back in 1999."

There was a moment of silence, and then Barb said, "I like it!" This was followed by a happy squeeze on those parts of my waist where extra calories are stored for emergency use.

I liked it, too. I've been riding mostly dual-sport, standard, and adventure-touring bikes for the past couple of years on the theory that they are easier on my back and wrists—which, of course, they are. But I'd almost forgotten how nice it is to tuck behind the fairing of a modern sportbike and lay it into a big sweeper with a little body weight over the front wheel and your legs tucked up and out of the way. It's one of the four or five classic physical sensations in motorcycling.

Did I say modern sportbike? Okay, the R1100S is actually going on 13 years old. But—like that other favorite of mine from the 1990s, the slightly more stiff-legged Ducati 900SS—you don't suffer much from the heartbreak of archaic technology. It has taut-yet-fluid suspension, great brakes, and a smooth engine with lots of satisfying torque. And both the R1100S and the 900SS are almost illogically inexpensive on the used bike market now.

As we came down out of the mountains and into the city of Bend, I found myself wondering if I didn't need one of these bikes. Yes, my wrists and butt were a bit numb at the end of a long day in the saddle, but one needn't always ride for a full day to have fun. . . .

Oh, Lord. The mental gears were turning again.

You'd think I would have learned by now never to borrow a good motorcycle, because I always end the ride by asking myself, "Why don't I have one of these?" It's a disease, but a harmless one, I guess. Except for the missing money in our IRA.

That evening, Ren and Marilyn had everyone over to their cabin and opened a few bottles of the eye-wateringly excellent cabernet from their own vineyard (Paradigm), and I accidentally magnetically wandered, glass-in-hand, out to the garage to look at the black R1100S.

A lovely bike to ride, and quite an impressive piece of motorcycle sculpture, I think.

Barb and I'd had some good times on these bikes. We rode that yellow testbike from Colorado to Wisconsin and back to California across Texas and the Southwest. Took a silver one through the Alps for a week, and Ren's black beauty through northern California a few years ago. And now this trip. All with the same group of people. But three of them are no longer with us.

This black one was special, of course. We'd ridden with Ren Jr. when he first got the bike, and it was a nice reminder of those times and the thing that had brought and held us together all these years, which was riding.

Sometimes it's hard to separate the symbolism and personal meaning of a bike from your attraction to it.

I guess that's because you can't, and shouldn't even try.

65

The Superslab vs. The Blue Highways

*O*NE OF THE CERTAINTIES OF LIFE IS THAT IF you make a doctor's appointment two months in advance, it will land on the worst possible day. And so it was last summer, as I was mapping out my backroad scenic route from our Wisconsin home to the MotoGP in Indianapolis.

The phone rang and a surprisingly cheerful recorded voice reminded me I had a long-awaited doctor's appointment the next day at 2:30 p.m.

This was not good.

Cycle World had a reception planned for our Rolling Concours at a downtown hotel that evening, and Editor Hoyer had asked me to join the gang. I knew from previous trips that it took about six hours to get to Indianapolis—via interstate—so I figured I could see the doctor and still get there with about 45 minutes to spare. See everybody, have a drink, and dine on small crackers with mysterious bits of crustacean and greenery on them.

Alas, my doctor is a competent and earnest young professional, so the next day's appointment was not a quick one. He spent so much time pondering the dosages of prescriptions needed that I was afraid my brain might explode: "We could give you 10 milligrams, I suppose, but then perhaps 7.5 would be better to start out, . . ." etc., etc.

I looked into his eyes, and all I could see was the sun going down over Indiana, with me searching for the hotel in downtown Indianapolis at night, peering through starbursts of light in my bug-spattered faceshield. I hate riding in unfamiliar cities after dark.

Finally, he released me from speculative pharmaceutical bondage, and I literally ran through the halls toward my waiting Buell Ulysses. If there had been a fire pole in the building, I would have used it. I vaulted onto the Buell like the Lone Ranger and all but burned rubber pulling out of the hospital parking lot. Outpatients with walkers took one step backward. A few minutes later, I was on I-90, hammering south at 80 mph, and watching for cops.

This was a far cry from the laid-back trip I'd planned, but I found—once settled into the saddle—that I was really enjoying myself. Perfect late-summer riding weather, with the Ulysses right in its zone at 75-80 mph, motoring smoothly and liquidly along with the muted purr of a good Chris-Craft.

There's a tendency among most motorcyclists (including me) to put down interstate travel, but when you really have to get somewhere, there's nothing like it. You can picture yourself moving relentlessly across the planet like one of those little model airplanes on a parchment map in an Indiana Jones adventure. The uninterrupted progress itself creates a specific kind of euphoria.

As it turned out, I got there in less than six hours, but it didn't do me any good. I'd forgotten about the time zone change, so I lost an hour. Also, I had to negotiate a maze of road construction on the outskirts of Indianapolis, not finding my hotel until about 10 p.m. I missed the reception, but it had somehow gone on successfully without my standing there holding a wine glass, as Editor Hoyer did just fine with the hosting duties.

We all had a marvelous weekend with the Rolling Concours and the MotoGP, and when I left for home early Monday morning, I finally had the whole day ahead of me. And I mean the whole day. I inexplicably woke up in my hotel room at about 5 a.m. and could think of no good reason to lie there like a dead fish, so I made a little coffee in my room and left Indy with only a faint trace of light on the horizon.

Taking the I-road out of Indy to put the city behind me, I exited on Highway 25 near Crawfordsville and then spent the rest of the day heading jaggedly northwest on small county roads. Red barns, silos, neatly mown farmyards, golden-tasseled corn, old bridges, small towns, yellow school buses, cemeteries with pioneer gravestones, American Legion halls congratulating Al and Irene on their 50th anniversary. Bingo Night!

Coming into Rantoul, Illinois, on Highway 136, I found myself passing the old original Bell helmet factory, still active, but with somewhat faded paint. I bought my first Bell helmet, a 500-TX, in 1966. Still have it. And I had one on now, a more modern open-faced version with a flat shield. I turned around and tried to visit the office to see if there was a small display or museum, but the only factory entrance appeared to be at the cargo gate, where several semis were waiting. I decided to press onward.

Late in the day, I crossed the Illinois-Wisconsin border near Rockton, Illinois, and took Paddock Road past the gates of Blackhawk Farms, a favorite racetrack of mine for both cars and bikes. Crossing into Wisconsin, I took the hilly Highway 213 home. The sun was just disappearing behind the trees when I pulled into our driveway after about 12 hours of riding. So the return trip took almost exactly twice as long. Yet it was a fun trip in both directions.

It's funny how entering and exiting an interstate can create almost the same sensations of relief, but for totally different reasons.

When you absolutely have to be somewhere, the slow progress on a two-lane road—stuck behind slow drivers, with a few detours thrown in—can almost reduce you to tears of frustration. When you finally hit the interstate and twist that throttle open, you feel like Superman bursting out of a phone booth. Free at last.

Conversely, when you have time to spare and can take that exit onto Farm Road 233, you feel like someone who's rocketed in from the coldness of outer space and landed on a new green planet. Everything slows down, color intensifies, noise is muted, and the world takes on a serene, life-in-a-fish-tank quality. Thousands of small details in landscape and architecture suddenly keep your brain occupied, and you stop calculating distance and looking at that digital clock on the instrument panel. Progress slows, but time flies.

I had a nice dose of both kinds of road on this trip and enjoyed the contrast. But I must say that if the day ever comes when I have all the time I need—and enough travel money for all those inviting small-town cafés and rustic cabins and motels—my tires will seldom touch the interstate.

The exits still have the on-ramps beat.

66

Lessons from the Glen

LAST WEEK, BARB AND I DECIDED TO SQUEEZE ONE last weekend of fun into late autumn before winter turned on us like a rabid dog, so we towed my 1978 Formula Ford 800 miles, from Wisconsin out to Watkins Glen, New York, for a vintage race.

The Glen, which sits in the hills along Seneca Lake in the scenic Finger Lakes region, is a legendary track that I'd never driven before, though I'd once been there as a spectator.

That was back in 1979, when my buddy John Jaeger and I rode our motorcycles out there from Madison, Wisconsin, to see the US Grand Prix for Formula 1 cars. It was the year a Ferrari, driven brilliantly by Gilles Villeneuve, won in the cold October rain.

And—wouldn't you know it—when Barb and I drove through the gates last week, it was yet another rainy October afternoon. I pulled over and walked up to the fence along the track, looking out on the downhill sweep of Turn 1.

"This is exactly where John and I stood to watch qualifying thirty-two years ago," I told Barb. "I think our bikes were parked right over there."

"Did you camp at the track?" she asked.

"Well, we had camping gear, but we were so cold and wet we got a cheap cabin somewhere near Watkins Glen. I can't remember where," I said. "I think my brain was frozen."

A few memories, however, remained clear. John was riding his nearly new silver-smoke BMW R90S, and I was on a metallic blue 1975 Honda CB750 Four. We'd been planning the trip all summer but, at the last minute, I concluded that my 1967 Triumph Bonneville was mechanically too tired to make a high-speed run all the way to New York in the company of an R90S, so I decided to sell the Triumph and buy a Honda 750.

I listed the Triumph in the classifieds, and the ad was answered by a well-known local motorcycle collector named Kenny Bahl. He asked me why I was selling the Bonneville and I told him I needed a newer bike for a long road trip.

"I have a nice 1975 Honda CB750 I could trade you, straight across," he said.

Done deal.

The Honda four-piper was in excellent shape and had low mileage, but it had been sitting for a while in a damp barn, so all the electrical ground wires had turned green and needed cleaning. Also, the carbs were full of grit, and the float needles and seats leaked. I took the carbs off and cleaned them—about three times—before everything worked right.

John and I left Madison on a dark Tuesday morning with temperatures hovering in the low 40s. By the time we got to Rockford, Illinois, we had to pull off at a restaurant called the Clock Tower and drink many cups of coffee, after running our hands under hot water in the men's room. On the way out, we stuffed newspapers into the fronts of our jackets. John had a leather jacket and a sweater, and I had a Belstaff jacket and a wool sweater Barb had knitted.

It wasn't enough.

After that, I don't remember much about the trip except holding onto the handlebars with a death grip and shivering. Only a few pleasant moments stand out in my mind, like slightly out-of-focus snapshots: a green, lovely stretch of farm road past huge yellow haystacks in southern Ontario; hot apple pie at a hilltop restaurant in the Alleghenies; an afternoon of perfect winding road through rural Pennsylvania, during which I kept thinking we should return sometime on a warm summer day. That's about it.

So when Barb and I got home last week, I called John to see if his memory was any better than mine.

It was.

"We draped all our wet camping gear over the chairs and bed in that cabin in Watkins Glen while we went to the track," he said, "and we were worried they'd throw us out for getting the furniture wet. Also, we almost crashed into a giant water-filled hole at a road construction site in Pennsylvania. We both did a lock-up slide on the muddy pavement and almost fell in."

I could picture it: our faceshields fogged up, both of us tearing along a little too fast to properly interpret the yellow flashing barrier lights in the mist. Also, our hands and brains were frozen.

"Why were we so cold?" I asked John. "Why didn't we plan better and take better riding gear along for the trip?"

"There wasn't any," he said flatly. "Or else we just didn't know about it. No heated grips or seats. No insulated touring suits. No good, rainproof touring boots. I don't even think we had any real rain gear," he added. "All we owned were hooded raincoats and baggy rain pants, and they flapped in the wind and leaked water down your chest and into your boots, so we didn't bother to take them. Anyway, nobody really planned anything in those days; we just did it."

True enough. I had a supposedly rainproof waxed cotton Belstaff Trialmaster jacket, but the rain always soaked into the fabric eventually, and you ended up as a giant Air Wick. The wind rushing over a rain-soaked Belstaff jacket could work quite nicely as a cooling tower for a nuclear reactor. I tried some cheap plastic rain pants, but they tore apart in the wind and, after much duct-taping, I threw them away.

My first bright yellow Dry Rider rain suit was still a year or two away. I might not have worn one anyway. We were way too cool to appear concerned about our comfort. As John says, we just did it, leaping into the unknown. These were the existential touring days.

"Okay, here's another question," I said. "Knowing it was probably going to be a wet, miserable week in October, why didn't we just take a nice warm car out there, like your MGB?"

John thought about that for a few silent moments, then said, "Probably because a car trip would have been too easy. We'd wanted to go to a real Grand Prix at Watkins Glen since we were 13, and the trip deserved a certain amount of effort and sacrifice. A car wouldn't have made it seem important enough."

Of course. That was it. I'd almost forgotten. The pilgrimage factor.

Still, a momentous event deserves only so much respect, and I wouldn't take this trip again without a windshield, heated grips, neck-warmer, waterproof boots, a decent rain suit, and an electric vest. And a credit card for motels.

All of which I now possess, thanks to Watkins Glen.

67

Directing Traffic

WELL, OUR SLIMEY CRUD CAFÉ RACER RUN WAS A big success this past fall. I've never been any good at estimating crowds, but those with adding machines behind their eyeballs assured me we had more than 1,000 motorcycles show up for this biennial ride from Pine Bluff to Leland, Wisconsin.

The perfect autumn weather helped, and bikes came pouring in from three or four surrounding states, if you count Illinois—which many of my Illinois friends do, even though they have no true hills or curves. It seems cruel to remind them, but sometimes I can't help it.

The starting point for this ride is about 30 miles from my home, so I got up early and took scenic backroads on my Buell Ulysses, cutting though swirls of yellow and red autumn leaves and inhaling the pure country air, which is supposed to be good for you. This theory may precede the advent of large "factory farm" feedlots, however. I can now hold my breath longer than a Navy Seal.

I hung out in Pine Bluff for a while, then headed for Leland through the woodsy hills.

Right after turning north onto Highway 78, I came upon an accident scene, with police cars and an ambulance. A cop was emphatically directing traffic, so I didn't stop to help—or slow down much to gawk. A passing glimpse, however, revealed a group of riders standing around, the bottom of a motorcycle on its side (Triumph Triple?), and—strangely—a neatly folded stack of riding gear on the roadside, with a helmet on top.

When I got to Leland, I mentioned this scene to a group of guys, and an old acquaintance named Ray said, "I'm the one who stacked that gear next to the road. I saw the whole accident."

Ray said a group of bikes had been stopped on the road with their left turn signals on when it appeared the about-to-be-injured rider tried to pass them on the left, just as they were turning. Bad idea. He T-boned the front end of one of the bikes and crashed, with some injuries, but apparently nothing critical.

I was glad to hear the rider was still with us, despite his apparent lapse of judgment. I was also glad not to be one of the first on the scene.

I really hate directing traffic.

That phrase, in fact, has become my personal code for impending disaster. If I'm on a group ride where the red mist sets in and people (especially me) start riding over their heads, I mutter to myself, "Before long, someone will be directing traffic."

I've done this unenviable job myself at least three times.

The first occasion was in late 1989 when Barb and I rode from *CW*'s Newport Beach office up to Laguna Seca for the USGP on our first Honda ST1100 testbike. On the way home, we took some backroads through the mountains and came across a group of Honda dealers trying out new Pacific Coast 800s.

One of them had collided with the left front fender of a car in a blind corner. The car was dented, and the rider had broken his leg, while the Pacific Coast had an ugly gash of missing bodywork down that side.

Japanese manufacturers seldom waste a lot of money making hidden parts look elegant, and I remember thinking the bike looked like something from *The Terminator*, where an android peels back the skin on his wrist and you can see all the hydraulic rods and wire bundles.

Barb and I directed traffic around the crash scene while the rider's friends looked after him. The man was in considerable discomfort, and it took forever for the ambulance to show up. When it finally got there, I had a tension headache from willing it to arrive. Empathy beats injury hands down, but it still takes something out of you.

The next episode was a lot more fun, just because no one—including the motorcycle—got hurt. I hope I can mention this one again without getting fired.

A bunch of us staffers were attending the Honda Hoot in Knoxville, riding on a winding mountain road near the Blue Ridge Crest. We were whistling along pretty good on our VFR800 Interceptors when Mr. Hoyer, our now-editor, glanced in his mirror briefly to make sure everyone was still behind him, then entered a tight corner too fast and went straight off a cliff, taking part of a rusty old barbed-wire fence with him.

I sez to myself, "Well, this can't be good."

But by the time I turned around, Mark's hand was already reaching over the edge of the precipice as he pulled himself back up onto level ground. It was like a Wile E. Coyote cartoon. I resisted the urge to hand him an anvil from the Acme Anvil Company.

Mark wasn't the least bit hurt, and his bike was down below, lying on top of a big bush, with hardly a scratch on it.

Some of us are just blessed. I'm surprised he didn't land in an inflatable swimming-pool chair with an umbrella drink in the armrest.

Anyway, I spent the afternoon directing traffic while a tow truck winched the bike back up to the road. Got to meet a nice couple who stopped on their

KTM 950 Adventure to see if we were okay. Their bike was just like my old one. After a few hours of staring at their parked bike, I was inspired to go home and buy another new 950.

So what happened to my old KTM?

Well, on a Saturday ride, I'd traded bikes with my friend Greg Rammel, who had a Ducati Multistrada. Greg went pretty hot into a tightening left-hander and, as an experienced roadracer, overestimated the amount of grip available from my spindly, semi-knobby adventure-touring tires—i.e., almost none. He skillfully slid both ends, then disappeared into the woods and broke his knee badly on a small tree.

I directed traffic that afternoon and got another migraine from wishing for the ambulance to come, as Greg was not feeling any too chipper. Luckily, this one got there a lot faster; cell phones had arrived.

So far, I've avoided having traffic directed on my behalf. All my injury/bone-breaking crashes have occurred off-road, on trails so remote I had to be my own ambulance and ride out.

I suppose this means I need a separate phrase for impending disaster in the dirt. One that might work is "I guess we'll soon be needing the Vicodin."

For those moments just after a dirt crash, I've found it's also useful to practice the phrase "No sense taking that boot off 'til we get to a hospital."

68

Windjammer Days

THERE'S AN OLD SAYING THAT COINCIDENCES ALWAYS COME IN pairs. Well, it's not an extremely old saying, because I just made it up a few minutes ago, but it seems to be true.

As a handy example, I went to the AHRMA vintage races at Road America last summer and, while wandering through the swap-meet area, noticed a very well-preserved old Windjammer fairing from the early 1970s. White in color, it was sitting on the ground, almost lost in the usual mix of rusty CB360 frames, slightly bent wheels, and rare two-stroke engine cases with blown crank seals.

I got down on one knee to examine the Windjammer and had one of those odd moments of delayed product lust and wistful longing that iconic motorcycle stuff always seems to generate.

I turned to my buddy Richard Sharer and said, "I wish I had a motorcycle to put this fairing on. I think I need another Honda CB550 or 750 Four."

Richard nodded without blinking an eye. He understood perfectly. "A classic fairing and bike combination," he said.

Then, lo and behold, shortly after Barb and I got home from Elkhart Lake, a large manila envelope arrived in the mail.

Seems a *CW* reader named Ken Cook of Smyrna, Georgia, had sent me an old book he thought I might enjoy, and it turned out he was right. It's a big soft-cover volume called *Motorcycle Camping and Touring*, published in 1972 and edited by Peter W. Tobey.

I'd never seen the book before, but the illustration on the cover was a pen and ink drawing of a Honda CB500 Four with a Vetter Windjammer fairing on it.

I looked at the illustration and experienced—for the second time that week—one of those odd episodes of arrested breathing where you find yourself caught in a brief moment of time travel. This usually happens when I see old photos of Elke Sommer or Julie Christie, but in this case, there was a motorcycle involved. Again.

Why the odd reaction?

Well, if anything on earth says "motorcycle travel in the early 1970s," it's a single-cam Honda 750 or 500/550 Four with four upswept mufflers and that big-yet-sleek Vetter fairing on it. Interestingly, the first ad for a Windjammer appeared in this magazine in November of 1971—just one month after the new Honda CB500 Four graced our cover.

For those of us who started riding in the 1960s, it was a combination that seemed to promise that we were finally on the brink of a whole new era in motorcycle travel. Here was an electric-smooth motorcycle that would ostensibly run forever without leaking oil or blowing up, coupled to a fairing that would allow you to ride across the Rockies in late autumn after most people had put their bikes away. The whole rig had "freedom" (and freedom from suffering) written all over it.

You could suddenly see yourself going anywhere. Got a girlfriend on the opposite coast? No problem. Hop on your bike and discover America en route. Take a tent and sit around campfires at night. That was the dream.

A dream in no way dampened when Robert M. Pirsig published his famous *Zen and the Art of Motorcycle Maintenance* (reviewed right here in our February, 1975, issue) and turned the idea of motorcycle touring into a virtual religion. Suddenly, you weren't just going for a ride; you were making a philosophical statement about the way to live and the correct way to see the world. It was like canoeing or mountaineering for the mechanically inclined.

I'd just made the leap into big-bike ownership then with the hopefully named "Interstate" version of the Norton 850 Commando, and of course, Barb and I had to take a long cross-country trip on it. And naturally, we needed one of the big fairings of the era. It was the way things were done. You needed the Zen-like calm behind that fairing to be fully aware.

I thought the Vetter Windjammer was the best-looking fairing of the era, but I seem to recall there was no mounting kit available for the Commando, so I ended up with a Daytona fairing. I also thought the Daytona fit the lines of the Norton well, because it looked as if a cherry bomb had gone off inside a classic English café racer fairing and puffed it out a few hundred percent. But it was nicely finished and had storage pockets for gloves, sunglasses, etc. built in. What luxury. Weather protection was pretty good, too, but the thing was heavy. The first time I hit the front brake, the Norton dived enough to put a fairing dent in the front fender. Some precision shimming (i.e., stack o' washers) required.

Like most of these big, frame-mounted fairings of the era, it had a sturdy, blacksmith-quality mounting platform held on with hose clamps, and a built-in headlight and turn signals that required some cobbling of the stock wiring harness. Quite the operation, installing one.

After our trip from Wisconsin to Montana (we were headed for Idaho but the Norton Interstate "refused the office," as the Brits say, and decided

Montana was plenty far enough), I took the fairing back off the bike and was amazed at the sudden rebirth of performance. The Norton felt like it had gained 40 hp and wanted to wheelie and leap around like a colt. I decided never to put a heavy fairing on a bike again and sold the Daytona to my friend Jim Wargula to put on his own 850 Commando.

We're still friends, but he sometimes goes all sullen on me for no apparent reason.

In any case, I've never had a bike with a true Windjammer fairing on it. Craig Vetter himself sold the company a few years later, as more motorcycle companies started to make their own touring fairings. And I was getting into roadracing at that point, moving away from weight and touring tranquility to more of a café-racer ethic in my bikes. As was Vetter, with his lithe and racy Mystery Ship.

Still, the Windjammer remains a nice touchstone to that era when many of us first went touring. And it's still a classic shape that has stood the test of time. Good looking, then and now.

When I see one, it makes me think of tents and campfires, the smell of bacon cooking, and open spaces in the West. That's a lot of freight for one piece of fiberglass to handle, but it still works its spell on the defenseless imagination— mine, at least—after 40 years.

69

To Café or Not to Café

OMETIMES WHEN YOU COME IN FROM THE WORKSHOP, IT'S best to go directly to the basement and throw your coveralls and virtually all your clothes straight into the washing machine. And I say "virtually" only out of modesty.

That's exactly what I did the other night, as I was pretty well saturated with parts cleaner, gasoline, and choke-rich exhaust fumes. If I'd lit a cigarette on the way in from the garage, I would have gone up in a green flash of smoke, like the drummer in *Spinal Tap*.

The source of the problem was a 1975 Honda CB550K I bought only two weeks before. I'd just removed the perfectly good aftermarket 4-into-2 exhaust system to put on a slightly café-racier 4-into-1 system made by Mac.

Nice pieces. The system fit perfectly (without heating and bending, for once) and was well-chromed and quiet, yet pleasantly woofy, allowing just enough of that famous Honda single-cam Four electrically smooth rustle and howl to escape. The sound of subdued rage, a civilian echo of the old Hailwood Hondas.

While I had the old exhaust system off and out of the way, I'd decided it was a good time to change the oil and filter and clean the bottom of the engine, so I'd been lying on the floor beside the bike with a pan full of parts cleaner under it, brushing away, with plenty of chemicals running down my sleeve and puddling on the floor around my shoulder. The finned oil-filter housing had road tar on it, so I'd soaked that outdoors in a pan of gasoline. Messy business for me, the lowly worker bee, but the queen was now spotless, and the new system was in place and ready to go.

With that project done, I'd put up with my own aroma and itchy skin long enough to open a bottle of Lake Louie Stout and kick back in my erstwhile Buell office chair (bought at the factory liquidation sale) so I could contemplate my night's work.

And it was beautiful. I love the look of the old Honda CB500s and 550s. As with the 400Fs and CB750s, I seem to be genetically disposed to admire them.

This was a great era for all Hondas, but there's just something about the 500s and 550s, a balance and a rightness of size. They are, as my journalist friend Rich Taylor once wrote, "ethereal."

As such, they are now much sought-after for café-racer projects and have been almost from the moment they hit the market in 1971. They aren't especially fast bikes by any modern (or even ancient) standards, but their sound and architecture lend themselves to dreams of purposeful modification, to the adding of lightness and simplicity.

I'd been looking for a CB500 or 550 café-racer donor bike for quite a while, as had my Colorado friend Mike Mosiman, and we'd been trading emails with Craigslist and eBay listings for a year or more. I'd seen a few prospects, but they'd been inconveniently far away, high in mileage, or already restored at great expense. Generally speaking, I like to find bikes in my own area, where I can go look at them and hear them run. There's also an element of serendipity in finding one close by, as if the Fates had intended it. Good for morale.

And this one had all the right credentials. I found the CB550K on consignment at Sharer Cycle Center near my home, with only 6,000 original miles on the odometer. The owner, an FBI agent, lived nearby. He'd bought the bike in Illinois and spent quite a bit of time and money bringing it back to good running condition.

The guys at Sharer's had cleaned the carbs, installed new jets, adjusted the valves, installed a new battery and vintage-correct tires, etc. They'd also sent the non-standard metalflake blue tank (no corrosion inside!) and sidecovers out for a stock paint job in "Candy Garnet (chocolate) Brown" with black side panels and gold pinstriping. Correctly speaking, this was a 1976 color option, but it's a paint scheme I've always liked. Actually, all the K-bike colors from this era are pretty nice.

We started the bike up, and it ran beautifully; clean revving, no cam-chain rattle, nice idle. Too cold and snowy out to ride it, but I bought the bike anyway, on faith and instinct. By coincidence, Mike was visiting his relatives down in Illinois that week and had swung by our place on the way home. We hauled the 550 back to my workshop in his pickup and spent a euphoric, coffee-fueled evening cleaning and polishing the bike and removing the slightly scabby luggage rack, backrest, and caseguards. As anyone knows, this is the most satisfying part of any restoration. The physical pleasure of tossing a rusty luggage rack almost pays for the bike.

When we were all done, we sat back for the requisite sacramental beer, and Mike said, "You know, this is really quite a nice original bike. I mean, it's got decent chrome and paint, a good seat, and no sun-fading on the instruments. Even the original decals are all there. You might want to think twice about turning this into a café racer. If you put the original four mufflers on this thing, it would look almost new. I don't think you want to be grinding the passenger peg brackets off this frame or chucking those nice chrome fenders."

I nodded. "Unfortunately, I've been thinking the same thing. It's too nice a bike to modify in any way that's irreversible. I think my café racer plans may end up as a mere change of handlebars, shocks, and tires. But I am going to put a 4-into-1 pipe on it. I've owned a couple of CB550s in the past and could never bring myself to remove those beautiful original pipes. On this bike, I don't have to worry about it. Also, a set of new OEM replacements costs about $1,000 . . . ."

So after Mike left for home, I ordered that Mac 4-into-1 system. While waiting for it, I spent some pleasant evenings last week cleaning and polishing the valve covers and other aluminum bits with a buffing wheel and various colors of metal rouge. The bike just keeps looking better and better. Every time I turn my workshop lights on now, it's like Christmas morning.

Naturally, the minute Mike got back to Colorado, he found a really original orange 1974 Honda CB550 on the Internet, and last weekend, he drove his truck out to Omaha to pick it up. In the pictures, it looks showroom perfect. Another survivor.

It's a peculiar kind of bad luck when you keep finding bikes that are too nice to modify. Maybe next year we can do worse.

70

Range Anxiety

ON ONE OF OUR TYPICAL LATE NIGHT PHONE CALLS, my brother commented recently that I spend quite a bit of time talking about weather in this column. He's probably right, but it's pretty hard to avoid the subject when you're a motorcyclist. You might as well expect a fish to ignore water quality. The weather is where we live.

And yesterday, we were really living.

It was 83 degrees here, the hottest March day in Wisconsin history—as recorded by European settlers, who first introduced clear-cutting technology and the exact science of weather forecasting to the local forest dwellers.

And it was almost as warm the previous evening as I rode into the city for our Slimey Crud Motorcycle Gang meeting. I was riding with my leather jacket unzipped, and this has never happened before in March. I can't tell whether we've got global warming or if I've accidentally thrown the earth off its axis by selling my '53 Fleetwood to that guy in L.A. and we're now on the same latitude as Panama. In any case, it was about 75 degrees on Old Stage Road at 7 p.m. as I rode along on my newly refurbished 1975 Honda CB550 Four, its new 4-into-1 exhaust sizzling electrically down the road.

A few miles from home, unfortunately, the Honda engine began that disheartening stumble that says, "You'd better start groping for your fuel petcock now, pal, or the Dodge Ram in your rearview mirrors will run you down like a ground squirrel." Hmm . . . kind of early for reserve . . . I'd just filled the Honda up for my very first spring ride the previous afternoon. I looked at the odometer, and it said I'd gone 92 miles.

Yikes! Short range for a bike with a 3.7-gallon tank, 1.3 of that supposedly being reserve, though I've found these figures always to be slightly theoretical, like the number of servings in a bag of deep-fried pork rinds.

But then I remembered that this was, after all, a CB550 Four. Not one of the most efficient engines ever designed.

Back in the 1960s and 1970s, Honda had a reputation for wringing incredible mileage out of a gallon of gas at a time when their Japanese two-stroke competition was fairly guzzling the stuff. Small-bore Hondas (50-160cc) would typically get anywhere from 80 to 200 mpg. Then the CB750 Fours came out, and they weren't too bad for a big, glamorous high-performance bike, but mileage dropped into the mid-30s to low 40s. Next, the 500/550 Fours were introduced, and, oddly, they were slightly worse. My previous 550—given a little spirited throttle twisting—would get around 33 mpg. I've never heard a good explanation of why this is. Probably just the vagaries of gearing and cylinder-head design.

Anyway, I switched to reserve and hummed along toward town. I had about 20 miles to go, and there was a convenient Shell station right near the Blue Moon Bar where we hold our meetings. Should make it just fine, I reasoned, and I did. The tank took a little over 3.1 gallons, with 112 miles on the trip odometer, for about 35 mpg. Not too bad for a 550. About the same as a modern Honda Civic (which the reader will note is a slightly bulkier object), but still livable.

Nevertheless, I made a mental note for any future 550 road trips that I should plan my gas stops around 100 miles apart—unless I wanted the suspense of running on fumes. This was the shortest range I've had on any motorcycle, except for the 883 Sportster I owned in the mid-1990s.

The Harley got better mileage than the Honda, but it also had a 2.25-gallon "peanut" tank. I think I could have carried more gas in my wallet. That bike went on reserve and then ran out of fuel in less than 100 miles on an empty stretch of Florida's I-95 while I was speeding to see my dad in Boca Raton after the Daytona 200. The bike rolled to a quiet stop about two miles from a fuel exit, and I was rescued by a couple with a Gold Wing who just happened to have a siphon hose. Blessed are the organized, for they shall save the feckless and dim.

I took this as a sign that, just as you should never play pool with a guy named after a state, you should never tour on a bike with a gas tank named after a small nut.

The fact is, I really like range in a motorcycle. Or a car, boat, or airplane, for that matter. To quote the world-circling Voyager co-pilot—and former fighter pilot—Dick Rutan, "I hate sweating gas."

I've been seriously low on fuel twice in my life while flying a small plane, and I must say it gives you a wonderful sense of alertness but tends to leave your neck muscles in a knot. Low fuel on a motorcycle, like a single error in flying judgment, tends to compound itself with progressively worse consequences. You skip a gas station; the next one is closed; there's an unexpected detour; then it's getting dark and now you're on Highway 50 in Nevada reading a sign that says "Next Fuel 63 Miles." On reserve.

The dirt-bike version of this happened to a bunch of us on a trip through Copper Canyon in Mexico a few years ago. We got some bad advice on a "shortcut" through the mountains and found ourselves way low on fuel, smack-dab in the middle of nowhere. Luckily, my buddy Dave Scott was riding his almost unmanageably heavy BMW R100GS with the huge Paris-Dakar tank. Soon, we were calling his bike "The Mother Ship." Without that P-D tank, our bleached bones would still be down there somewhere, picked clean by buzzards. (Which brings up my favorite line from *Dances with Wolves*: "Someone back East sayin', 'How come he never writes?'")

Anyway, my idea of good range on a touring bike is about 250 miles, including reserve. Our old BMW R100RS would do that—and did once, in the lonely Four Corners neighborhood of Arizona, with a good tailwind and much fervent prayer. But hitting reserve at 92 miles is a little disappointing.

Still, I like riding that 550 a lot and will probably do some touring on it this summer. Humans have survived worse hardship than stopping every hour and a half for fuel and a nice cold drink in an air-conditioned convenience store.

Which I'll probably need. If it's 83 degrees here in March—40 degrees above normal—I think we can safely extrapolate that it'll be about 143 degrees here by the end of July. But there I go again, talking about the weather. Which probably has nothing to do with fuel mileage.

71

The Two-Buck-A-CC BSA

SO, THERE I WAS, MINDING MY OWN BUSINESS THIS week with life going pretty well, when the phone rang. It was my old friend Scott Dell, a Vincent buff who lives in New Jersey. I met Scott at the Mid-Ohio Vintage Festival about 12 years ago when he kindly let me take a ride on his beautiful Series A Vincent Rapide. A rare treat, and we've stayed in touch ever since.

Anyway, Scott called me this week and said, "Hey, you like BSA Victor 441s, don't you?"

"Yes . . ." I said, guardedly. This is kind of like having someone ask if you are interested in a blind date with a really neat woman he just met at the methadone clinic. You've got to think. The date part sounds all right. . . .

Which is to say that the 441 Victor has always been, to my eye, one of the most clean and starkly beautiful shapes in British big Single scramblerdom, but friends who have owned them always warn me that they are not exactly paragons of anvil-like reliability. Not for nothing, apparently, were they called "441 Victims" when I was in high school. But back to Scott's phone call.

"Why do you ask?" I said.

"Well, my friend Kenny is cleaning out his garage, and he's had a Victor sitting there for many years. He was going to sell it to a couple of neighborhood guys who have no idea what it is, but I told him we should find an owner who appreciates its history. And I'm coming out your way in a couple of weeks to drop off a Vincent in Wisconsin. If you're interested in the BSA, I could drop that off, too."

"How much does Kenny want for the bike?"

"Two bucks a cc. So I guess that would be $882. That's what he paid for it some years ago when he bought it used from a local dealer."

"Does it run?

"No, but it turns over. It's missing its front fender, chainguard, and muffler. Otherwise, it looks complete and in pretty good shape. It's a 1969 square-barrel

model. It has all its original decals, and the frame doesn't even look like it needs repainting. Might be an easy restoration. Are you interested?"

"Sure," I said. "Always wanted one, and this is my big chance."

After I hung up with Scott, I went over to my massive wall-o'-bike-magazines bookshelf on our front porch and started digging out old, well-thumbed issues with Victor road tests and cover photos. I also pulled out my three or four hardcover BSA history books by Roy Bacon and Don Morley for a quick refresher course in 441 Victor lore.

Strangely, the old *Cycle World* and *Cycle* magazines in my 1960s repository of great literature didn't spill a lot of ink on these bikes, given their popularity at the time. The only full road test I could find was in the April, 1966, *Cycle World*, which ran a very cool cover photo of the 441—a close-up of the engine, distinctive yellow-and-polished-aluminum tank, and a rider's buckle-style motocross boot, with speed lines coming off them.

The road test was reasonably enthusiastic but not effusive. The editors were a little disappointed that the production bike was not a closer replica of the factory GP models on which the great Jeff Smith had won back-to-back world motocross titles in 1964 and 1965. Smith's bikes, of course, had many special alloy parts, a hand-built frame of Reynolds 531 tubing (later, titanium), and an aluminum barrel with a liner of chrome instead of cast iron. In order to be affordable to the general public, the road-legal "Enduro" model understandably had to be made from less-exotic materials.

Still, the guys here at the magazine liked the bike pretty well—except for the cursed Lucas Energy Transfer ignition system, which required perfect adjustment between contact points opening and crankshaft position for the bike to run at all. They said it was a "beast" to start, and more or less echoed author Roy Bacon's comment that "if it starts it won't run, and if it runs it won't start."

Even in high school, I was amazed that England could build Merlin V-12s for Spitfires in 1939 but couldn't come up with a better ignition system for a single-cylinder pushrod engine in 1966. There was no explaining British technical progress.

But, with a 302-pound curb weight and 34 horsepower, the medium-big Single did a fairly respectable quarter-mile of 15.5 seconds with an 83-mph terminal speed. Its most notable trait, though, was instant throttle response and big torque from almost zero rpm.

And that was my lasting impression of the Victor when I'd ridden one, just once, in the summer of 1968. My girlfriend's cousin was dating a guy who had one, and we both showed up at her cousin's house on our motorcycles—me on my Honda Super 90 and him on his 441 Victor. Somehow, my manhood survived this withering contrast, and he let me take the BSA for a short ride. I happily lunged down the street and couldn't believe the arm-jerking, big bang nature of the engine. I told him, "This thing only fired five or six times going all the way around the block."

So, if I ever get this new project bike running, it'll be interesting to see if it still exudes that same aura of awesome grunt, or if it just seemed impressive after riding a Honda Super 90 all day.

In any case, the 1969 square-barrel version of the 441 Victor I'm buying is a somewhat improved version of the early round-barrel model we tested in 1966. For one thing, it has battery-and-coil ignition instead of the dreaded ET system, as well as a larger front brake, a good-looking dual seat with the classic BSA bum-stop, and various other small technical improvements. The best-developed of the series, essentially, right at the end of the era. And almost at the end of BSA's existence.

I don't have any illusions that this BSA will be a daily rider, a long-distance touring bike, or even a rational replacement for a good used trail bike, such as a Suzuki DR350. But the 441 is a blessedly (we hope not deceptively) simple bike that should be fun and rewarding to restore. It'll also be great to look at in the garage, whatever its state of tune.

To me, it's one of those special old bikes—like the Bultaco Metralla or Ducati Mach 1—that can easily double as both art project and transportation. And sometimes, you just have to take the leap and invest in art. Especially at two bucks a cc.

72

Adventures in Retro-Touring

WHEN I HOPPED ON MY BUELL ULYSSES LAST TUESDAY evening to head in to our Slimey Crud meeting, the bike fired right up as usual. Or maybe "exploded into action" is a better description. That big Sportster-based motor always starts with the calm precision of a couple of mortar rounds going off and then settles into a pounding and violent "Hey, lemme outta here!" combustion cycle. All part of the charm.

This time, it once more started instantly, but the Check Engine light came on and did not go off. I took the bike for a very short test ride and the light stayed on.

Hmmmm . . . Low oil? No, the oil was fine. I "visually inspected" the bike—which does about as much good as staring at your refrigerator—and could see no glaring problems. This is my idea of checking the engine.

I used to be a professional auto mechanic but am pretty much defeated by Check Engine lights these days. Unless there's an obvious hole in the crankcase, I don't know where to start, so I usually just call the dealer, who has a diagnostic computer.

Last week, however, I couldn't take a day off to run the bike into a shop, and we were leaving on Friday for the AMA SuperBike races at Road America. What to do?

Slowly I turned . . . and looked at my 1975 Honda CB550 Four. Nice bike, great seat, running fine. Why not take that?

Back in 1977, Barb and I rode our Norton Commando out West and ended up riding for a few days with a guy named Tom, who had a Honda 550 just like the one we now own. He rode with us from the Badlands to Yellowstone Park, and I remember listening to the reassuring hum of his Honda Four on the highway and wondering if maybe we'd made a mistake, buying a big, vibratory British Twin. Which—unbeknownst to us—was about to swallow an exhaust valve and leave us stranded in Montana.

The morning we were leaving our campground near Yellowstone, my Norton was uncharacteristically hard to start (valve already beginning to seize in its guide, no doubt), so I was cursing and working up a sweat with the kick starter. At that moment, Tom walked over and hit the starter button on his CB550 while brushing his teeth. The engine instantly hummed to life. Hot and tired as I was, I had to laugh.

Not hard, mind you, but I still had to laugh.

The next day, after we'd sent our broken Norton home in a Bekins moving van and continued our vacation by bus and train, I wondered what it would have been like to take that trip on Tom's 550.

Maybe our ride to Road America—35 years later—would be a chance to find out. Barb was fine with the concept, so I set about preparing the bike for our little 300-mile round trip.

First, I strapped on my tankbag, but we'd obviously need more luggage space. There were no hard bags, and even my soft bags wouldn't fit, as the 550's stock, forward-mounted turn signals (which are about the size of small frying pans) prevent you from slinging anything over the rear seat. So, I did the unthinkable and retrieved the old, rusty luggage rack from the scrap-metal pile in my garage.

The luggage rack came with a severely ugly bolt-on passenger backrest— one of those 1970s jobs with an S-curve in the back that makes it look like part of an aluminum screen door. A stylish leftover from the era of lamb-chop sideburns and chocolate-brown riding leathers with huge, floppy collars. I took the backrest off and tossed it. I have my standards.

After throwing a duffel bag across the reclaimed luggage rack and strapping it down, Gulliver-style, with plenty of bungee cords, I jacked up the rear springs, checked the oil, aired the tires, lubed the original non-O-ring chain, and off we went, wearing our vintage Belstaff jackets—still with Norton and Isle of Man pins on them.

And it was . . . not bad. The 550 actually rides better with a passenger and luggage—more settled, not as stiff and jouncy—as if the springs were intended for two-up touring all along. The engine, which is no ball of fire even solo, was nevertheless quite torquey and unfazed, pulling easily at anything over about 3,000 rpm. We flew along the backroads at 70 or 75 mph (5,000-5,500 rpm) with a serene, electrical hum. Even the dual seat, which felt a little too soft on first sitting, was surprisingly comfortable for touring. We got off about every hour and a half to stretch, but seat pain was minimal.

Range was the only real shortcoming. We had to get gas about every 100 miles and got 32 mpg on the trip. But low fuel was timed about right for coffee stops. Anyway, the bike ran like an electric train and made the trip just fine. Great weekend ride.

So: would we want to take this thing to Montana, two-up, on a modern-day road trip?

Well, if it were the last motorcycle on earth, I'd do it without hesitation. But it's not, and time has marched on. What we mostly get with modern motorcycles is vastly improved suspension and brakes, more precise handling and—most of all—real horsepower.

When we got home, I fired up the Buell again and—guess what?—the Check Engine light went out immediately. I love problems that are self-curing. I took the Ulysses for an evening ride, and the immense horsepower and torque almost brought tears of gratitude to my eyes. After riding the Honda 550 for three days, it was like trading a Remington electric shaver for a McCulloch chainsaw. Pull the trigger and rip.

When I unpacked last night, I realized my lower back was just a bit sore from leaning forward on the Honda—one of those wishful-thinking leans, as if your posture would make the bike accelerate harder. Back when Barb and I flew our 65-horsepower Piper Cub, we used to stretch our necks trying to make it climb faster. This is the same thing. Bare adequacy brings on its own tension and fatigue.

So, I would say that as an all-purpose tourer, the Honda is a sweet bike, but it's not quite, well, bad enough to be continuously entertaining on a cross-country trip.

It suddenly occurred to me that this was exactly why I'd bought my Commando back in 1975. It was bad, in the best sense of the word. And if you ride one now, it still is.

Nevertheless, there's much to be said for arriving at your destination and getting back home. Without a bus.

73

The Vision Thing

I'VE NEVER UNDERSTOOD WHY CLAMS ARE THOUGHT TO BE happy, as they seem rather expressionless to me. But this past spring, I was certainly as happy as any of these fabled bivalves, and the reason was a change of faceshield and helmet. Yes, my needs are simple.

I have a good friend in Colorado, you see, who has an old pal named Thom Parks, who now works for Bell Helmets, and they both conspired to send me a new full-face Bell Star in bright silver. This is a shapely thing with good venting and a trailing-edge spoiler that helps pull air through the helmet and also gives it a hint of velociraptor-like menace. It fits quite well, considering I have what used to be known in motorcycling as an "Arai head," meaning my skull is long and narrow rather than round.

I had an anthropology professor in college who told us that this skull shape is a throwback to the now-extinct Neanderthals. Apparently, I had a primitive ancestor who sneaked into a campfire sing-along with a bunch of modern Homo sapiens and fathered a child who, for some reason, was not immediately killed, despite his odd appearance. He may have been launched down the river in a reed basket and adopted by a band of roving Gypsies on their way to Ireland. I know it sounds crazy, but that's my theory.

Anyway, the new Bell Star looks sharp and fits well, but by far its best feature (for me) is that it came with an accessory, $120 "Transitions SOLFX" faceshield. Like Transitions lenses in eyeglasses, the SOLFX is clear in low light but automatically darkens in sunlight. The best part of having this technology in a faceshield, however, is that it's out-of-doors, where it can react immediately to sunlight rather than being hidden behind another windscreen. I hate to make too much of it, but for a person like me who wears glasses and has had his clip-on sunglasses fall off inside the helmet a few times, this is a revolutionary development.

Now I can leave on a trip with a single faceshield instead of storing one in my jittering tankbag where it gets all scuffed up. Or head out for our Tuesday

Slimey Crud meeting in bright sunlight and return through the dark forest at night without opening my smoke-tinted shield and ingesting mosquitoes while watching for the deer that are trying to kill me. This shield really works.

So, all is finally well in the vision department, right?

Not exactly.

About three months ago, I was riding in town and, while stopped at a red light, flipped up my new faceshield to rub my right eye. While doing so, I glanced down at my odometer and realized I couldn't read it with my left eye.

At all.

There was just a foggy blur where the numbers should be. Odd. And it didn't improve on the rest of the ride. When I'd shut my right eye, I could see vague shapes and colors but not much detail.

Was it possible that a single 16-ounce margarita, consumed the night before, could cause bleary vision in just one eye? Would two of them have made me stone blind? Unlikely.

Over the next few weeks, this condition seemed to be getting worse, so I finally went in for a thorough eye exam. When it was over, the doctor said, "Well, you've got a pretty bad cataract in your left eye and the beginnings of one in your right eye. You need surgery in both eyes so we can implant matching lenses."

I sat back in my chair and said, "Cataracts? Me? Seems like I'm kind of young to have cataracts. I'm only sixty-four."

He shook his head dismissively and said, "Lots of people younger than you have problems with them."

That made me feel better. Still, I couldn't remember anyone in my Cub Scout troop having cataracts. . . .

"It's a fairly quick day-surgery procedure," the doctor said, "and we can put in lenses that should give you 20/20 distance vision. You might have to wear some light-duty drugstore glasses for reading, though."

Well, this was certainly good news. I really hate wearing glasses—and I especially dislike trying to shove those flexible bows back over my ears inside a helmet. Alas, there was a time when I wore only reading glasses and could ride and drive without them. We have photos of me just 15 years ago doing trackdays with my Ducati and racing a Reynard Formula C car at Road America, sans glasses. And wearing cheap (yet dashingly stylish) drugstore sunglasses at trackside instead of $400 prescription sunglasses that I seem to misplace with some regularity. Those were the days.

So, I'm actually looking forward to surgery, for once, and getting my eyes fixed. The only downside is that the VA (my only source of medical insurance at the moment) won't pay to have both eyes done, since my right eye isn't quite bad enough yet to qualify for surgery. They want to put in a lens that matches my current bad vision in the left (since your brain won't tolerate just one bifocal) and then fix the other one the same way a year or two down the road. No cataracts, but no improvement in basic vision.

I told them I don't want to go through double eye surgery so I can retain my crappy, 64-year-old vision and bifocals. I'd rather have it done right at a private clinic and pay for it myself.

"Ha, ha!" they said. "Wait until you find out what that costs!" I did, and it's about $15,000—after a 10 percent discount for cash payment.

I came home, thought about it for a while, and decided to sell my beloved '34 Ford to pay for the surgery. Yes, that's how much I dislike wearing glasses. I'd rather be able to see clearly than have a great old car in the garage. Which looks kind of blurry these days and may actually be a Studebaker, for all I know.

Before I left the eye doctor's office after my exam, he asked, "What do you do for a living?"

I told him I ride motorcycles and test cars and write about them for a couple of magazines. I said I also race a vintage car for a hobby, an old Crossle Formula Ford.

"Well, I wouldn't go out on the track with your vision," he said. "You don't have much depth perception, and you're almost blind in your left eye. Also, you might want to think twice about riding your motorcycle."

The '34 Ford goes on eBay this week.

74

Zen and the Art of the Oil Change

*T*HESE DAYS, A LOT OF YOUNGER, LESS EXPERIENCED RIDERS come up to me and say, "Mr. Egan, you have an almost legendary reputation for being able to change the oil and filter on your motorcycles without spilling more than about thirty percent of the oil onto the garage floor or your own clothing. How the heck do you do it?"

I tell them, "Well, kids, part of it is experience. I worked for almost a decade as a foreign-car mechanic, and I've also owned and maintained a lot of motorcycles in my life. But basically, it's a Zen thing; you have to work thoughtfully and carefully, planning every move and wasting no motion. You have to be at one with your motorcycle and the molecular flow of lubricants in the universe."

I've been asked this question so often, I thought it might be beneficial to our readers if I walked them through the stages of one of my typical oil changes. Let's take the case of my Buell Ulysses, whose oil I changed just last weekend.

Naturally, I didn't have an oil filter on hand, so I rode 60 miles to Mischler's Harley-Davidson/BMW in Beaver Dam to get one.

There are Harley dealers closer than this, of course, but they don't have BMWs to look at, as well as Harleys. And it's important to remember that at least 60 percent of the reason we ride is to go look at other motorcycles. I'm told some people do it just for the scenery and fresh air, which I suppose is possible, but it seems rather shallow.

So I arrived at Mischler's and—after confirming that they didn't have a good, used black BMW R1100S for sale—went straight to the parts counters and asked my friendly parts-man Aaron if he had an oil filter for a 2009 Buell Ulysses. Harley is long since out of the Buell business, as we know, but I was told when I bought my bike that parts and service would be available for the next nine years. This sounded fine to me.

When you're in your mid-60s, nine years sounds like eternity, which it very well may be, depending upon the results of your last EKG. And if, for some reason, you happen to live longer than that, there are always parts on eBay. No worries here.

Anyway, Aaron looked up the filter and said, "Do you want just one?"

He asked it in a tone that implied that most wise shoppers buy at least two filters at a time or maybe a six-pack. "Better give me two," I said grandly, privately mourning the lost opportunity to take another long, pointless ride to a motorcycle dealership.

So I took my filters and headed home. I could have bought some genuine Harley-Davidson oil, too, but I use 20W50 Valvoline racing oil (with mystical ZDDP) in a racing car and have a couple cases of the stuff stacked in my workshop. Should be okay for the Buell, I figured.

Back home, I followed the oil-change instructions in the owner's manual and began my sublime work. Here's where the specific instruction kicks in. Pay careful attention.

Step 1: Place a "suitable container" under the sump or oil reservoir—which, in the Buell's case, is in the hollow swingarm above the end of the muffler—and remove the plug. A stream of scalding hot oil will run down over the rear of the muffler and cascade into the pan, like Niagara Falls in a nightmare. Some will run down to the far end of the muffler and onto the floor. Or trickle warmly down your forearm and into your sleeve.

Step 2: While oil is dripping from the drain hole and muffler, remove the small chin fairing and place another pan under the oil filter. Remove the filter with a web-type tool, and stand back as oil from the engine and filter run over the front of the muffler and into the pan. Much of the oil will follow the bottom of the muffler and run onto the floor. Expect some to drip off the filter wrench onto your blue jeans. Accidentally drop the slippery, hot filter into the pan for a nice splash effect.

Step 3: Carefully fill the new filter with oil, spilling hardly any at all, then screw it into the engine and put the drain plug back in. Here's where you give the drain pan an accidental kick so that a small tidal wave of oil flops onto the floor. Then refill the reservoir using a funnel with too small an opening so that it overflows immediately and burps oil onto the swingarm. Before putting the chin spoiler back on, use massive amounts of contact cleaner/degreaser to clean up the muffler and floor, along with ecologically friendly piles of oil-soaked paper towels.

Step 4: Carry the main oil drain pan across the workshop and dump it down a large funnel into a disgustingly filthy, oil-streaked, red plastic five-gallon gas can with the words "DRAIN OIL" scrawled across it so people don't accidentally drink from it.

Step 5: Check to make sure this can isn't already almost full. Otherwise, about two quarts of dirty drain oil will well up around the sides of the funnel and run onto the floor, as mine did. Expect some oil to run down the back side of the pouring spout on the drain pan and drip onto your running shoes.

Step 6: Mop up the oil spill with more paper towels and wring them out over your drain pan. Clean the whole area with half a spray can of contact cleaner, but don't breathe any of the fumes. When everything is cleaned up, start the bike and check it for oil leaks. Mine was fine; not a sign of a drip.

Step 7: Wipe your tools carefully, put them away, and then go into the house. Throw all your clothes—including the running shoes—into the washer and then take a shower. Put on clean clothes and return to the workshop to have a beer and ponder the evening's work. Now, you're done.

The sharp reader will note that some oil was actually spilled during this process, but that the majority of it ended up in either the bike or some kind of container.

Is there a truly perfect, Zen-like way to change your oil, working calmly and logically, without spilling a drop?

I suppose somebody somewhere can do it, but not me. There's a remote possibility that I'm too impatient and impulsive or just too unskilled.

In any case, I've found the best substitute for skill is to work alone. That way, no one knows you're not at one with the serene, clock-like machinery of the universe. Or how much you swear.

75

The Great Plains Triumph Exchange

THERE'S AN OLD SAYING, "BE CAREFUL WHAT YOU WISH for, because you just might get it." And this is never truer than when you mention to my friend Mike Mosiman that you're thinking about buying another motorcycle. His computer is on full Internet alert all day long (picture the boiler room of the HMS Royal Oak preparing for the Battle of Jutland), and he's never more than a few key taps away from total knowledge.

And so it was with my search for another Triumph Bonneville T100 in claret and aluminum silver. When I told Mike what I was looking for, he immediately found a 2008 model at Erico Motorsports in Denver with only 1,400 miles on it. "I'll drive down there tomorrow from Fort Collins and take a look at it," he said.

He did just that and pronounced the bike "perfect." A few days later, I'd negotiated a deal, and my cashier's check was on the way. Mike said he'd pick up the bike with his Ridgeline and keep it at his house until I could figure out how to get it back to Wisconsin.

The obvious and fun way would have been to get a cheap one-way flight from Madison to Denver and ride the bike home. And if it had been early autumn, I would have done just that. But in August, the temperature everywhere between Wisconsin and Colorado was hovering at 104 degrees—or higher. When you stepped out of our house at noon, the sunbeams felt like death rays from outer space. Nietzsche said that which does not kill you makes you stronger, but sometimes that which does not kill you just melts your boots on the exhaust pipes. It was too hot on the Great Plains to be fun.

So, not wanting to wait for cool weather to ride the new Triumph (that would be wrong), I was about to call a shipping company for a quote when my phone rang. It was Mike.

"Okay, I've got your Triumph in the back of my truck, and I've got a couple of days off. So, I thought rather than unload it at my place, I'd just head for

Omaha tomorrow morning. That's about halfway between your place and mine. If you get up early and jump into your van, we could meet there late tomorrow afternoon. I'll pay for my gas if you get the motel rooms."

"Not only that," I said magnanimously, "but I insist on buying you dinner at one of the best truck stops on the Interstate, within reason."

By "Omaha," of course, Mike actually meant Marne, Iowa, which is about 30 miles east of Omaha.

Marne (locally pronounced "Marn-ee," like the Hitchcock movie rather than the French battlefield) is a small, shady village just south of the Interstate and famous among motorcyclists as the home of Baxter Cycle. This shop, owned by Randy Baxter, is a modern Triumph dealership that also buys, sells, restores, and repairs vintage British bikes. The back room is filled with classic Triumphs, Nortons, and BSAs, with the occasional Vincent or Velocette lurking in the mix. If you like British bikes, it's kind of like agreeing to meet at the candy store. Or maybe a more adult analogy would be an opium den. The British have profitably fostered many addictions.

So, Mike and I jumped in our respective trucks and headed east and west, like one of those old algebraic story problems (if one train leaves Boston at 9:00 . . . etc.). Luckily, I didn't have to make this long drive alone, as my retired buddy, Lew Terpstra, agreed to go with me. Lew himself has two Bonnevilles, a modern T100 and a 1972 version that he's actually taking to Bonneville this fall in a record attempt.

Westward we wafted van-wise across the mighty Mississippi into Iowa at Dubuque, then down through Cedar Rapids and Des Moines, pressing on regardless of corn fields, subsisting only on gas station health food and energy drinks that contain something called "taurine." All jacked up on this beneficial amino acid, we arrived at Baxter's in Marne just 20 minutes before Mike got there. Good algebra.

The claret and aluminum silver Bonneville gleamed in the back of Mike's pickup and was indeed perfect. I took it for a ride and searched in vain for the reasons I'd sold my last one. Randy Baxter himself came out of the shop and took it for a ride, pronouncing it flawless in throttle response, even with the stock jetting and pipes. Randy helped load the bike, running it up into the back of my van and assuming the dreaded cave-crouch while we tied it down. This is a true bike guy.

While at Randy's shop, I bought a centerstand kit for the Triumph (a must-have for proper garage viewing) and an exhaust system for my BSA 441 Victor project. Unfortunately, I also went into the back room full of British classics and fell for a 1970 Bonneville that Randy was preparing to sell. Dark red and silver ram's-horn paint scheme, almost exactly like the '08 I'd just loaded in my van. To my mind, the most beautiful of the era and the last of the great Meriden Bonnevilles. Oh, Lord, another temptation, and me fresh out of money.

I resolved to go home and re-read both Thoreau ("Simplify, simplify!") and the Dalai Lama, who points out that happiness cannot be found in material objects.

But then I thought, *Hey, what do Thoreau and the Dalai Lama know about the eternal and timeless appeal of Triumph Twins?* Next to nothing, as far as I can tell. I resolved to eventually complicate my life in the form of a 1970 Bonneville.

New bike in van, we found lodging at a glamorous Super 8 motel nearby, and then had dinner at a family restaurant next to the motel. Excellent home-smoked ribs, good beer selection.

Lew and I headed east in the morning and made it home that afternoon. Long drive, but it had been a productive and eventful two days that would otherwise have probably been lost to memory in the dog days of summer. And I suppose you could say this is what motorcycles do best. They eliminate the dangerous tendency to sit perfectly still, stare out the window from your air-conditioned house, and contemplate the meaning of life. Which we now know to be meaningless without motorcycles.

Mike's invitation to jump in the van immediately and drive 500 miles west fit perfectly with a favorite motto of mine, which I'm going to have translated into Latin just as soon as I find someone smart enough to do it:

"Without motion, nothing."

76

The Moon of the Slippery Wet Leaves

*I*T COULD HAVE BEEN A BAD MOMENT FOR A new rider. But luckily, I'm an old rider who's already fallen on his elbow in a situation exactly like this, so I stayed off the brakes, took the gentle "rain line" through the corner, and slithered through without incident. Holding your breath helps.

Wet, new-fallen autumn leaves were the problem here. Seems we had a wild spell of wind and rain last night, which pretty much stripped the woods of their last vestige of fall color and pasted all those red and yellow leaves to the road surface. And these babies are slippery, belonging as they do to the banana peel family of deciduous foliage. I hit a patch of them while riding my CB160 to class when I was in college and learned to see the world from a whole new angle.

Incidentally, I see here in my dictionary that *deciduous* comes from the Latin verb *decidere*, which means "to fall off." I guess this also means some of us are deciduous riders. One fall begets another.

But I did not fall off this time, and it was a beautiful day. The morning after our big storm dawned sunny and warm, so I hopped onto my '08 Triumph Bonneville and turned off Highway 59 onto County H, a nice little winding road along the Rock River. I was headed for Team Triumph, our nearest Triumph dealer, in Janesville, Wisconsin, ostensibly to buy some oil. Or maybe I was just going there to take another look at their new green 2013 Thruxton with gold stripes. No one knows. Sometimes our motives are inscrutable, even to ourselves.

Anyway, there I was, headed south along the Rock River toward the Triumph shop with some kind of semi-contrived excuse to be riding somewhere on what may be one of the last warm and beautiful days of autumn.

I slowed for the little town of Fulton and passed a sign for Indianford, a small village situated nearby on the banks of the river. It's best known now for having a nice little café and a bar with a great fish fry, but 180 years ago, Indianford really was a place where Indians forded a shallow spot in the river.

Chief Black Hawk and his band of Sauks and Foxes supposedly used this spot to cross while being pursued by the Illinois volunteers (among them a young Abraham Lincoln) in 1832, during the last big fight to hold onto their territory in what is now Wisconsin. Their original trail probably lay beneath the very blacktop I was now riding upon.

I swerved to miss another patch of damp yellow leaves in a corner and suddenly thought, This is the moon of the slippery wet leaves.

Perhaps it was the ghost of Chief Black Hawk whispering in my ear. Whispering quite loudly, it would seem, as I was wearing a helmet and earplugs. Maybe I was just hearing voices again.

In any case, as I rode along, it occurred to me that the traditional Native American custom of naming months for some seasonal phenomenon made a lot more sense than our system of naming months after Roman gods—many of whom seem to be either retired or slacking off on the job. I mean, when was the last time Janus or Mars answered your prayers for anything? Never happens, even when you sacrifice an owl.

So, during my ride, I came up with possible motorcycle-related names for our months to replace the ineffective, non-descriptive old ones. Depending upon what climate you live in, you may have some of your own names, but this is my personal upper-midwestern take on the calendar.

October: I'll stick with The Moon of the Slippery Wet Leaves, as mentioned.

November: The Moon of We Should Have Taken This Trip a Month Ago.

A sure sign that you're touring a little late in the season is the sight of jack-o'-lanterns that are all caved in and withered on the front porches of farmhouses. If they're turning black, it means they have frostbite.

Incidentally, if you're riding around the north shore of Lake Superior, you may want to move this lunar phase back to October, or even September. Last time I made this trip was in early October, and I came to think of it as The Moon of the Steaming Wet Gloves on Heated Handgrips.

December: The Moon of the Shrinking Leather Jacket.

The lunar cycle here starts with Thanksgiving dinner and ends with New Year's Day football snacks. Also sometimes called The Moon of the Christmas Cookies.

January: The Moon of the Blinking Battery Tender.

Here in the rural Midwest, we also call it The Moon When Mice Eat Your Wiring Harness and Put Corn Nuggets in Your Air Cleaner.

February: The Moon of Looking at Property for Sale in Arizona and New Mexico on www.Realty.com.

Also called The Prozac Moon in some depressive cultures with a strong peyote tradition and no Internet access.

March: The Moon of I'm Sure It Won't Snow This Year if We Ride to Daytona Instead of Taking My Van.

April: The Moon of I Should Have Drained My Carburetors During the Moon of the Slippery Wet Leaves.

Also called The Moon of Soaking Your Jets in Carb Cleaner. If you still have a bike with carburetors. T.S. Eliot said April was "the cruelest month," but this is only true if you've neglected to prepare your bike properly for storage. Or if you try to take a ride.

May: The Moon of Waiting Endlessly for One Good Rain to Wash Away the Sand and Salt.

Also known as The Moon of Premature Enthusiasm and Unpleasant Surprises at Nearly Every Apex.

June: The Moon of Now I Remember Why I Bought All These Motorcycles and Have a Closet Full of Riding Gear.

July: Moon of the Greasy Tar Snakes.

August: Moon of the Mesh Jacket.

Some also call it the Moon of Pretending to Shop for Sunglasses at the Gas Station While You Soak Up Their Air Conditioning and Pour a $2 Bottle of Mountain Spring Water on Your Head.

September: The Moon of the Adult Vacation.

Yes, children are back in school, and the Mount Rushmore parking lot is blessedly empty of minivans. The weather is dry, clear, and still warm, and the first hints of fall color are just beginning to hit the aspens and maples. Sometimes simply called The Best Moon.

77

This is Your Life

BREAKING A LONG TRADITION OF ALWAYS BEING IN A hurry and accomplishing nothing, I finally managed to slow down last week and smell the roses.

Okay, there weren't any roses because it was late autumn, so I had to smell the bare brown fields of the Great Plains, some recently spread with fresh manure, but I still managed to engineer one whole extra day into a cross-country trip so I could take two-lane backroads instead of blasting down the interstate.

Alas, I was not on a motorcycle this time, but driving home with a nice, inexpensive "winter" car, an older BMW 325i I bought from a friend in Denver. Flew in from Wisconsin and drove it home.

And on my meandering three-day drive, I magically found myself stopping for gas in Anamosa, Iowa, right next to the National Motorcycle Museum, which is housed in a large building at the center of a mall.

Now, I've been past this place at least a dozen times in my life but never had time to stop. Always miles to go or people to meet. But this time I looked at my watch, realized it was still morning and I was only about 150 miles from home, so I walked right in and bought an $8 ticket. Map in hand, I passed through the entrance into a big, remarkable motorcycle wonderland, with only a few other tourists wandering around on this cold weekday in the off-season.

A strange calm descended upon me as I realized that—for the first time in my life—I was by myself in a motorcycle museum, with all the time in the world. I could spend the whole day here and still make it home that evening.

The first section I happened upon was an Evel Knievel display, which was fascinating, even though I was always a little too old for the lunch-bucket and coloring-book phase. Opposite that sat the last existing Captain America chopper from *Easy Rider*.

A placard explained that the bikes Fonda and Hopper rode through most of the movie were stolen right after filming was completed, but a second

Captain America bike used in the final redneck/shotgun scene was saved, and this was it.

I looked at the bike for a long time and recalled that I first saw it projected against the yellow plaster wall of a latrine at a base camp called Than Hai. I saw another motorcycle-intensive movie, *Alice's Restaurant*, on the same wall that year. I was not a big fan of the Vietnam War while I was there, but it occurred to me—even then—that a less tolerant country than the United States (North Vietnam, for instance) would probably not show movies with these anti-establishment themes to its troops.

So, for some riders, the Captain America bike may represent freedom of the road, but for me it's more symbolic of freedom of expression—and a country worth coming home to. An odd twist, I admit, but there you have it.

I passed a display dedicated to the really bad biker movies of the 1960s and watched a trailer from *The Mini-Skirt Mob*. Babes with big hairdos and tall white boots riding the usual mix of small, mismatched motorcycles. Fistfights and wrasslin' matches between girl bikers in tiny skirts. Summer outdoor movies so bad and so funny you just had to go. Where are they now? We need to make more movies like this. Yes, moguls, it's retro time.

I turned a corner and ran into a bunch of mannequins wearing motorcycle-club uniforms from the 1940s and 1950s—one of my first impressions of motorcycle riders in this life. Uniforms of a radium-green not found in nature, cowboy pockets, and yellow stripes down the legs, part military and part service-station attendant, with a hint of a country-and-western band.

The monogrammed uniforms were from a club in Chillicothe, Ohio, with a father figure "John" standing next to a uniformed child with "Little John" embroidered on his green shirt, both of them talking to a woman mannequin named "Vickie." Small people, by our standards, thin as rails. They'd survived the Depression and World War II and were celebrating life with motorcycles and friends who understood them, at a time when not many people did.

At another display sat Steve McQueen's Indian Scout rat-bike with the old sleeping bag strapped to it. On the wall, the "Halt" Triumph poster from *The Great Escape*, the same one I've got on my garage wall. Off to the side, a continuous running of *On Any Sunday*, one of the few movies I will watch at the drop of a hat, anytime with anyone. They were showing the desert-racing section, and I got a brief glimpse of our late off-road editor, Ron Griewe, coming into a checkpoint. Ron was a great guy to work with, and desert racers like him and McQueen did a lot to make riding in the dirt seem like a wonderful idea in that era. I'm not ashamed to say that I got a little watery-eyed watching this film clip, the way you do when you truly glimpse the steady passage of time, if only for a few moments.

What else? A Bridgestone 7, the Sport 50 model, exactly like the first motorcycle I owned. I saved the money for it by mowing the local cemetery all summer and stared so hard at this bike in the window of Lee's Hardware store that I'm surprised it didn't melt. Pure desire, condensed into a single object. To paraphrase John Prine, if desire were lightning, that shop would have burned down a long time ago.

And over there, an original, unmolested 1913 Henderson Four on display. I went over and stared at the engine for about 20 minutes, looking at its open valve gear, polished aluminum intake manifold and beautiful flowing exhaust header. I traded a go-kart for one of these engines in 1963 because I wanted to use it in a home-built airplane—one I never got built at home or anywhere else. I got part of the wing done, and that was that. Out of money, time for football practice. But what a beautiful engine. Just to have owned one erases all regrets.

There were many, many other bikes, of course, and the museum seemed to have at least one version of every motorcycle I've ever owned or longed to own. Nortons, Triumphs, dirt bikes, roadracers. For me, taking my time and walking through these displays was kind of a slow unfolding of life and experience, from the earliest moments I can remember to the present.

We're lucky, I thought as I drove away, that we have such a good way to measure time. Motion, memory, loss, and desire, all contained in metal castings and the shapes of tanks.

78

The Spark of Life

I DON'T THINK I'M EXAGGERATING MUCH WHEN I SAY MY BSA 441 Victor ran last weekend.

Yes, the thing actually carried me up the hill to the nearest stop sign and then roared back down again. Exactly two miles under its own power.

It was a little brisk out there—almost too cold for combustion—but I hardly noticed because I was drenched in sweat from kicking for 20 minutes and then physically running the bike up and down the driveway to break the clutch loose and bump-start it.

This is something I do every few years to see if I'm overdue for a massive heart attack. It's a lot cheaper than having a stress test at the hospital, and it allows you to perish right at home, with your loved ones nearby. In any case, the second I popped the clutch in third gear, the Victor fired up and took off like a bazooka round, only with more smoke. This is a bike from England's black-powder era.

Running. For the first time in 20 years.

Granted, it wasn't what you'd call smooth running. There still seems to be something clogging the idle circuit, so the engine was hammering along on the main jet, bellowing and surging. It sounded just like one of those Le Rhône rotary aircraft engines from World War I, where there's no throttle so the pilot has to control his speed with a ground switch. If you want to hear this stuttering effect, check out Errol Flynn and David Niven in *The Dawn Patrol*, landing their ever-mutating Nieuports and Scouts on that mythical corner of France that is forever Orange County, California, a few miles from the *Cycle World* offices.

Oddly, working on this bike wasn't what I'd planned to do at all on a cold Saturday morning. I'd walked out to the workshop carrying my tweed Fender guitar case, intending to do a little practice in our beautifully carpeted (indoor/outdoor, in slag gray) band corner. While waiting for the place to warm up, I idly walked over to my Handy motorcycle lift to gaze upon the elevated BSA.

It was poised there waiting for that special dark, dull day in midwinter when I'd inexplicably find the gumption to roll up my sleeves and start restoring it in earnest.

But as I stood there examining the side of the engine at eye-level, it suddenly occurred to me that it might be fun to kick the Kroil-soaked piston over and see if I could make that spark plug spark. I'd bought the bike with no battery and no ignition key, so I installed an old Spree scooter battery, plugged the coil wire into the hot side of the switch, took out the spark plug, laid it on the cylinder head, and gave the kick-start lever a shove with my hand.

Spark!

Not just a spark, but a big, blue fat spark that made an audible snap. Amazing. This BSA had been sitting around in the back of someone's garage in New Jersey for two decades, and I hadn't even cleaned the points.

It's hard to know which metaphor to use in describing that spark. I suppose it would be sacrilegious to mention Michelangelo's Adam receiving the spark of life from God on the ceiling of the Sistine Chapel, so I'll go with Dr. Frankenstein channeling the energy of the heavens into his monster, after first running it though a Van de Graaff generator for a little added scientific hocus-pocus factor.

Either way, I was suddenly energized and immediately forgot all about guitar practice. If I had spark, all I needed was fuel and air, right? What if I just dumped gas in the tank and the bike started?

Probably not a good idea, after all these years of sitting. I decided to take the Amal carb off and clean it, and a good thing, too. It was full of dry white aluminum powder and other crud, so I got out an old can of carb cleaner and set the carb parts aside to soak for an hour.

And when they came out of that cleaner they looked . . . exactly the same. Someday, I'll find a brand of carb cleaner that actually works. If I do, I'll let you know. Better yet, if you find one, you can let me know. All this stuff did was smell really bad.

Five days later, the fumes emanating from my hands are still waking me up at night, even though I've bathed, done dishes, washed the car, and stolen some of Barb's lilac-scented hand cream. I swear, when I die, there'll be some old deaf guy in the back row at my funeral shouting, "Emma, do you smell carb cleaner?" This stuff just doesn't quit.

Anyway, I went to Plan B and cleaned the carb parts with lacquer thinner and a stiff-bristled brush and got most of the stuff off. Blew out all the jets and passages and put the carb back on the bike. I installed a fuel line, added gas to the beat-up-but-clean, old aluminum tank, and was theoretically ready to go.

I tickled the carb, eased it over TDC, pulled in the compression release, held my mouth just right (as CW's late contributor Henry Manney used to say) and kicked.

And kicked. Got a classic BSA oil-cap bruise on the back of my leg, had the engine spit back a few times and try to throw me over the moon, but it wouldn't start. Sounded like too much ignition advance to be safe for further kicking, so I did that bump-start down the driveway and it fired right up.

Took my short, two-mile ride and discovered the brakes work, the clutch works, the transmission shifts smoothly, and the bike goes right down the road. It's also a wonderful size for a motorcycle—light, agile, and fun. Still needs a second carb cleaning (or maybe a new carb; the old one's pretty worn out), the timing set correctly, and a bit of cosmetic restoration, but I'm on the job.

Yesterday, I drove down to a vintage British motorcycle shop called Morrie's Place in Ringwood, Illinois, and managed to spend about $450 on a bunch of parts the bike needs. Got a new throttle cable, a better headlight bucket, and a pair of new Dunlop K70 tires for that correct period street-scrambler look. Next, I have to find someone who can do a proper yellow-and-polished-aluminum paint job for the tank.

Amazing what a single spark will do to a human being. Adam got himself kicked out of Eden, Frankenstein's monster had to flee from a bunch of angry villagers with torches and pitchforks, and my guitar case is still sitting over near the amp. Also, I'm $450 poorer and something smells like carb cleaner.

79

Return of a Cult Classic

WHEN I WAS IN HIGH SCHOOL IN THE MID-1960S, dazzling my way to a perfectly mediocre scholastic record, my parents used to drive 70 miles down to the University of Wisconsin in Madison to visit my smarter older sister, Barbara, who was a student there. Whenever possible, I would bum a ride and go with them.

I hate to admit it, but the main reason I came along (not that I didn't like my sister) was to visit motorcycle shops. Particularly a Triumph—and other brands—dealership called Cycles Incorporated, on University Avenue. I'd have my folks drop me off there, promising to join everyone later for dinner.

My usual routine was to lurk around Cycles Incorporated drooling over all the bikes I couldn't afford, then hike down to the Student Union to visit the Rathskeller, a big Germanic-style beer hall where all the beatniks hung out.

There, I would buy *The New York Times*, get a cup of coffee, light a cigarette, and try to blend in, peering over the top of my paper to see how real beatniks behaved. I'm sure they thought I was one of them.

Of course, an apprentice beatnik can't read *The New York Times* forever, so I'd also kill time reading all the motorcycle brochures I'd snagged.

Triumph brochures, mostly, but there were others, as well—from what you might call the second tier of unrequited motorcycle desire. Yes, I speak here of Royal Enfields. And one model I found quite riveting to my teen eyes was the 250cc Royal Enfield Continental GT.

Beautifully proportioned, with clean café-racer styling, it looked like a legitimate, almost affordable alternative to the larger and more expensive Triumphs—and to the fearsome Royal Enfield 750 Interceptor that perched in the front window of the shop.

The Continental GT appeared to be only moderately fast, with an advertised (possibly optimistic) top speed of 86 mph, but it certainly looked the part with its clip-ons, fly-screen, racing seat, and oversized front brake fins. And it had a five-speed transmission, which was rare at the time.

Unfortunately, the engineers had jammed five gears into the old four-speed box, and there were said to be reliability problems. Also, even though the GT was relatively inexpensive, it still cost more than a Honda CB160, which had similar performance and no threat of transmission trouble. When you lived in a small town without a motorcycle shop, reliability mattered a lot. Without it, you were walking. To the bank, to pay off the foolish motorcycle loan your reluctant dad had co-signed.

And here we have the Japanese success story in a nutshell. They knew the first job of any machine is to stay running. After that, the design can become as alluring as it likes.

So I ended up riding inexpensive used Hondas instead. But the appeal of this English small-bore classic has never gone away. And now that I'm well over 16 and no longer need one as my sole means of transport, its appeal is considerably enhanced. Same for the handsome but sometimes-maligned BSA 441 Victor Special, one of which I finally acquired last summer as a project bike.

Strangely, a recent acquaintance of mine named Lee Potratz dropped by this week bearing gifts: three cardboard boxes of random used Victor parts to help me with the restoration. Lee, it turns out, has a nice Victor himself, plus the rare competition GP version of the same bike. I asked Lee if he was restoring anything himself at the moment, and he said, "Just an old Royal Enfield Continental GT."

Twenty minutes later, we were standing in his neat, heated workshop, looking at the GT on its lift. Faded and a bit tired-looking, but all there. Lee had just started disassembly work on it. Big project, but well worth doing.

We later retired to his kitchen to drink coffee and talk about bikes, and discovered we'd both been in the army in Vietnam, our tours almost overlapping in the same province of II Corps. Lee had been a helicopter pilot, and I'd flown all over the province in helicopters. We knew all the same mountain ridges, rivers, temples, roads, and other landmarks in this distant little spot on the globe.

When I left, we pledged to get together some evening and look at each other's dusty slide collections, which we hadn't dug out in decades. Neither of us had ever run into another person who cared very much about that particular corner of Southeast Asia.

Or Royal Enfield Continental GTs, for that matter. The only other guy I'd ever known who had one was my friend Jim Buck in Idaho. So I drove home from Lee's thinking it was nice to find out that at least three of us on planet Earth seemed to remember these rare, short-lived bikes and place some value on them. Maybe we were the world's smallest cult.

Or maybe not.

When I got home, I went online to see what the parts supply looked like for a bike as arcane as the Continental GT. Googling "Royal Enfield," I was greeted by full-color photos of a new model, called simply the Café Racer, that Royal Enfield of India had just introduced at the Long Beach Motorcycle Show. On a slightly larger and more muscular scale, it's almost a dead ringer for the old Continental GT and absolutely stunning.

Long red tank, clubman bars, 535cc four-stroke Single putting out a claimed 36 horsepower, Harris-designed frame, hump-back seat, classic café-racer styling. The projected price, when the 2014 model is released this summer, is $7,295.

Every bit as appealing in style as the old Continental but with the added benefits of Brembo disc brakes, fuel injection, modern sport tires, more than twice the displacement, piggy-back Paioli shocks, electric and kick-start. Also, nothing on the bike seems to need bead-blasting, powdercoating, re-spoking, reaming, boring, plating, or gapping.

The old India Enfield company had a pretty spotty reputation for quality control, but the reborn high-tech Royal Enfield plant in Chennai is bent on banishing that legacy. I sincerely hope they have. A classically beautiful bike that starts and stays running may be modern technology's finest gift to the past. And the present.

Perhaps I should print out the online brochure, run down to the Rathskeller, get a cup of coffee, and pore over the details. Maybe there'll be some younger beatniks around. Continuity is a wonderful thing.

80

Resurrection of a Superbike

WHEN THE PICKUP PULLED INTO OUR DRIVEWAY, THERE WAS a large, mysterious oblong object in the back, wrapped in blue plastic tarps held together with bungee cords. My first thought was that it might be a stolen surface-to-air missile, but then I realized the driver was my Colorado buddy Mike Mosiman, and he's too nice a guy to be dealing in rogue weapons. Also, there are almost no recorded instances of terrorist activity among avid motorcyclists.

Why? Because we have hobbies and are therefore too busy and sociable to participate in the dark and brooding cruelties that always accompany ideological purity. Still, Mike was a missile technician in the Air Force . . . . But that was a long time ago, and in the past 4.2 decades, he's shown absolutely no interest in anything but the 60-plus motorcycles he's owned since his reasonably honorable discharge.

And now, he had another one. Mike jumped out of the pickup to reveal that the carefully wrapped lump in the pickup was his newly acquired 1976 Kawasaki KZ900. Yes, a classic four-cylinder Universal Japanese motorcycle from the 1970s and the immediate successor to the mighty Z1, which was launched in 1973. And predecessor to the 1980 KZ1000 Mk. II I once owned.

Mike bought this bike about four months ago from its original owner in Monroe, Wisconsin, which is only about 30 miles from my home, and he drove all the way back here from Colorado to pick it up. Before returning home, he stopped by for a visit on a very cold day in late October, and, of course, we had to unload the KZ so we could inspect it in the heated comfort of my workshop.

After the oil uncongealed itself, Mike actually took the bike for a ride in 35-degree weather. He wore his classic open-face helmet with sunglasses and came back with his face so red and wind-burned he looked like he'd been shaving with a blowtorch. To my eternal shame, I turned down a chance to ride it myself, but then I don't go scuba diving through a hole in the ice with the Polar Bear Club on New Year's Day, either. I have my standards, and they all involve temperatures above 50 degrees.

The KZ, with 25K on the odometer, was in very nice shape, but showing a few signs of age. A couple of nicks in the dark green paint on the tank, light corrosion on bolts here and there, and a little surface rust on the Kerker 4-into-1 header that had, at some point, replaced the original 4-into-4 factory system. A good rider, with a great exhaust sound, just as it was.

And when Mike got home to Fort Collins, he did ride the thing. Like, all the time. I got almost daily reports of riding ecstasy, detailing the joys of a perfect riding position, comfortable seat, killer motor, rugged character, nice handling, etc. And when it finally snowed in Colorado, he took the bike off the road and decided to put big bucks into restoring the KZ back to showroom condition.

He sent the gas tank, sidecovers, and tail section to a painter named Mike Kukura in British Columbia, and they came back stunningly redone in the original dark green, with hand-painted bright green and yellow pinstripes. The fork went out to Race Tech for new springs and cartridge emulators, and an original 4-into-4 factory exhaust system ($1,600!) was ordered from the supplier in Japan.

And when he stopped by our place with that big blue lump in the back of his pickup, he was on his way to Skokie, Illinois, to drop the bike off at a shop called Redline Cycle, where they specialize in Z1s, KZ900s, and Z1-Rs. There, they checked his engine over and said no rebuilding was necessary, just a new timing chain and carb cleaning. The valves, compression, and bottom end were all good.

It's interesting to me that Mike, who has spent so many years refurbishing mainly European bikes—older BMWs and Ducatis, mostly, with a few British bikes thrown in—is going full tilt on this Kawasaki restoration. But then all of us who go to bike shows have, in recent years, noticed a strong resurgence of interest in the great UJMs of the 1970s and early 1980s. These are the bikes guys like Mike and I actually rode during that period, and they're the bikes a slightly younger generation lusted after in high school.

And they were really good motorcycles. Still are, if they haven't been beaten to death. Especially the old Kawasaki Fours, whose soulful, straightforward ruggedness and bulletproof bottom ends are legendary. That 1980 KZ1000 Mk. II I mentioned was my only streetbike for about six years (before I added another Norton to the garage) when we lived in California. I strolled into Champion Kawasaki in Costa Mesa one fine day, intending to buy this black and gold beauty, and found a SOLD tag hanging on the handlebars. Turned out, Barb had bought it for my birthday—a fact I only discovered when a set of Kawasaki keys showed up in the melting ice cream next to my birthday cake.

We rode this bike everywhere—up the Coast Highway to the USGP at Laguna Seca every year, on vacations through the Gold Country, and on Sunday-morning rides over the Ortega Highway. I also commuted with it much of the time. After we moved back to Wisconsin in 1990, I eventually sold it to help pay for a new Ducati 900SS—another great bike, certainly. But so was the KZ1000. It went to a Japanese UW student who took it home with him. Gone, far across the sea.

Do I miss this bike?

Yes. One of the four or five I truly do. Given a chance to rewind the videotape of life, I'd never sell it again.

For better or worse, I admitted this to Mike, and he—The All-Knowing Master of eBay and Craigslist Who Misses Nothing—has started sending me listings of bikes for sale, particularly the black 1980 Z1-Rs to which I am vulnerable. These things aren't particularly cheap anymore, so it wouldn't be a casual purchase, and I have to ask myself if I really need to spend that money when I have a couple of other perfectly good bikes to ride.

Perhaps I should ponder the very advice I recently emailed to my guitar-playing buddy Doug Harper in Pittsburgh, who, like me, turned 65 this week. He told me he's always wanted to buy a Gibson ES 335 electric guitar but doesn't know if he should spend the money. I sent back a simple reply: "What are you waiting for? After you're dead is no time to take action."

81

Downward Spiral

ABOUT 23 YEARS AGO, WHEN BARB AND I MOVED from Southern California back to Wisconsin because we were nostalgic for freezing sleet and mosquitoes the size of bats, we went to a village picnic and met a few of our new rural neighbors. One of them, an older gent who lived just down the road (and is sadly no longer with us), turned out to be a former motorcyclist who'd owned a few dirt bikes. While we were eating lunch, he caught my rapt attention with a single sentence.

"I have an old Ducati Single from the late 1960s I'd like to sell," he said casually while munching on a bratwurst.

"What is it?" I asked, carefully setting my white plastic fork full of German potato salad back down on its paper plate.

"A 350 Scrambler," he said. "I'll probably never get around to restoring it, so I should move it out of my garage. I'm hoping to get a couple grand for it."

Hmmm. I guess that seemed reasonable, if the bike was in fairly good shape. When we left the picnic, I followed him home.

The old Ducati was in the shadows at the back of his large workshop, leaning against a wall. When he turned on the lights, I was speechless, for once. The whole bike was a mass of rust, crusted over with dried mud. The chain was rusted into a solid object, like an oval piece of welded sculpture, and the engine didn't turn over. Luckily the fenders and instruments were gone, so they were probably fine. Somewhere. But the motorcycle itself was ruined.

"Wow," I said. "What happened to this bike?"

"Oh, one autumn I was riding across the creek down by our marsh, and I fell over and got it stuck in the mud. It was really stuck, and I was kind of banged up. It was so cold out I just left the bike there until the next spring, when it thawed out."

I looked at the Ducati for a few minutes and honestly couldn't see a single part or component that could be restored—or sold at a swap meet for more than a dollar. What a relief, I thought. I've finally found an old Ducati I'm not tempted to buy. Now I'm free to spend that $2,000 on something else!

This is what passes for "business sense" in my reptilian brain.

Anyway, I went home somewhat saddened, contemplating the fate of that poor old Ducati. I tried to picture what combination of cold weather, minor injury, or lethargy would induce me to leave a functioning motorcycle lying on its side, frozen in a bog for the winter like an Ice Age mastodon. No combination I could think of, but then I'm cursed with a tendency to withdraw venerable objects from a bog rather than make deposits.

I mention this extreme case of the frozen Ducati only because the relative condition of old bikes has been much on my mind lately. Blame it on the Internet.

As I mentioned last month, my buddy, Mike, is in the middle of a 1976 Kawasaki KZ900 restoration, and he's been preying on my own weakness for these older KZs by e-mailing me photos of those he finds on eBay or Craigslist. And I'm amazed, as I study the close-up photos of these bikes, by the huge variation in their condition.

Some, even though they have 10,000 or 25,000 miles on them—and are now about 33 years old—look like they just rolled out of the showroom. Others, with equal miles, look rode-hard and put-away-wet, as we say. They have dented tanks, oxidized aluminum castings, rusted chrome, sagging chains, missing sidecovers, amateurishly carved-out seat foam, scabby aftermarket mufflers, etc. Kind of like the motorcycle version of a T-shirt Sid Vicious would wear. If he were still alive. Or still dead, for that matter. A little rough, in other words.

This always makes me wonder: when was the exact moment some previous owner decided that a perfectly good and previously undamaged motorcycle was no longer worth cleaning or repairing? Or putting away for the night, or throwing a tarp over in a snowstorm. At what point in a bike's life is it no longer worth it to replace a damaged speedometer or a lost sidecover? Where's the tipping point?

Obviously, economics figure into this. We've all had hard times when "funs are running low," as John Lennon used to say, and we just can't afford to fix something right away. Or any time in the foreseeable future. Which is why I used to commute to school in the snow on a Honda CB160 with a bald rear tire and a dead battery.

And then there's the "I gave this bike to my little brother while I was in Afghanistan" factor, which can cause serious setbacks in cosmetic excellence. Luckily my little brother was only eight while I was in the army, but I had my parents sell that CB160 anyway, just to be safe. Statistics show that 80 percent of all damage is caused by younger brothers.

And then there's creeping decay. When a bike gets to be 10 or 12 years old and goes through a couple of owners, it can get incrementally frayed around the edges until the next dent or oil leak doesn't seem all that critical, usually because the bike is toward the bottom of its downward value curve.

Our former CW editor, Allan Girdler, always maintained that it took at least 20 years for a basically good design to come back around and be appreciated again after a period of public indifference. And I'd say that's still pretty accurate—stretching, perhaps, to 30 years, in some cases. Seems we have a cultural tendency to forget good stuff and then suddenly remember it.

So I guess the trick we face as motorcycle owners is to nurse them through that slump in order to create the next generation of survivors, and to remind ourselves that honest utility will generally outlast the whims of fashion. Compared with so many other things (a house, for instance), a motorcycle seems like such a simple object to preserve. It's so easy to store, cover, wipe down, and just save from casual damage that there's no one factor—short of crashing—that should turn it into junk. Other than sheer laziness.

And no one is lazier than I am, or so my mother used say. That's why these Kawasaki e-mails from Mike are good for me. I carefully examine the ruins of what was once a nice new 1980 Z1-R, and it automatically makes my hair stand on end. I'm then inspired to get out of my chair, go out to the garage and wipe down my most recently ridden bike with a soft cloth, clean the rims, get the bugs off the fork tubes, etc.

A lot of things can go wrong in the life of a motorcycle, but it looks to me as if the downward spiral generally starts with nothing more exotic than a mixture of moisture and dirt. They're the foot in the door that leads straight to the frozen bog.

82

The Parental Consent Form

SOMETIMES I WONDER IF I'D HAVE ANY SOCIAL LIFE at all without old motorcycle parts. Yesterday morning, for instance, I was staring forlornly into the kitchen cupboard, trying to decide whether to have Cheerios or Grape Nuts, when the phone rang. It was my friend Lee Potratz.

"I found a really good Victor 441 chainguard in a box of old BSA parts in my workshop," he said. "I could drop it off at your place or we could meet for lunch at the bakery in Brooklyn."

Lee was speaking here not of Brooklyn, New York, but of the small nearby village of Brooklyn, Wisconsin. You can tell the difference because the Wisconsin version has no bridge. Also, the police force used to consist of just one officer, who was known by the name of "Radar Bob." I believe he's retired now, but I still ride very slowly when I enter that village, like a cowboy expecting an ambush in a narrow canyon. In his prime, Radar Bob cost me plenty.

Nevertheless, I fearlessly headed toward Brooklyn through the rain in my elderly green Jeep Wrangler. When someone says he's found a good used Victor chainguard, you don't hesitate. BSA Singles tend to gnaw both their chainguards and front fenders in half from engine vibration, so a good original one is a rare thing, indeed. It's like finding an undamaged U-boat after World War II. They almost don't exist.

So Lee met me at the bakery for lunch, and we sat at a table in the front window drinking coffee and talking.

Somehow we got onto the subject of our first motorcycles, and Lee mentioned that his parents had absolutely no interest in them and forbade him from owning one while in high school. He didn't buy his first bike—a Honda XL350—until he came home from flying helicopters in Vietnam in 1973.

I told Lee my parents took an extremely dim view of bikes, as well. My dad had been on exactly one motorcycle in his life, and it hadn't left a good impression. He was temporarily stationed at the Brooklyn Navy Yard during World War II and billeted in an old ship. When he returned to base one rainy night, another sailor gave him a ride on the back of a Harley. My dad said the guy swooped back and forth between piles of cargo and loading cranes at high speed, and the whole thing was terrifying.

So when I told my dad I'd like to get a motorcycle, he looked at me as if I'd expressed a sudden interest in the occult.

"Dad, how come we never celebrate a black mass around here or sacrifice a goat?" That sort of look. My mom seconded that emotion.

But I was not to be dissuaded, and both my parents finally caved in—under intense lobbying—and allowed me to buy a new Bridgestone 50 because I convinced them it was just a harmless little scooter and not a motorcycle at all. And that, as they say, was the camel's nose under the tent.

After that, I escalated to progressively larger bikes, and they hardly noticed the difference. But, as I recall, none of my motorcycle buddies in high school had parents who had ever ridden a motorcycle, either, or even wanted to.

I think there were three things going on here, culturally speaking. First, our parents had all lived through the Depression and the War, and they didn't believe in spending money on frivolous things (to include electric guitars, I soon learned). Second, the 1950s and early 1960s were a time when most Americans aspired to a cleaner, brighter, and more sophisticated future, and motorcycles of that period—mostly loud and shuddering oil-leakers—looked like some kind of throwback to a darker time. It really took the "You Meet the Nicest People on a Honda" advertising campaign to turn that perception around with the older generation.

And third, our parents thought motorcycles were dangerous. The basic job of parents from time immemorial has been to keep children alive until they're old enough to develop a glimmer of common sense, and a lot of parents saw bikes as a threat to that plan.

And, of course, motorcycles are somewhat dangerous, as are most things worth doing—flying, mountain climbing, horseback riding, defending your country, skydiving, arresting felons, football, auto racing, boxing, firefighting, scuba diving, etc. You don't do these things to be safe; you do them after deciding what kind of life you want to lead, careful or exciting. An exciting one can easily take you out of the gene pool early, and that's a difficult choice for parents to make on someone else's behalf.

Even now, friends will say to me, "Our son wants a motorcycle. Do you think he should have one?"

I just smile and fall back on the Sergeant Schultz from Hogan's Heroes defense: "I know nothing!" I almost always tell them it's between them and the kid. I already fought that fight and won, but I'm not going to tell anyone else what to do. If the kid wants a motorcycle badly enough, he or she will get one. Eventually. If not, the kid can take up golf or some other perfectly nice pastime. It's not my decision.

After lunch, I took my excellent new/used BSA chainguard home. While driving, I began to wonder if I knew anyone (other than my wife, Barbara) whose parents actually encouraged him or her to buy a bike. When I got home I called a couple of the usual suspects, riding buddies Mike and Lew, to see what their story was.

"Are you kidding?" Mike said. "My dad was a doctor and he called them 'murdercycles.' I joined the Air Force specifically so I could leave home and buy a motorcycle. I bought a Kawasaki Trail Boss 100 when I was stationed in Okinawa. Two weeks after I got there."

Interesting. Bikes are unsafe at home, so Lee becomes a helicopter pilot in Vietnam and Mike ends up installing bombs on F-4 Phantom jets in Okinawa. I think this is called the Law of Unintended Consequences.

When I called Lew, he said, "My parents absolutely didn't want me to get a bike. My dad was a skilled auto mechanic who owned his own shop, but he had no use for motorcycles—or the people who rode them. I finally talked my folks into letting me buy a Cushman scooter."

"What was your first real motorcycle?"

"A BSA 650 Lightning."

"Wow! How did you manage that?"

"I traded my beautiful black 1951 Cadillac hearse straight across with a friend who had the BSA. My dad was actually very glad to see the hearse go."

Brilliant strategy, I thought to myself. Just plain brilliant.

83

Good Vibrations

WHEN I HEARD MY FRIEND ROB WAS GOING TO haul his T-shirt trailer to the Madison BMW Club's Great River Road Rally in Soldiers Grove, Wisconsin, I decided to ride up there for a visit. It was supposed to be a beautiful day, and the loop from our house to Soldiers Grove and back takes you through 250 miles of green, hilly farm country, with lots of curves, ridges, and hollows. If we were a little closer to the Appalachians, they'd be called "hollers" and Dolly Parton would live there. Alas, we don't and she doesn't. Nice roads nevertheless.

My one reservation in visiting the BMW rally was that I don't have a BMW right now. I've owned four but am sadly Boxerless at the moment. As a soulful alternative, I thought I'd take something British, so it was a toss-up between my 2008 Triumph T100 Bonneville or recently refurbished 1969 BSA 441 Victor Special.

The burning philosophical question was should I take my Triumph and buy a BSA shirt from Rob, or ride the BSA and buy a Triumph T-shirt? I already have about 12 Triumph shirts and no BSA shirts, so the decision was easy. I've long admired those shirts with the winged red BSA emblem across the front, as they always make me think of Dick Mann in his prime, which is a good memory.

Of course, there was another obvious reason to pick the Triumph: it's a modern, bulletproof bike with faultless electrics, a smooth counterbalanced crank, and a top speed above 100 mph, and the BSA is not.

I've been riding the Victor quite a bit lately, mostly on those short evening jaunts where you chuff around the countryside and watch the sun go down—making sure, of course, to get home before dark. The bike is kind of a vampire in reverse; it has a special darkness-sensing headlight that starts to flicker and dim just about moonrise, as if it wants to fold its cape and return to the crypt for the night. So most of these twilight rides last only about 25 miles, which I've found to be just the right amount of time to spend on the bike, anyway.

Why?

Well, vibration.

An old *Cycle World* road test from April of 1966 shows the Victor running the quarter-mile in 15.5 seconds at 81 mph, with a theoretical top speed at redline (6,500 rpm) in fourth gear of 93 mph. This was on a brand-new testbike, of course, and mine is old, but I would no more attempt to squeeze 81 mph out of this engine than drop our favorite cat out of an airplane to see if it lands on its feet. Not without a Carrillo rod, anyway. As for 93 mph, well, it's like hearing your Chevy Sonic will hit 215 mph, if you can just reach redline. No need to go there.

I've discovered this bike is happiest at about an indicated 45 mph. And I say "indicated" because the speedometer does seem to be reading slow, so it might be 50 mph, for all I know. Smiths instruments have always been vague, which some would say is a serious shortcoming in a precision instrument designed to measure things. But I would estimate the BSA's "sweet spot" is somewhere around 50 mph. Beyond that, it starts to vibrate in ways you instinctively know can't be good for coil brackets, light bulbs, fender stays, and other metal parts. Or your kidneys.

This bike, after all, was designed as a street-legal scrambler, so it's geared (and cammed) for flexibility in the dirt rather than droning down the interstate. It is, in fact, that easy torque and spare, dirt-bike simplicity that define its character and make it such a charming cruiser on our quiet farm roads.

But it does vibrate some, even in that sweet spot. When I first got the BSA running last month, I rode it six miles into the town of Stoughton to put some fresh fuel in the tank, and when I came home, I told Barb proudly, "I made it all the way into Stoughton and back with no trouble!"

She smiled an uncertain smile, not quite sure what all the fuss was about.

I then parked the Victor in the workshop next to my 1976 Honda CB550 Four, and, contemplating the two of them, had to grin at the contrast. Last time I took the 550 out for a ride, I came home and told Barb, "I would honestly ride this thing to California and back without hesitation."

And now, I was proud to have made it home from the gas station.

Hardly a fair comparison, of course, as these bikes, though close in age, were designed in different parts of the 20th century. Still, the most glaring difference between them is really just the electric smoothness of the Honda Four. I've often thought the greatest single technical advance in motorcycle design in my lifetime (other than brakes that actually retard your speed) has been the conquest of destructive vibration.

BMW seems to have been the first company to tackle this problem at its root, Max Friz's Boxer Twin having a natural balance that produced only a rather pleasant rocking motion at idle. I haven't ridden any of the historic longitudinal inline-Fours, such as the Henderson or the Indian, but I'm told by those who have that they're quite smooth. After that, we have a mixed bag of jitters with various Singles and Twins, most fixes revolving (literally) around rubber engine mounts.

Other than Honda's rediscovery of the inline-Four (and sublime Six), we really didn't make much progress until Yamaha came up with its "Omni-Phase Balancer" for its 500cc and 750cc four-stroke Twins in 1973. I remember a great debate about this at the time. Some thought this was cheating because these chain-driven dual counterbalance shafts added complexity to the bike without furthering its measurable performance. What would we have next? Cannibalism in our schools? The end was near.

Well, two of my favorite modern bikes, the Bonneville and the Suzuki DR650, have counterbalancers in them, and I don't mind a bit. I can't see or hear them, they never wear out, and my hands and feet aren't humming like tuning forks at the end of a ride. Headlight filaments light up the night, and the exhaust pipes never fall off.

And I had a serene 250-mile Bonneville ride to Soldiers Grove, a beautiful little town in the Kickapoo Valley, swarming with lots of those naturally smooth BMWs. And Rob gave me a T-shirt with that classic winged BSA logo across the chest.

Now, I look just like Dick Mann, but without the riding talent. Or that tingling sensation in my hands and feet. When I got home, I still felt good enough to take a 25-mile ride on my BSA. Wearing the T-shirt, just before dark.

84

Thirty-Three and a Third Revolutions

CHANCES ARE, IF YOU'RE OLD ENOUGH TO UNDERSTAND THE title of this column and its reference to vinyl albums (which I see have made a comeback among audiophiles), you may also have been around when I got hired by this magazine. That would be in the first week of January in 1980. Yes, more than 33 years ago. And the idea that led me here actually took root a little before that.

In the late 1970s, I was working as a mechanic at a place called Foreign Car Specialists in Madison, Wisconsin. Nearly all of us at the shop had graduated from the nearby University of Wisconsin with degrees for which there was little (i.e., no) demand at the moment. Journalism, in my case. And nearly all of us liked sports cars better than our chosen disciplines, anyway. We were a shop full of racers, working on customers' cars during the day and our own race cars at night. The owner of the place, Chris Beebe, raced a Lotus Super Seven and was a national contender in the SCCA.

But there was also a strong motorcycle contingent in the shop. Chris and I both owned Norton Commandos and Honda 400Fs, and I was increasingly being drawn into motorcycle roadracing. In 1977, I sold my fun but finicky Lola Formula Ford and started racing the bulletproof 400F in WERA Box Stock events.

One day, while riding in a Chevy van to a race at Grattan, Michigan, I had an interesting conversation with my fellow racer, Howard Sprengle. I confessed that I still hoped to get back into journalism someday but hadn't had much luck. I'd written two books and numerous articles and short stories, only to have them rejected, returned with a dull thud on my doorstep. I told Howard, "I seem to be destined to go through this life without getting one word published by anybody."

He said, "Instead of inventing fictional characters, why don't you write about something you're actually interested in. Like motorcycles. That's what Phil Schilling did, and now he's working for *Cycle* magazine. He was working here in Madison as an editor at a book company, and then he wrote a nice color story about Daytona Speed Week and sent it to *Cycle*. They liked it so much they hired him."

I stared wondrously into space, struck by the possibilities. Write about something I was interested in? What a concept! And, until that moment, it had never occurred to me that a would-be writer from the Midwest could possibly get a job with a magazine in California. I thought you'd have to know somebody.

So, I sat at my Olivetti portable typewriter for three months of evenings and weekends, working on a touring story about a trip Barb and I had just taken on our Norton Commando. Seems we were riding out to visit relatives in Idaho when the bike swallowed an exhaust valve near Missoula, Montana, and we had to ship the Norton home in a Bekins moving van and make the rest of the trip by train and bus. I wrote the story of this trip over and over again until even I liked reading it. This was apparently another concept that had never occurred to me before.

When I'd finally "perfected" the story, I sent it to the former *Road Rider* magazine because they published more touring stories than anyone else. And they rejected it. Another thud on the doorstep. I tossed the manuscript into a bottom desk drawer and decided to give up.

But then, over beers one night several weeks later, my friend Lee Heggelund said, "Aren't there any other motorcycle magazines?"

"Sure," I said, in my best hangdog tone. "There's *Cycle World* and *Cycle*, but they're big-time glossy magazines, and they don't publish many touring stories. *Cycle World* does once in a while."

"Why don't you send the story to them? You've already got it written. What can you lose?"

What, indeed? So, I shipped the story to *Cycle World*. And it came to pass that Associate Editor Tony Swan liked it and recommended it to Editor Allan Girdler, who also liked it and sent me a nice letter saying they were accepting the story—and would like to look at anything else I wrote.

That Friday evening, when I came home from work and opened the letter, we had friends over for Mexican food. I read the letter aloud and then we drank margaritas until all the tequila in Madison was gone, just before the sun came up.

I did four more touring stories for *CW*, and then Allan asked me to fly out to California for a job interview just before Christmas in 1979. Miraculously, he hired me, and I asked when I should start.

"I suppose you need to go home first," he said.

"Well, Christmas Eve is the day after tomorrow, and I'd kind of like to be home with Barb."

"Can you leave early on Christmas Day?"

"Yes, I can."

So I flew home, left Barb to sell our little cottage in Madison, and, with the help of my friend John Oakey, drove our rusted-out 1968 Volkswagen

Beetle through several blizzards to Newport Beach, California. I started work the first week in January of 1980, just before my 33rd birthday and have been here ever since, as either a full-time staffer or a contributor, while also working for *Road & Track*, which used to be our sister publication in the same office building.

Other than meeting Barb, opening that letter from *Cycle World* is the best thing that ever happened to me. The staff has always been like family, and I've been privileged to work for four great editors and good friends: Allan Girdler, Paul Dean, David Edwards, and Mark Hoyer. Production Editors Dee Winegardner and Robyn Davis are two of the finest and nicest people I've ever worked with. It's been the best of times, with no worst of times at all, ever.

But now I'm almost 66, and I've been meeting three or four copy deadlines a month for fully half of those years. I've also had a few minor setbacks in health recently (plus a healthy level of the usual laziness), so it's only natural for me to dial it back a bit and spend less time sitting in front of the computer screen.

While that means you won't see my column every month, I'll still stay connected to *CW*, writing the occasional "Leanings" and contributing stories from time to time. In fact, Editor-in-Chief Hoyer and I are already cooking up a long road trip of an epic nature for an autumn comparison test, and I'm looking forward to it. Got the maps all over my desk. Which is always my favorite view of the possible future.

SECTION II

The Features

85

New France at Long Last

*I*T WAS AN OLYMPIAN ENTRANCE INTO THE OLD FRENCH-CANADIAN city of Trois-Rivières on the Saint Lawrence River. Thunder clapped and lightning struck hills on both sides of the highway. But as we followed signs for the Centre Ville, the clouds parted and the sun came out, bathing the tall church steeples and the slate roofs on the old stone houses in soft evening light.

We turned left near the river on a street called the Chemin du Roy.

"What does that mean?" Barb asked over my shoulder as we paused at a stop sign.

"It means 'Way of the King'," I replied.

"I thought *king* was spelled r-o-i in French."

"It is," I replied authoritatively, "but in this case they are referring to Roy Rogers, King of the Cowboys. French Canadians love Westerns. They consider Dale Evans to be their queen."

This would not be the last time my masterful command of college French came in handy on this trip. In fact it was a college course, taken 36 years ago, that prompted this trip in the first place.

It was all Dr. Loudon's fault.

Loudon was my freshman Geology 101 professor at the University of Wisconsin, a guy who might have been the prototype for Indiana Jones. He taught college in the winter, but in the summer he was a highly paid oil geologist who worked for Sun Oil and traveled all over the world in search of this vital black fluid. He'd canoed down the Yukon River, paddled into the jungles of British Honduras, and flown his own float plane into the wilds of northern Canada. And he had the Kodachrome slides to prove it.

In one of his lectures, he showed us images of rock formations on the shoreline of Québec's Gaspé Peninsula, that lobster claw of land that follows the Saint Lawrence River northeast and juts out into the Atlantic. His pictures showed a rustic land of sweeping coastal roads, lonely stone cottages, and small fishing villages that looked like something from Brittany or the north coast of Scotland.

The people, he said, spoke only French and were descended from the earliest European settlers in North America.

I was stunned.

Here was a chance to exercise your pathetic French skills and visit a place that looked like Europe without actually buying an airline ticket and flying to Europe—something this starving student couldn't begin to afford. And you could ride there on your motorcycle!

My roommate, Pat Donnelly, was equally thunderstruck by the irrefutable logic of this concept.

So in the autumn of 1968 we loaded our two motorcycles (mine a Honda CB160, Pat's a Honda 305 Dream) and headed for the Gaspé. Barb, who was then my girlfriend, knitted me a warm scarf to take along. I still have it.

Pat and I rode for days in the cold autumn Canadian rain—with no raingear, because that wouldn't look cool—and slept on the ground in a leaky tent. We made it as far as Montreal before we ran out of time, money, calories, and body heat simultaneously, and had to turn around. We arrived home in Wisconsin like prodigal sons: wet, cold, and broke.

No Gaspé Peninsula. A failed quest.

And all these years, I have nursed an unfulfilled desire to see the place, partly out of curiosity and partly out of revenge on the past, to let the other shoe drop, as it were.

So when Barb and I were looking for a touring destination last summer, I said, "Let's go see the Gaspé Peninsula. Limber up our rusty French, see Québec, eat some seafood in small fishing villages, and come down through New England on our way home."

Barb looked at the map and said, "Wow! It's way out there! That's a long way to ride. . . ."

I nodded and said nothing. Now, as back in 1968, I didn't want Truth to interfere with Destiny.

We loaded up our BMW R1150RT and on a hot, sultry Wednesday morn headed north into threatening skies toward upper Michigan and the Canadian border at Sault Ste. Marie.

By lunchtime that first day, four equipment failures had occurred.

First, we discovered that the stock BMW seat that felt so good in the showroom was almost unbearably uncomfortable after four hours in the saddle. By noon, we were both standing up on the pegs every few minutes.

Barb made me stop at a Wal-Mart, where she bought a small child's pillow festooned with stars and moons and planets. It looked like artwork from *The Little Prince*. Very cosmic.

Then it started to pour, and I discovered that my trusty old Gore-Tex touring jacket—perhaps a victim of one too many washings—had suddenly decided to soak up water like a sponge. Also, my plastic rain pants leaked in the crotch. So did Barb's. We looked like poster children for incontinence. Backtracking to Nick's BMW near Green Bay, we Mastercharged about $200 worth of new raingear.

Suitably pillowed and waterproofed, we thrummed up the Lake Michigan coastline as far as Manistique, and then hit Canada the next morning, crossing the bridge at Sault Ste. Marie. The border crossing was friendly and easy, a far cry from the one Donnelly and I had endured in 1968. Fearing the endemic draft desertion, drug culture, and motorcycle hooliganism of 1960s youth, the border authorities had run us through the mill, checking our police records, patting us down, pawing through our duffel bags, and sniffing our toothpaste.

No such trouble this time. We are old and respectable. We have hard luggage, credit cards, and bifocals. It's hell not being a threat to anyone.

On Canada's Highway 17, we soon discovered a pleasant fact. Canadians drive like bats out of hell. Their roads are seriously under-posted (90 kph, or about 55 mph, even on four-lane segments), but no one pays any attention. They all go 70 to 90 mph, speeding along politely without aggression, keeping right except to pass. And you never see a cop. Pure heaven.

We made it through the north woods and lakes to Mattawa that night, a pretty little town on the steep banks of the Ottawa River. Our view from the Valois Motel could have been a painting from the nineteenth-century Hudson River School, except for the satellite dish and the oil-head Beemer with ABS in the foreground.

Early daylight found us descending the river valley on winding scenic roads through Pembroke. I looked for a place called Wright's Cabins, where Pat and I had pooled our dwindling money for a cabin one night so we could avoid shivering to death in our soggy sleeping bags. Old Mrs. Wright had made us tea, dried our clothes, and brought extra blankets. A miraculous find, fondly remembered. But now I couldn't locate the place. It was either bypassed with

the new four-lane around Pembroke or buried under a shopping center. Everything looked different. Time marches on, while memory simplifies and condenses. Also, brain cells are killed off by tequila.

Barb and I cruised through Ottawa and then up the freeway to Montreal, where we hit rush hour. Montreal has a beautiful old city center, but the surrounding suburbs are what I call a Ruined Zone. Too much traffic, too many people, houses, franchises, malls, and car dealerships. You look around and say, "Lord, get me out of here."

We zoomed northeast on increasingly more rustic two-lane roads along the Saint Lawrence and soon found ourselves in Trois-Rivières, a picturesque city that is still human in its size and scope. Motoring straight into the old downtown on the Chemin du Roy (Rogers), we found a beautiful bed and breakfast called the Auberge-Gite de Fleurvil, right on the river.

Barb checked on a room while I waited outside, fearing rejection. We were wet and dirty. The owner, a Monsieur Yves Adams, came out, shook my hand enthusiastically, and directed me to park our bike in the family garage, next to his Harley Springer Softail. He had a copy of *Hog Tales* on the antique coffee table in the living room.

Sometimes you stop for the night and drive right into the dead center of Nirvana. Other times, the bear eats your tent.

We walked around town in the evening, and suddenly everything was very French—menus, signs, and architecture. The houses in Trois-Rivières are right out of France, a curious mixture of ungainly proportions, wrought-iron porch railings, and metal roofs of bright red or green. As in Paris, all old architecture is charming, while nearly everything modern is hideous beyond all comprehension, as if two different races of humans had inhabited the country, before and after World War II.

Cruising up the Saint Lawrence on the river road the next morning, we began to see a lot of touring motorcycles and bicycles. Things were getting more scenic and vacationish by the mile.

Using our proven method of following signs that say Centre Ville, we rode steeply uphill into the lovely old city of Québec, which was originally built as a mountaintop fortress to protect French Canada from the ambitions of British, Indian, and Yankee marauders. It was here, on a high plateau called the Plains of Abraham, that the British under Wolfe defeated Montcalm's French forces and ended France's power in North America.

If the battle had gone the other way, people in Winnipeg would be eating snails and drinking decent wine at this very moment. Both Montcalm and Wolfe were killed in this battle, incidentally, and never saw the outcome of their struggle.

Old Québec is a wonderful city, full of great restaurants, charming old hotels, narrow streets, and sidewalk cafés—a Paris in miniature, easily walked. I was right in my suspicion that Donnelly and I could have visited Europe right here in North America. Too bad we never made it.

On the other hand, we couldn't have afforded it anyway. Cities—even beautiful ones—can be hostile to young people without money. When Pat and I left for Canada in 1968, we each had $60 to last us for two weeks. Québec would have eaten us alive. We'd still be there, washing dishes.

Barb and I, however, had a paid-up credit card, so we checked into the Hotel Le Clos Saint-Louis, parked our bike in the courtyard, and chatted with our friendly concierge, who said she used to tour all over Canada on a Gold Wing. You have to love a country where hotel managers don't stare sullenly at the bugs on your jacket while you check in.

Climbing the narrow stairs to our antique-rich second-story room, we kicked back to wait for photographer Brian Blades to join us for dinner. He was supposed to fly in from California and call us when he got to the hotel.

At 7:30 in the evening, Brian still hadn't called, so we phoned California to find out when his flight was arriving. His wife, Wendy, answered and said, "I'll let him tell you. He's standing right here." "Hi, Brian," I said. "I guess this means you'll be late for dinner."

"I couldn't get a Saturday flight," he said, "so I'm taking the red-eye. I'll be there tomorrow around noon."

I was secretly delighted because this gave Barb and me a leisurely morning to look around Québec City and enjoy Sunday breakfast at an outdoor café, where the chairs were a lot better than our BMW seat and there was no helmet buffeting.

We met Brian at the airport, where he snagged a rental SUV the size of Idaho and followed us up the highway into the fabled and much-imagined Gaspé Peninsula.

I'd made it at last.

For the first few miles, however, this was not the cliff-hanging shore road I'd expected, but rather a busy highway through rolling farm country. It was still quite populated until we got to Rimouski, where the road narrowed and finally began dipping in and out of small villages and harbors on the shoreline. The Saint Lawrence River starts out narrow at Québec (which means "a narrowing of waters" in Iroquois) and gets wider, like an opening funnel, as you head toward the Atlantic. By the time you get to Cap-Chat, the opposite shore has disappeared.

It was Cartier who first charted this shore, in 1534, looking for that elusive western route to the Far East. Europeans were desperate for a way to bypass the steep trade markup imposed by Islamic potentates. An urge that persists to this day, as anyone filling up at a gas station will tell you.

In the United States, I'd been keeping track of our mileage, which was always between 48 and 50 mpg on the big Beemer, regardless of speed. In Canada, trying to figure out mileage using liters and kilometers proved difficult for a person of my math skills, so I gave up computing our mpg at every gas station and ate a Butterfinger instead.

From 5 to 6 p.m. we started scanning the small coastal towns for a motel and finally lucked out at a place north of Rimouski, called the Auberge Marée Douce (Hotel of the Gentle Sea). Yet another discovery, a nice old hotel with big porches and quaint cottages on a hillside overlooking the coast. At night the place was lit up like a Mandarin palace, and it had a fine dining room with excellent food.

Funny how the French preoccupation with good cuisine made the transition to the New World and is still in force, more than 300 years later. I always wonder why the English never noticed all this highly edible stuff, right across the Channel. Or north of Maine and east of Toronto.

Incidentally, the couple who ran this hotel, Marguerite and Fernand, spoke very little English, so we got a chance to exercise our rusty language skills. You don't need a lot of French in Québec Province, but it helps to know a few common phrases, such as "Have you a bottle of absinthe and two glasses?" or "The shaft of my blue umbrella is afflicted with doleful malfunctionings."

As we headed up the coast in the morning, the road was alive with touring motorcycles, mostly bearing Québec provincial plates. A loop around the Gaspé Peninsula seems a popular getaway for Canadians, just as circling Lake Superior is for midwesterners. And I would say that 85 percent of the bikes you see touring now are big V-Twin baggers—Harley Road Kings and their imitative Japanese brethren. Black beanie crash helmets rule.

The central spine of the Gaspé Peninsula is a heavily forested mountain ridge, and as you go northeast, the foliage changes from central Eastern to North Woods and it starts looking like Sergeant Preston or Nelson Eddy country. There are few internal roads on the peninsula, but at Sainte-Anne-des-Monts we turned inland to see the Parc de Conservation de la Gaspésie, a camping and hiking area in the mountains.

Alas, we had no hiking boots or tent, so after lunch at a costly and strangely sterile little hotel complex in the park, we headed back down a scenic valley full of sweeping roads and turned right. As we headed east along the shore, the towns got more remote, the coastline prettier, and the road curvier. The place was beginning to look like Doc Loudon's old Kodachromes.

Late in the afternoon, the road began to turn southeast along the cliffs, and I realized we were suddenly at the farthest end of the peninsula. My odometer said we were exactly 1,900 miles from Wisconsin. Twice as far east as Donnelly and I had gone with our little Hondas. At Montreal, we were only halfway here. What were we thinking back then?

And even now, as we stopped at a scenic lookout to gaze at the Atlantic, Barb said, "It feels like we're a long way from home . . . ."

Truly, as you turn away from the Saint Lawrence and along the Atlantic cliffs, the ocean suddenly looks vast, with nothing but Europe out there somewhere. Even the road feels lonelier, and there's less traffic and tourism. The roller-coaster pavement makes steep climbs and descents, sweeping down on the coast and briefly inland at small bays, like California's Big Sur. The curves are all sweepers—no scorch-the-edge-off-your-tires stuff. Everything can be taken at 70 mph. Symphonic riding, with the cymbal crashing of waves.

With the sun setting, we finally turned into Gaspé Bay, where Cartier first set foot on North America, 471 years ago. We looked around the slightly seedy (but lively and jumpin') town of Gaspé and found an old, partly restored hotel called La Maison William Wakeham at the edge of town. The place was still being renovated but had Norman architecture and a beautiful wood-paneled lobby and dining room (closed Mondays, wouldn't you know).

After dinner at a good local restaurant called the Café des Artistes, we returned to our hotel, where I think we were the only guests. As we made our way through the silent, dimly lit lobby, Barb said it felt slightly creepy, like a scene from *The Shining*, so I thoughtfully resisted the temptation to shout "Here's Johnny!" as we entered our room.

In the morning we found a man wandering around the lobby, inspecting the place. He was a French Canadian named Jacques who had rented one wing of this hotel 40 years ago as a family dwelling and had returned to look around. He told us he now worked for a government agency that promotes Gaspé development. I asked him how the economy was doing.

The fishing industry, he said, was essentially dead, what with the near extinction of cod from overfishing. "But we're doing okay with tourism," he said. "Still, the peninsula is big and far from any urban center. Far flung. It's a commitment to come here."

I nodded. "I tried to come here 36 years ago myself and didn't make it. It was too far."

As we rode away I was troubled by a recurrent thought. Everywhere we go now, the traditional local economy is half-ruined by some environmental meltdown, but there's always said to be tourist or real estate money coming in from "the outside." I worry about shrinkage of the outside.

We crossed the York River and swept down a coast studded with light-houses to the tourist town of Percé, so named because it has a huge Gibraltar-like rock off the coast with a hole pierced in it by waves. Just off the coast sits Bonaventure Island, famous as a sanctuary for thousands of wild seabirds and no good place to sit down.

Percé is a beautiful spot, with lots of seaside motels, restaurants with porches on the ocean, gift shops, etc., but it was absolutely swarming with tourists. We had lunch on a sun deck and then left before terminal claustro-phobia uncorked my penchant for sudden violence. As we crawled out of town in bumper-to-bumper traffic through a sea of pedestrians, I turned to Barb and said, "Never underestimate the power of a rock with a hole in it. Erode it, and they will come."

We rounded the peninsula and headed back west along Chaleur Bay into increasing population, prosperity and farming along the shore. More meadows and fields, less forest. The coastline was still pretty, but the wild part of the Gaspé was behind us.

It had taken us three days to round the peninsula, and our last stop for the night was in Carleton. We stayed at the Hotel Baie Bleue, a clean, modern place with an upstairs dining room overlooking the bay, where we sat down to the best seafood stew I've ever had. Every tour has its Meal of the Trip, and this was it. After dinner we said goodbye to Brian, who was getting up early to head back around the peninsula for Quebéc City and home.

Barb and I left early in the morning, too, rolling down into the forests of New Brunswick on Highway 17 through pockets of ghostly morning fog.

Suddenly the signs were in English again. We crossed into Maine at Van Buren and began a wonderful backroad journey diagonally across New England, upstate New York, and western Pennsylvania.

We passed Maine's Mount Katahdin, the state's highest peak, and then spent three days crossing the White Mountains, Green Mountains, Adirondacks, and Alleghenies, winding through one lovely old colonial town after another, across stone bridges, around white-painted churches and pausing to explore Revolutionary War cemeteries, Fort Ticonderoga, and Watkins Glen.

Riding pleasure? For endless curves and sportbike roads, this was the best part of the trip. The northeastern United States doesn't have the exotic French flavor or the lonely, edge-of-the-world atmosphere of the outer Gaspé, but it's great riding in a setting of deep antiquity and charm.

Maybe this is where Pat and I should have gone. It was closer to home, cheaper to get to, and had more curves. We also understood the language and the money.

But that wasn't the point, really.

Back on that first motorcycle trip, we wanted desperately to go somewhere else, somewhere that didn't look or feel or sound like the place we lived. We were driven onward by those exotic Kodachromes, images of ocean and fishing villages, of stone huts and slate roofs, of a place where people spoke French and had menus filled with things that were new and hard to pronounce. We had to go there.

Or at least try.

And now, 36 years later, on the last day of our tour, Barb and I found ourselves in a fast-food joint along the Indiana Toll Road, making tracks for home and drinking iced tea to rehydrate ourselves from the suddenly crushing midwestern summer heat.

Barb looked tired. She'd come a long way—4,000 miles in 12 days of riding without a day off—while sitting on that cosmic little Wal-Mart pillow with nary a word of complaint. She gazed out the tinted window at the passing traffic and said, "Well, was the Gaspé Peninsula what you expected?"

I thought about it and shook my head. "No," I said. "It's not as poor and remote as I pictured. It's greener, more vast and mountainous. Still rustic and beautiful, but more prosperous and complex. Also, much farther away. From our place, it's like going to California and back."

Barb nodded. Apparently she'd noticed.

As we rode toward home I pondered Barb's question further and realized that no place I'd ever been turned out to be exactly as I'd imagined it while sitting at home. Not Vietnam, Paris, Katmandu, or Yellowstone Park. Nothing is ever what you expect. Maybe that's why we travel.

86

Ride a Crooked Road

*N*O WONDER THERE ARE SO MANY BLUEGRASS REFERENCES TO fog," I mumbled, wiping off my visor with one hand and peering blindly into the pure whiteness. "'Foggy Mountain Breakdown' . . . the Foggy Mountain Boys . . . these mountains are full of it."

A gas station and convenience store loomed out of the ether as I crested a ridge, and I pulled in for a warming cup of coffee. "What's the name of this village?" I asked an old boy who was climbing out of a nearly invisible pickup truck.

"Whitetop," he said.

I nodded approvingly. "Good name."

On the downside of the mountain, things got better. My Buell Ulysses suddenly dropped out of the clouds on a steep, winding road along a beautiful valley with small pockets of pure white fog stuck in its hollows like balls of cotton. Rays of sunlight broke through the overcast, and suddenly you could see one of those views that only Appalachia offers, a descending vista of increasingly distant mountain ridges in shades of gray and green, all bathed in soft light. Corners came at me one after another on the valley road, and the Buell flicked through them effortlessly.

If this road were a drug, I thought to myself, it would be illegal.

The road, in this case, was a route put together by the State of Virginia to stimulate tourism in the back country. Dubbed "The Crooked Road," it looped through the pointy western end of the state, linking all kinds of famous musical sites in Appalachia.

Some alert member of the state tourist board sent a map and brochure to *Cycle World* in California, and the equally alert Editor Edwards called me in Wisconsin and asked how I felt about doing a musical tour of Virginia on the just-released Buell Ulysses.

"You live close to the Buell factory in East Troy," he pointed out, "so you could pick up one of their early testbikes and ride down there. Also, you know a lot about Bluegrass and traditional music."

Well, sort of. I'm not exactly a mountain music scholar; my expertise is pretty much limited to a veneration for Bill Monroe and Ralph Stanley, along with a deep suspicion that Patty Loveless and Alison Krauss secretly wish they'd met me in high school.

And, like millions of other Americans, my interest in old-time mountain music was reinvigorated by the sound track from *O Brother, Where Art Thou?* And, before that, *Bonnie and Clyde* and *Deliverance.*

But to a hard-core Bluegrass fan—the kind who plans his vacations around the annual Bean Blossom Festival—I'm just a piker. I have, however, squandered lots of money on books and exploratory CDs, so I guess you could say I'm a student of the art form.

And what better thing for a student than a class trip like this one? Also, I was keen to put some road miles on a Ulysses, as it's one of a small handful of new bikes on my ownership radar.

Off to East Troy.

I picked up the Buell with my van, brought it back home, packed the voluminous saddlebags and a duffel bag with enough riding gear to theoretically survive all the variations of mountain weather in October, said goodbye to Barb, and rode south at sunrise on a Tuesday morning.

It took me two days of steady riding to reach Virginia. I left Wisconsin, blitzed down the Interstate to Bloomington, Illinois, and then headed diagonally across Indiana on two-lane roads. I stopped for the night in Madison, Indiana, a beautiful old town on the Ohio River. After checking into a hillside hotel, I walked downtown for dinner and a movie.

The theater was showing the highly acclaimed documentary *March of the Penguins* in one auditorium and *Dukes of Hazzard* in the other. A recent review of the latter in our local paper had called it (and I quote here from memory) "a really bad movie made from one of the dumbest TV shows in history."

I looked at the posters in front of the theater and noticed there were no '68 Dodge Chargers or girls wearing short shorts in *March of the Penguins*, so I naturally went to *Dukes of Hazzard*.

It wasn't as bad as I expected, and it had Waylon Jennings in the soundtrack. Some things you have to do for art.

On a foggy morning, I crossed the Ohio and climbed into the warm, sunlit hills of Kentucky. Farm stands along the road were laden with Indian corn, yellow squash, and pumpkins almost the same color as the airbox cover in front of me.

The Buell was booming along nicely, the 1203cc Twin cranking out tons of easy torque. The engine shows its Harley heritage at idle, shaking up and down in its rubber mounts, but transforms itself into a smooth runner when you start rolling. It revs freely and easily to its 7,500-rpm redline but seldom needs to be revved past 5,000, with all that midrange wallop. And the sound is deep and throaty.

Gears are well-spaced, but you rarely have to shift and can dial speed on and off with the throttle in fourth or fifth on a twisty road. When you do shift, clutch pull is light and the thing changes gears with quiet, well-oiled precision. Nice gearbox. Superb brakes, too.

Typical of most Buells, the Ulysses' handling is quick, effortless, and reassuring. Erik Buell makes much of his engineering efforts at mass centralization (short exhaust canister under the engine), low unsprung weight (perimeter brake rotor on a very light wheel), and weight-saving cleverness (oil reservoir in hollow swingarm), but it all pays off in agility, handling, and ride. This is a really fun bike that works with you on a backroad. The ride is compliant, well-damped, and civilized.

It ain't bad on the interstate, either. The bike is a little windy at 70-80 mph with its short, snap-on-and-off windscreen (a larger optional one is on the way), but the roomy riding position is just about perfect for all-day travel. So is the seat, which may be the best-designed, most comfortable perch available on any modern motorcycle. I spent seven days and 2,200 miles in this saddle and never gave it a thought.

Note to BMW, Ducati, and KTM: quit fooling around and just copy this seat.

The Buell carries its 4.4 gallons of premium unleaded in the perimeter frame/gas tank, and range can vary widely depending on how and where you ride. On the interstate, I averaged about 41 mpg and the fuel light came on around 155 miles.

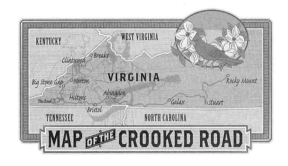

Following coal trucks through mountainous West Virginia on the way home, I averaged 57 mpg.

Any downsides?

Riders with short inseams will find the bike tall and a bit clumsy at stop signs and in slow maneuvers. Also, a noisy electric fan that cools the rear cylinder stays on for about a minute after you shut off the ignition. When you stop to ask for directions, it roars away.

The engine probably needs it, though. On a hot day, the frame/gas tank gets quite hot to the touch, particularly on the right side, even with the fan running.

And the weather stayed warm and beautiful all the way into Kentucky on Highway 421, a zone of old cabins, deep valleys, and tobacco barns. I turned onto Highway 460, and the state morphed into horse country, with huge estates and miles of white fences. Places where big pillars and gates say, "Hey, look over here! I'm rich!"

That evening I crossed into Virginia to the official starting point of the Crooked Road. This was a mountaintop park that straddles the Kentucky/Virginia border, called Breaks Interstate Park. I stayed at the park lodge and took advantage of its deck looking out on a gorge with rock chimneys and a river far below. In the morning, I was supposed to meet Brian Blades, our photographer who had flown in from California and rented a car at the Bristol airport.

The steep mountains precluded cell phone service—which was lucky, because I don't own a cell phone and Brian's was broken—so we agreed to meet at the Breaks village post office at noon. Brian was a little late, so I got to talk to dozens of people who came to pick up their mail.

One older gent by the name of Tom Blankenship told me he'd been a coal miner for 24 years until the local seams played out, then built Cadillacs and Chevys in Detroit. Now he was picking ginseng in the forest for a living. He asked where I was heading and I said, "Down to Clintwood, which is Ralph Stanley's hometown."

He nodded. "I know old Ralph. Everyone here knows him. He's kin to my wife. Her mother was a Stanley. Ralph and the Clinch Mountain Boys are playing tomorrow night at the theater in Clintwood. You might want to see 'em."

Good tip.

Brian hove into view with his rental car, and soon the Ulysses was descending into legendary Dickenson County on tight, winding Highway 83 in a light rain. I rumbled into the small town of Clintwood and stopped on Main Street at the Jettie Baker Center, which had "Ralph Stanley and the Clinch Mountain Boys" on the marquee. Friday night.

This was only Thursday, so I decided to continue south and somehow backtrack the next night for the show. I took a wrong turn leaving town and did an accidental 70-mile loop through Appalachia and ended up back in Clintwood two hours later. It's hard to sense your direction in these mountains when the sun's not shining. I'm surprised Daniel Boone didn't end up in Newark.

I finally rode into Norton, the next star on Virginia's Crooked Road map. Outside of Norton was a famous old place called the Country Cabin, built in the 1930s as a community recreation center for dances, music, cakewalks, hoedowns, box suppers, and other entertainments whose allure has been partly lost to youth since the invention of the Marshall 100-watt stack and the reign of Sid Vicious.

Across the street from the original site is Country Cabin II, a larger log hall that holds more people. Unfortunately, the place was closed until Saturday's Bluegrass night, so I looked in the darkened windows, hoping that bad timing would not turn this into the Closed Building Tour.

On the door were rules of behavior for music nights: no drinking, guns, or other weapons, unruly behavior, harassment of others, vulgar language, etc.

This train don't carry no gamblers, this train. Bluegrass is essentially a culture of modesty and good manners, the flip side to Rock's experiments in sullen nihilism. You'd be just as likely to see a space launch at a Bluegrass festival as to hear the F-word spoken.

Near Norton I motored down a deep valley behind a coal truck and suddenly realized the road was covered in fine coal dust. Along the highway I saw my first big coal processing plant and stopped for a look. Glancing in the mirror, I saw a face with a raccoon mask of carbon looking back at me. You could get black lung here just reading the fine print on someone's bumper stickers.

As I headed through the valley, a small drive-in movie theater appeared (*Bad News Bears*), tucked into a small parcel of flat land. On both sides of the road, old houses and mobile homes clustered in deeply shaded hollows and ravines, and it occurred to me that opportunity here is pretty much proscribed by valleys, channeled by ridges. That isolation is a good part of what made—and preserved—the old music.

It being too dark and late to search out rustic charm, Brian and I

got generic hotel rooms on the highway outside Norton and ate at a generic steak house. Other than that, I remember nothing. Another case of amnesia through modern comfort.

The next day the Ulysses threaded its way through old coal towns around Big Stone Gap, then headed for the next big star on our route, the little village of Hiltons, Virginia. Home of the Carter Family Fold.

You might call this spot the cradle of modern Country music.

A tall, thin man named A.P. Carter lived here with his wife, Sara, and they sang songs with Sara's guitar-playing sister, Maybelle. In 1927 they got into their car and drove down to Bristol for a trial recording session in an old warehouse with a talent scout named Ralph Peer. He discovered, to his amazement, that this "hillbilly" music was immensely popular with record buyers all over the country. Their songs, "Wildwood Flower" and "Will the Circle be Unbroken," are the dual anthems of Country music.

Maybelle's daughter June married Johnny Cash, and A.P. and Sara's daughter Janette still emcees music nights at the family home. The Carters are the Royal Family of Country music, only without the tweeds, Wellingtons, and big ears.

Peer also recorded a guy with a bluesy yodeling style named Jimmy Rodgers, "The Singing Brakeman," and he too became a star. I still listen to his records myself. These sessions are called "The Big Bang of Country Music."

Anyway, the old Carter family home and grocery store is still there on a quiet rural road in Poor Valley near Hiltons, at the foot of the Clinch Mountains, and there's an open-sided music theater built next door. I got there on a drizzly afternoon, and there were workmen renovating part of the theater.

One of them was a CW reader and avid motorcyclist. He said Janette Carter usually performed with Bluegrass groups on Saturday nights, but she'd been in the hospital and probably wouldn't be there that weekend. Once again, I'd have to backtrack the next night to make the show. I'd see.

Motoring into the big town of Bristol, Brian and I got motel rooms for the night. We then jumped in his rental car to retrace our route back to Clintwood to see Ralph Stanley. It was a dark and rainy night, and I didn't feel like riding over the mountains again on the Buell. I like to pay my dues, but only once.

When we got to Clintwood, Stanley's tour bus was in front of the theater. As we stood under the marquee to keep out of the rain, Dr. Ralph Stanley himself climbed down from the bus, and I got to talk to him for a while. A nice man, alert and quick for his 78 years. Now that Bill Monroe is gone, he is really the last performing legend of mountain music, one of the greats.

Before the show, I wandered across the street to the Ralph Stanley Museum. I got there 10 minutes before they closed, but that didn't keep me from loading up on rare Bluegrass CDs and DVDs. I got a feeling the Buell's luggage was going to get heavier on this trip, perhaps approaching black hole density.

The show that night was terrific. Stanley has a high, lonely ache in his voice that Dwight Yoakam once called "ancient, in the most flattering sense of that word, and timeless." It really is the sound of the mountains. He sang "O Death" in his haunting a cappella, a performance that brought him national fame in the soundtrack of *O Brother, Where Art Thou?*

I should mention, too, that the opening act, The Reeltime Travelers, was one of the best bands I've ever heard, and they all looked to be under 30. They had a stunning woman fiddle player who blew everyone away, as did the woman who played guitar. I think there were also some guys in the group.

Brian and I careened back down the mountain to Bristol in the fog and rain. In the morning we headed to the Birthplace of Country Music museum, which is located on the basement level of the huge and modern Bristol Shopping Mall. As we crossed the parking lot, I said to Brian, "This is where the Carter family did all their shopping during the Depression. They'd come in here and pick up calico and biscuit flour and then get a latte at Starbuck's."

The museum, however, turned out to be well worth the risky mall exposure, and the woman running it told me the mall had been kind enough to donate space until they could move into a larger and more appropriate site. Also, the place was full of music fans, even at 10 in the morning.

I unholstered my Visa card and spent a small fortune on more CDs and DVDs. The Buell saddlebags quaked in the parking lot; flocks of birds took flight in alarm; Alan Greenspan tossed in his sleep.

Winding roads, all day long. Beautiful roads with endless corners along Highway 58. We stopped first at Abingdon, a rather upscale town full of beautiful old homes and architecture, to look at the famous Barter Theater, then swung on to Galax, Virginia (pronounced "Gay-Lax," like an over-the-counter medication). This is a pretty town in a broad valley, famous for its Old Fiddler's Convention, held each August since 1935, and the Rex Theater, home to a nationally popular Friday night radio show called "Blue Ridge Back Roads."

There was no Bluegrass at the Rex that night, but something completely different: a Gospel celebration to raise money for Hurricane Katrina victims, organized by the local fire department. Performers and audience were mostly black, from nearby churches, and it was one of the best nights of music I've ever heard. Everybody sang and clapped and swayed. The local talent was amazing; Aretha Franklin meets Percy Sledge.

With volunteer work and personal donations, these small-town citizens raised hundreds of dollars and presented the money to a young white family from New Orleans who'd lost their home. Meanwhile, American oil companies raked in billions of dollars in profits from high fuel prices after Katrina and got an enormous tax break from our government.

Nice to know part of this country is still great.

From Galax, Highway 58 just got better and better. The music may hold this route together, but it needs no such justification to the motorcyclist. It's all curves, scenery, mountains, ridges, and subtly changing landscapes, down to Stuart and all the way up to the hilltop town of Floyd, where a famous record shop and the Floyd Country Store (home of the Friday Night Jamboree) were both closed, as you might expect on a Sunday afternoon.

And that's the main problem with this tour. You need at least two weekends to do it right, rather than just one, and most things happen on Friday and Saturday nights. You have to be too many places at once. Regardless, you still hear a lot of good music, as we did, and to a motorcyclist the music is just a sidelight anyway. The Crooked Road is exactly that, and you'd have a great ride if you didn't know Bluegrass from Shinola.

Brian and I motored up to the end of the Crooked Road at Rocky Mount, had lunch at a good Italian restaurant, and split our separate ways for home. He was driving back to the Bristol airport, and I was 1,100 miles from home, mostly by winding two-lane roads through Appalachia. The return trip took me two and a half days.

I rode through the stunningly beautiful and rugged mountains of West Virginia, more raw and wild than Virginia's and studded with gritty coal towns. While passing a coal truck on a mountain road, my Check Engine light came on. The engine was running fine, but I pulled over and checked the oil, which was okay. I noticed the rear cylinder cooling fan hadn't come on, as it usually did. Maybe it was running hot, and this fan was the Achilles heel of the Buell. (Achilles heel on a Ulysses from East Troy? Isn't this too much Greek literature in one paragraph?)

But the engine didn't feel hot, and the Buell continued to run well all the way home. Still, the engine light came on intermittently, giving me one of those dull headaches of doubt. Erik Buell later told me the first 40 bikes left the factory with defective threading on a screw that opens the exhaust system's power valve, and this tripped the light. Didn't hurt anything; just reduced horsepower slightly above 5,000 rpm. Now I know.

Except for that, the bike never gave me a moment of trouble. It was a good partner on this trip: quick, agile, and comfortable with an engine that pulls like a truck—but much better than the trucks you pass in the mountains. Every morning, I looked forward to getting on it. Which is the big test of an adventure-touring bike.

Is it a dirt bike as well?

Not really. I ran up some rutted dirt-and-gravel roads (to look at a cabin for sale) and found the 17-inch front tire too easily deflected for serious off-road work. You can make it through, but it's not all that much fun. What we have here, really, is a roomy, comfortable, and charismatic sportbike that lets you travel long distances and carry luggage while you sit up and enjoy the scenery.

And there was plenty of that on the Crooked Road.

If you showed the public some good color photos of rural Virginia and said they were NASA pictures from a distant planet, people would sell everything they owned and pay a million dollars for a one-way ticket on a space ship. Their hearts would ache with a desire to move there. It's that beautiful.

But it's not on a distant planet. It's right here on Earth, in a quiet corner of Virginia, haunted with old cabins, half-forgotten villages, brooding forests, and the echoes of ancient Celtic music with a high and lonesome sound. And the occasional motorbike on some kind of odyssey. You can ride there from your home.

87

Looking for Lindbergh

"SEE ANYTHING INTERESTING AT THE CHICAGO BIKE SHOW?" EDITOR Edwards asked me last winter.

"Well," I admitted, "once again, I spent half my time hanging around the Ural sidecar display. You just look at those things and you want to be on a cross-country trip somewhere, motoring along the backroads of America."

"Yes, they're very cool," David agreed.

"There's a lot of interest in the Urals," I said, "but everybody wants to know if they're reliable. The guy at the Ural booth said they've drastically improved since the company was privatized a couple of years ago. They have Brembo brakes and modern electrics now. But you still have to wonder about a Russian product, especially when it's essentially an updated copy of a World War II BMW."

"Maybe you and Barb should take one on a road trip next summer and find out how it works," David suggested.

Everyone has a favorite sentence in the English language, and that's mine.

So I immediately called Ural's US headquarters in Seattle and talked to a very nice woman named Madina Merzhoyeva, who assured me they could provide a Ural Patrol—their best-selling model—for testing when summer arrived.

All set, then. But where to go?

Barb suggested picking up the Ural in Seattle and riding to Alaska, but my friend Mike Mosiman, who owns a Ural in Colorado, nixed that idea.

"The Ural will go sixty-five mph, but it's a lot happier at fifty-five. If you drive to Alaska, you'll be looking at truck radiators in your mirrors all day long. Take a trip on scenic backroads with light traffic. That's what the Ural was made for."

Out came the maps, and I was soon reminded that some of the most scenic—and quietest—country roads in America started right at our front door in southern Wisconsin and meandered northwest toward Minnesota. Red barns, dairy cattle, small towns, ridges and hills, winding roads with nothing on them but hay wagons, horse-drawn Amish buggies, and farmers in old pickup trucks. The world as it used to be, when sidecars were real transportation.

"Let's go up the Mississippi Valley," I said to Barb.

"Where to?"

"Right here," I said, stabbing the map with my finger. "Little Falls, Minnesota. Hometown of Charles Lindbergh."

Barb looked at the map and nodded approvingly.

Like me, she's a pilot and vintage aviation buff, and we have a whole shelf of Lindbergh books in our library. Back in 1987, we spent six weeks circumnavigating the United States in our very slow and archaic 1945 Piper J-3 Cub. We flew over Cape Canaveral, landed at Kitty Hawk, and got to the Oshkosh Fly-In but never made the detour north to Little Falls. We just ran out of time. But now we had some.

Lindbergh, often named by historians as "the most famous American of the twentieth century," is best known for making the first non-stop solo flight from New York to Paris in 1927 at the age of 25.

Less known, however, is his enthusiasm for motorcycling. In 1920, he rode his 1918 Excelsior V-Twin from Little Falls 350 miles down to the University of Wisconsin, in Madison. As an Army ROTC candidate, he also rode his bike to Camp Knox, Kentucky, for summer training, and afterward took a 19-day road trip to Florida and back to Madison, arriving home "with a motorcycle badly in need of repair and nine dollars in my pocket."

One can only imagine what these roads were like in the early 1920s. Lindbergh eventually dropped out of college in the middle of his sophomore year with failing grades. He confessed that all he really wanted to do was shoot on the rifle and pistol team and ride around on his Excelsior. That March he rode his bike out to Lincoln, Nebraska, to take flying lessons. Good decision. He later bought himself a World War I–surplus Curtiss JN-4 "Jenny" biplane for $500 and went barnstorming all over the United States.

"We could retrace Lindbergh's ride to Madison," I suggested to Barb. "It's the perfect trip for this bike. The Ural almost looks like it belongs in the 1920s."

So on an August morning I drove to Steve's Service Center in the Milwaukee suburb of New Berlin (since moved to Phillips, Wisconsin) to pick up a new Ural Patrol. The Woodland-Green Patrol, priced at $9,795, is one of Ural's pair of two-wheel drive models, along with the more military-styled Gear Up version. They also make three one-wheel-drive rigs, the cheapest being the Tourist, at $8,595.

The Patrol looked very jaunty sitting there in the shade of a tree: flawless green paint and deep chrome, nice polished valve covers on its ohv Boxer heads. Much evolved from its flathead ancestors in World War II, the Ural now sports a Denso alternator, Ducati-style Italian switchgear from Domino, and an automotive-grade American wiring harness with modern blade fuses and connectors. It had 500 break-in kilometers on the odometer, with the valves adjusted and fluids changed, ready to go.

Shop owner Steve Krings, a certified sidecar instructor, took the time to give me a few pointers. I'd driven (not ridden, sidecar buffs tell me) a Harley sidecar rig 1,200 miles through Baja a few years ago, but sidehacks are so oddly different from motorcycles, there's no such thing as too much helpful advice.

"Pull out the choke knobs on both Keihin carburetors," he said, "hit the starter button, and go. Push the chokes back in after about a four-minute warm-up. Push down on this little chrome lever beside your right boot for

neutral and reverse. The lever behind that engages two-wheel-drive, but don't ever use it on pavement. There's no differential, so unless you're on a loose surface like snow or mud, you can't turn."

I took a short test ride with poor Steve in the sidecar, and in my first right-hander nearly ran his wheel over a curb. "You sit over the road as if you were driving a car," he reminded me, "and give the sidecar plenty of room in corners. It has width.

"If a right corner tightens up on you, apply some front brake but keep the power on. Always lean your weight to the inside of a corner, in either direction. And always carry your passenger in the car, never on the rear seat of the motorcycle. You need to keep a low center of gravity."

I'd forgotten how reluctant a sidecar is to turn at low speed, and how odd it feels to have your bike lean slightly outward in a right-hand turn. Unnerving at first, but after 15 or 20 minutes you adapt. I remarked that the four-speed transmission felt stiff and notchy. "It takes about 2,000 miles for these transmissions to break in," he said.

Steve stepped out of the car, shook hands, and wished me good luck. "Keep it under 50 mph for the first 1,000 kilometers to break the engine in properly," he said. "After that, you can cruise above 60."

Escaping the clamor of suburban Milwaukee, I dissolved into the backroads toward Madison, and the ride was uneventful. And fun. The 750 Boxer engine, rated at 45 horsepower, is smooth and civilized, thrumming along happily at 50 mph. It idles nicely at stops, pulls away with broad, torquey ease and light, normal clutch action. That front Brembo brake hauls the bike down right now. It stops straight, hard, and predictably, especially with a little bit of rear brake. It tracks straight and effortlessly over the landscape. Everything feels modern, smooth, and surprisingly refined—except for that clunky transmission.

Barb and I loaded the bike that evening. The roomy sidecar trunk easily swallowed Barb's duffel bag, the Ural factory toolkit, and a tonneau cover for the car. My duffel went across the back seat of the bike. And to the top rack we bungeed our old khaki Duluth bag full of raingear, survivor of many Canadian canoe trips. It was the only luggage we had that looked right on the Ural.

In keeping with the vintage/aviation theme, we decided to leave our modern riding gear home and take our A-2 flying jackets. Open-face helmets seemed right, too. With my sidecar skills, I drew the line at leather flying helmets and goggles. It's one thing to tempt Fate, and another thing entirely to spill its drink and step on its blue suede shoes.

We left early on a beautiful August morning, our first cool, clear day after almost a month of oppressive heat. On the backroads, cruising at 50 mph—or 35 mph on long, steep climbs—we quickly discovered that there's an entire American subculture of drivers, mostly polite older people in modestly priced sedans, who have probably never passed another licensed vehicle in their lives and absolutely don't know what to do when presented with the opportunity. So they follow you forever, even when the road is wide open. Eventually you have to pull over and wave them past.

Or maybe they just like following sidecars and watching them. I would.

We cruised through small farm towns on county alphabet roads, stopping for fuel at mid-morning. The five-gallon Ural tank went on reserve somewhere between 110 and 120 miles, and averaged right around 28 mpg on most of our fill-ups. Not spectacular mileage, but then there's a lot of weight (736 pounds dry) and frontal area here.

Stopping to look at Taliesen, the architectural school founded by Frank Lloyd Wright (another famous UW dropout), I was quickly reminded of one of the great sidecar joys: easy parking.

You just pull off the road anywhere, hit the kill switch with the bike in gear, turn the key, and step off the bike. No looking for a level spot or firm soil for your sidestand, no searching for a flat rock or wondering if the wind will blow your bike over. You just stop. The Ural is also good at U-turns. Stop, crank the handlebars, and do a hassle-free, perfectly balanced 180. Park, get off. Never on any trip have I been so willing to turn around and go back to look at something we'd missed. It's a new kind of freedom.

I was also pleased that the ride quality was so good, both on the bike and sidecar. Spring and shock rates seem perfectly worked out to handle hard bumps and undulations in the road, and Barb said the sidecar seat was comfortable and roomy. Her only complaints were a moderate amount of turbulence around the sides of the windshield and a closer-than-usual acquaintance with clicking tappets and whirring gears.

The noise made conversations nearly impossible. We spent a lot of time shouting "WHAT?" at each other, and the answer was always unintelligible. Our hand signals became more refined.

My own riding position was ideal: great seat, well-placed handlebar, and roomy footpeg position. I haven't been this comfortable on a bike since 1980, when Suzuki GS1000s and Kawasaki KZ1000s ruled the world and seats were not tilted downhill or sculpted to look like the mark of Zorro.

Another nice advantage of sidecars is fearless traction. When you barrel around a blind corner and find loose gravel, sand, or manure on the road, there's no cold sweat or panic. On the Ural you just grin and motor through it. Unless, of course, you're going too fast in an off-camber, decreasing radius downhill corner. That will get your attention, and not in a good way. "Enter slowly, accelerate out" was Steve's well-considered advice.

Late in the afternoon, we descended into LaCrosse and crossed the Mississippi into the hills near La Crescent, Minnesota, where Barb's parents are buried in a lovely cemetery overlooking the valley. Her dad's grave was flying a veteran's flag. As Lieutenant Fred Rumsey of the 2nd Infantry Division, he landed on Omaha Beach on D-Day, fought the hedgerow battles of France, and survived against all odds to liberate a concentration camp deep in Germany. He told me he rode in Harley sidecars and flew in Piper L-4 Cubs as a forward observer. Fred would have loved the Ural.

We crossed back over to LaCrosse, where Barb was born, and motored north on Highway 35, stopping at the little river town of Trempealeau. We got a room at one of our favorite places, the old Trempealeau Hotel, which has a four-star (but inexpensive) restaurant downstairs and clean, simple $35 rooms upstairs, where you share a bathroom down the hall. It's the kind of place Lindbergh might have stayed.

In 1920, it never would have occurred to most Americans that you would replicate your plumbing system, over and over again, for every hotel room. It's only our modern refusal to share that keeps the consumer economy thriving. That, and a growing population. At the time of Lindbergh's trip, the US population was 106 million. It's about three times that right now, but you don't see much change on the backroads around Trempealeau. Time almost stands still.

That night we had our windows open and about every hour a Burlington Railroad train blasted by in a shock wave of noise and clatter, heading up or down the Mississippi. Some people don't like railroad noise, but I'll take all I can get. I grew up in a railroad town, so for me it's the romantic echo of prosperity and travel to far off places.

We followed the river north in the morning and detoured inland at Pepin to see the childhood home of author Laura Ingalls Wilder, a favorite of Barb's, then crossed the river bridge into Red Wing, Minnesota, famous for its Red Wing Boots and Red Wing Pottery. I bought boots and Barb bought pottery, and all this loot fit easily into our trunk. Then we cruised up to Stillwater, Minnesota, to visit our old friends Bruce and Linda Livermore.

Bruce is a mechanical engineer who, like Lindbergh and yours truly, dropped out of the University of Wisconsin to "try other things." I tried Vietnam and Bruce worked as a car mechanic. Years later, we both returned to UW and finished school. Lindbergh didn't, of course, and you can see how a lack of diploma held back his career.

Interestingly, Bruce's grandfather, Professor Joseph D. Livermore, was Lindbergh's advisor in mechanical engineering at the University of Wisconsin in 1920.

As we came into Stillwater, I heard a cyclical groaning sound and felt a vibration from somewhere within the sidecar rig or motorcycle. Bruce and I jacked it up at his house and spun the wheels to check the bearings, but couldn't find anything wrong. A small amount of gear oil was misting out from the rear drive unit around the brake drum and spokes, but no other problems were evident.

We continued on the next day and the noise gradually went away. Transmission break-in pangs, perhaps?

We paused in the little village of Mahtomedi, Minnesota, my own birthplace (yes, there are a lot of birthplaces in this story; too many, some would say), and then zig-zagged north into Minnesota farm country. Past cattail marshes, redwing blackbirds, and flat farm fields, we ran on geometrically square Minnesota roads all afternoon, then slowed for the "Welcome to Little Falls" sign.

Little Falls is a pretty little place of about 8,000 that has a nice old downtown and straddles the Mississippi at the falls—which are now a dam. It's one of those just-right-sized cities where everything is built on a humane scale and easy to find—hospital, school, working movie theater, restaurants—all with light traffic and easy parking.

The old Lindbergh farm is just south of town on the west bank of the river. Lindbergh's father was a successful lawyer, farmer, land agent, and congressman, and his mother was a high-school chemistry teacher.

Young Charles was an avid outdoorsman, as well as a natural mechanic who was allowed to drive the family Model T when he was 11. He also drove his mother and uncle to California in a Saxon Six touring car when he was 14. Police in Los Angeles ticketed him for driving underage, when he'd just navigated 2,300 miles of the worst roads in America. This offended young Lindbergh's always-powerful sense of logic. He ignored the ticket and drove everyone back to Minnesota, in the age before computers and reciprocity.

A few years later, in 1918, he bought his Excelsior from Martin Engstrom's Hardware in Little Falls. In photos, it looks like a Model 17-3E, a 998cc V-Twin with a three-speed transmission. In 1918, Excelsior was one of the "Big Three," third in sales after Harley and Indian, and it was considered a very advanced and road-worthy bike, with a reputation for setting cross-country speed records. Excelsior bought Henderson in 1917, adding the luxurious Henderson Four to its showrooms.

In an odd personal footnote here, when I was 15, I traded my go-kart for a 1917 Henderson engine to use in a Pietenpol Air Camper, a home-built airplane for which I'd acquired plans. I ran out of money after building the wing and sold the Henderson Four to Mr. Neumann, my shop teacher, for $40 so I could afford to go to the prom.

It's deals like this that have kept me from becoming a household name in aviation.

We pulled up in front of the Lindbergh farm and paid $7 each to go through the excellent museum and take a tour of the nearby house. In the museum we found a large photo of Lindbergh on his bike and an exhibit of his motorcycle memorabilia, including his wood chest of tools and spare parts, and both his Minnesota and Wisconsin license plates.

There were various quotes from Lindbergh about his Excelsior. He wrote, "I liked the mechanical perfection of the motorcycle and took pride in the skill I developed riding it. I liked the feel of its power and its response to my control. Eventually, it seemed like an extension of my own body."

There was also a display of Lindbergh's probationary academic report from the UW, signed by a Professor Joseph D. Livermore.

We toured the home, a very nice two-story house with a big screened back porch—Lindbergh's summer bedroom—facing the river. Under the porch was a garage containing the original Saxon touring car, now restored after being, literally, pulled apart by souvenir hunters in 1927.

Before leaving, we naturally toured the gift shop and loaded up on books and DVDs, which joined our Red Wing boots and pottery in the ever-more-densely-packed trunk of the sidecar. We got rooms at a local motel, ate dinner at an excellent roadhouse called Cabin Fever, took in *Talladega Nights* at the local theater (alas, *The Spirit of St. Louis*, with James Stewart, which I saw about six times as a kid, was no longer playing), and then rolled south in the morning.

We debated what route Lindbergh might have taken to Madison—I know of no written record—and decided he probably would have taken the river road right from his front door down through Saint Cloud, the Twin Cities, and Red Wing, then cut over into Wisconsin. And that's what we did, stopping, of course, at my dad's birthplace on Breda Street in Saint Paul.

Leaving Saint Paul on a short stretch of interstate I tried for top speed and hit an indicated 67, flat out. The Ural could cruise okay in the right lane of the freeway but felt overstressed and unhappy in that environment, like a small dog in a large airport. Its RGS (Range of Greatest Serenity) was between 50 and 55 mph, at which it hummed happily, generated minimal wind blast for the pilot, and felt as if it could go on forever.

Highway 61, on the Minnesota side of the Mississippi, was a little too hectic and crowded for our laid-back Ural state of mind, so it felt good when we crossed into Wisconsin for another night in Trempealeau.

I know this sounds like the worst kind of state chauvinism, but when we stopped at a scenic overlook near Fountain City, I said to Barb, "No matter which way you come into Wisconsin, from any other bordering state, things are always just a little nicer here. Greener hills, quieter roads, more curves, prettier farms. Lindbergh knew where to ride."

There, I've offended all our neighbors, but I'll stand by it.

At one point, we turned off on a heavily graveled country road to see how the two-wheel-drive system worked. I flicked the lever and the Ural motored easily through the deepest gravel, straight as an arrow. It turned normally in the loose stuff, but not at all when we got back on dry pavement. It's a system you don't need very often, but it makes you fearless in the face of road construction, mud, deep puddles, and dirt roads.

From LaCrosse we took Highway 33, a beautiful ridge road and old pioneer route, southeast through the green hills. Barb made me stop at an Amish farm and craft shop where she bought three quilts and managed to stuff them over her legs and lap in the front of the sidecar. "An Amish airbag," I observed. Just then, a horse-drawn buggy clopped by with surprising swiftness, and another team of horses pulled a hay rake into the farmyard. I narrowed my eyes and thought about the $3.26 we'd just paid for a gallon of premium unleaded. A wind-driven water pump creaked in the breeze.

There was a joke here somewhere, and I felt it was on us.

We dropped down to Highway 14 and rolled into Madison late in the afternoon with the UW campus and State Capitol in view. Ceremonially, we pulled up at 35 N Mills Street, the house, now remodeled to be exceedingly plain and ugly, where Lindbergh had a student apartment (with his mother, no less) on the third floor. While I took photos, a student was moving out after summer school, loading his car. I asked if he knew Lindbergh had lived in his building, and he said no.

The place had a For Sale sign on it, and I wondered if this was our chance to become student slumlords and historical preservationists, all at once. We decided to pass; there are limits to our Lindbergh fixation. Barb and I headed 22 miles south to our home and got there just before sundown.

When we got home, the Ural had covered 1,015 miles in our meanderings, consumed only a trace of oil on its dipstick, and averaged 27.7 mpg. There was still a little oil misting out of the rear hub, but no other problems had occurred. Steve Krings later told us the rear hubs will do that if they are even slightly overfilled during servicing.

The transmission had loosened up a little bit but still wasn't a paragon of precision. (Ural says there are newly designed gears coming next year.)

Otherwise, the bike ran beautifully for the whole trip and started instantly with a prod of the button, almost before you could hear the starter motor engage. I started it once with the side-mounted kick-starter, though it took about six quick swings of the lever to get it running.

We ran out of gas once, going on reserve at 107 miles and running flat-out at 125 miles, half a block short of a gas station in Red Wing. A pedestrian named Rob, who said he owned both a Guzzi Ambassador and an Eldorado, helped us push it to the Marathon (of all things) station. It took exactly five gallons, the claimed tank capacity. Fuel mileage was better on backroads than running fast and straight on major highways.

The fun factor was better, too, even if the trip took a little longer. Which was okay with us, as a sidecar rig isn't about making time so much as the suspension of time. It's a comfortable and charming observation platform that forces you to slow down slightly and look at where you are. This little five-day journey might be the most pure, relaxing fun I've ever had on a motorcycle trip. Not the greatest speed, distance, or cornering thrills, just the best time. In a world of biz-jets, it's a Stearman biplane.

Or maybe a Curtiss Jenny, tastefully updated and with modern electrics.

88

Ducatis and Cigarettes

BACK WHEN I WAS A FULL-TIME TECH EDITOR AT *Cycle World* during
the early 1980s and lurking in the roomy but windowless office now
occupied by Editor Edwards, I had a small quote from a British bike magazine
taped to my door.

It read, "Ducatis are like cigarettes; you may quit for a while, but you
always come back to them in the long run."

This little gem of wisdom struck a chord with me because both addictions
seemed related in some strange way.

I was then trying, with only limited success, to quit smoking and had several
times ceremoniously thrown my last pack of Camels (a fine blend of domestic
and Turkish tobaccos) into the trash, only to have the urge for a nicotine hit
return at the least opportune time. Usually while I was working alone in the
office over the weekend.

I'd be sitting there typing my deathless prose about rejetting a Honda 400
Hawk with midrange stumbles when, suddenly, a red message would light up
in my brain saying, "You must have a cigarette." And I couldn't concentrate
until I did.

Well, I've long since stopped smoking—quit cold turkey on my 50th birthday—
but the instinctive urge to own a Ducati has remained as persistent as that old
cigarette habit used to be. I've owned nine of Borgo Panigale's finest over the past
28 years, and the occasional gap in ownership has always set off a motorcycle
variant of that same red message light: "You must have another Ducati."

The problem goes back quite a few years.

While I admired the small Ducati Singles that hit our shores in the 1960s
(even if they weren't Triumphs), the first stirrings of genuine desire came with
the arrival of the exquisite round-case 750 SS V-Twins. These were expensive,
however, and seemed virtually unobtainable, as any Ducati dealer lucky enough
to get one simply kept it. They were always on display in showroom windows,
but I never saw one on the street.

It was the square-case 900SS, built in much larger numbers, that finally made the sleek desmo Twins available to mere mortals. And it was here that the real addiction took hold.

It started about the first week I worked for *Cycle World*, early in 1980, when I arrived in California from Wisconsin just in time for the Los Angeles Motorcycle Show. A bunch of us rode up there from the office, and when we walked through the doors of the main pavilion, the first thing we encountered was a black-and-gold 900SS rotating on a raised, round platform under the lights. It looked like a wedding cake with a black widow perched on top.

Except the Ducati was better looking than any deadly arachnid. Equally dangerous, but much better looking. It had gold wheels, an anodized chain, and bodywork in ebony black with discreet gold trim to stir the Anglophilia of those of us who misspent our youths lusting after Vincents, Velocettes, and AJS 7Rs.

But this was no dusty old British classic. This was the most potent production track weapon of the moment, its immediate antecedents having recently won (in variously tweaked forms) both the Isle of Man and the Daytona Superbike races. And the bike was cleaning up everywhere in production club racing. Spartan, purposeful, and uncluttered.

While the other *CW* guys wandered off, I stood there transfixed by the beauty and rightness of the design, sort of like Wayne (or was it Garth?) staring at that white Stratocaster in the window of the music shop. Anticipating that movie by a couple of decades, I said aloud, "Oh yes, it shall be mine!"

As luck would have it, a few weeks later I won a $5,000 editorial prize from CBS Magazines (which then owned *Cycle World*) for a story I'd written about

my Triumph Bonneville. It was clearly a case of mistaken identity or some bizarre corporate foul-up, but I wasn't about to ask any questions.

The check arrived at 11:45 on a Friday morning, and at noon I ran down the block to Champion Kawasaki-Ducati and bought a used 1978 900SS from shop owner Lee Fleming. When I signed over the check, the money had been in my hands for exactly 15 minutes.

This bike was a runner. It had been Lee's personal streetbike, and he was then the AFM Open Production class champ on his racing 900SS. The compression was up slightly, and Jerry Branch had reworked the cylinder heads.

I remember my own first ride as being somewhat disorienting. Compared with, say, a Honda CB750F or Suzuki GS1000 of the day, the Ducati was slightly harsh and uncomfortable, with a severe shortage of steering lock. Your feet were tucked up behind you in a full racing crouch, and the exhaust note sounded like Muhammad Ali working a speed bag with forceful, rhythmic deliberation. You looked down at the engine and wondered if it had enough aluminum around the cylinder bores to contain all that violence.

Getting off my Honda 750 and climbing onto the Ducati was like leaving the Hilton and entering a Trappist monastery, a dark place lighted by torches where you slept on a stone floor.

No mini-bar in this room, pal. We're looking for salvation through austerity.

But out of the crowded city and on the back mountain roads of California, the bike transformed itself. Fast, composed, and easy to ride, it clicked smoothly along like a runaway freight train compacted into a highly precise instrument of speed. Pure pleasure, a mechanical drug that seemed to mix some kind of opiate with an equal amount of caffeine.

Nearly every Sunday morning my buddy John Jaeger (on his R90S Beemer) and I would take a ride over the Ortega Highway to Lake Elsinore for breakfast. The road was nearly empty in those days and largely unpatrolled.

Or so we thought. On a long downhill straight coming out of the mountains toward San Juan Capistrano, we got side by side and held our throttles to the stops. We'd just hit an indicated 135 mph when two cop cars materialized out of the rapidly approaching distance and turned on all their lights and sirens. We pulled over, feeling suddenly busted and financially ruined, but the cop cars kept going. I think they were on their way to investigate a minor fender-bender we'd passed earlier and were too busy to turn around.

John and I looked at each other, shrugged, and split for home. We spent the rest of the day hiding out in our respective garages, staying away from windows.

After a couple of years, I sold the 900SS to buy something more practical (a category that includes nearly all other objects in the universe), then started twitching like a dope fiend and bought another 900SS in the late 1980s.

Since then, I've owned a long string of Ducatis, old and new, including yet another bevel-drive 900SS. I sold that last bike to a friend in Colorado seven years ago and just bought it back last summer. It is now sitting in my garage, and here it will stay.

I guess I've finally reached the age where I'm not looking for anything more practical. I have a couple of modern bikes that work better for normal daily use, but I've come to realize that Ducatis are important not just as great machines, but as symbols of a healthy resistance to compromise.

In a world where everything gets dumbed-down, fattened-up, or over-civilized, Ducati has managed to keep a focus of purpose—what my friend Jeff Craig calls a "core idea of what they do best." They don't try to be all things to all people. Ducati makes racing and sportbikes that are light and charismatic, and that's it. We don't want Eric Clapton doing the best of Justin Timberlake, and we don't want Ducati making cruisers or 800-pound touring rigs.

Also, if you like Italy and things Italian—which I do, despite being largely Celtic, from a family that was notoriously undemonstrative—Ducatis are a way of celebrating everything distinct about the Italian approach to life, as filtered through a spare-yet-flamboyant mechanical sensibility. Motorcycles project a cultural force field upon your life, and Ducatis do it better than most. The bikes have Emilia-Romagna written all over them, and seem to have been made for narrow Apennine roads lined with Lombardi poplars and old stone buildings. Which is why you don't want to go off the road in that country. And why Ducatis generally don't have floorboards.

Another key quality in Ducatis is presence. Whether you're riding along on a 250 Mach 1, an old 900SS, or a new 1098, you never forget for one moment what you're riding. You keep looking down at the tank and instruments and thinking consciously about where you are—both literally and in the flow of history. Remaining oblivious to my 900SS while speeding down the highway would be difficult indeed, like sitting across the dinner table from Hilary Swank and trying to forget who she is, or that Clint Eastwood may have taught her how to box. The mind doesn't wander much.

But enough of these show-business analogies. Back to smoking.

Like those cigarettes I gave up a decade ago, Ducatis also carry with them a bracing touch of fatalism. The owner has to be somewhat willing to dive into the unknown (or at least be willing to endure a desmo valve adjust) in order to make life more interesting and less predictable. The bikes serve as a kind of compensation for putting up with everything safe and mundane in this world, a thumb in the eye of caution. All motorcycles do this to some extent, but Ducatis are the image on the recruiting poster.

I took my black 900SS for a long ride this weekend (maybe the season's last, as it's supposed to snow tonight) and sat in my workshop, warming up and looking at the bike for a while when I got back.

I happened to glance over at my glass trophy case, where I keep memorabilia—odd souvenirs, old tank badges, models, etc. —and noticed that I still had a spare set of silver velocity stacks left over from my first 900SS, as well as a 1/12-scale Tamiya model of the black Ducati, carefully assembled years ago by my late father-in-law, Fred Rumsey.

Behind the velocity stacks, on the middle shelf of the trophy case, was an ancient pack of crumbling Camels. They'd come out of the zippered tail compartment of my 900SS seven years ago, when I sold the bike to my friend in Colorado.

I always carried them there—for scenic roadside stops and reflective episodes of bike appreciation—along with two spark plugs, a tool roll, and a Zippo lighter. The Zippo, which I'd purchased at a military PX in a place called Phan Rang in 1969, was in the trophy case as well. Right near the cigarettes.

A small red light came on in my brain, but I ignored it—for the time being—and opened a Diet Coke. The kind with caffeine.

89

Rare Birds; Vincents in Texas

DANGEROUS BUSINESS, FLYING DOWN TO AUSTIN TO RIDE A Vincent. Last time I made this trip was 14 years ago, and I ended up buying the 1952 Vincent Black Shadow featured in a story I cleverly entitled "To Ride a Vincent." Came home, sold everything I owned that anyone would want to buy, and purchased the bike from collector/restorer Herb Harris. The Shadow is gone now—I parted with it about 10 years ago when I realized I could sell it and pay off our house—but I'm still friends with Herb.

And when he invited us back to Austin this time, I figured I'd be in a little less peril, as the two rare Vincents featured here are way out of my price range. Actually, all Vincents are way out of my price range now, unless we sell our house and move into an abandoned cardboard box. Next to the railroad tracks. Time, collectability, and inflation have marched on. While I, apparently, have not.

Herb Harris is an Austin lawyer who retired a couple of years ago to open a new business (Harris Vincent Gallery, Inc.), one that would allow him to concentrate on his favorite things in life, which are tracking down Vincents and/or restoring them.

He and his wife, Karen, have a nice home in the Texas Hill Country on the west side of Austin, with a guest house attached. Upstairs is a comfortable apartment, with a refrigerator full of Guinness, and the downstairs looks exactly like a traditional English pub, with a dark wood bar and a shining row of great British bikes lined up on the varnished (and surprisingly oil-free) floor. Vincents, vintage Triumphs, BSA Gold Stars, AJS 7Rs, etc.

When you pour a cup of coffee and walk downstairs into the pub in the morning, you automatically find yourself repeating that famous line from *Field of Dreams*: "Is this heaven?"

"No," you tell yourself, "this is Texas. And what we have here is a very fine collection of motorcycles."

Though many of the world's great Vincents—including the Rollie Free "bathing suit bike" of Bonneville record fame—have passed through his hands,

Herb says he's not really a collector. He enjoys having the bikes for a few years and working on them, but feels no need to hang on to them in the long run. As is the case with so many of us, it's the hunt that matters. He's really more history detective than collector.

And, without Herb, it might have taken Sherlock Holmes himself to track down the big Series B Vincent engine that's nestled in the heart of the first bike we're looking at today. It's the very first Series B engine, introduced just after World War II.

Long since separated from its original chassis and passed around for various factory experimental projects, it was discovered by Herb in an English eBay ad, and he's now returned it to a proper chassis—one it might have had when it was introduced to the English press in 1946—with an overlay of appropriate patina.

To explain where this all fits in the Big Scheme, perhaps we should do a quick little review of Vincent History.

Philip Vincent came from a wealthy English family and went to good schools. While at Harrow and Cambridge, he was an avid motorcyclist with a trouble-prone BSA , so he did what serious scholars (such as you and I) have always done with their study hall time, which is sketch motorcycle frames. He wanted to start his own motorcycle company, but his wise old father convinced him to buy a defunct but prestigious brand—H.R.D. This company was named for Howard R. Davies, a famous motorcycle racer who'd started building his own high-quality bikes (out of frustration with other brands), but had gone broke by 1927.

Yes, here we have a prime example of the "Frustration with Other Brands" school of motorcycle design, which appears to have propelled British ingenuity through much of the twentieth century.

Anyway, Phil Vincent started building his own Vincent-HRD Singles with purchased engines (J.A.P., Villiers, Rudge, etc.) and his own stoutly triangulated frame designs. Frustration with some of these engines (J.A.P., mostly) drove him and his famous partner in crime, Australian engineer Phil Irving, to design their own big Singles, the Meteor and the hotter Comet.

These engines had a number of clever features, including high cams and rocker-arm fingers operating on collars at the center of the valve stems, which shortened the pushrods to lighten the valvetrain and reduce overall engine height. Valves were carried in two guides, with a gap between them for the rocker arm. In 1936, the Two Phils quite logically joined a pair of these cylinders at the hip and introduced the Series A Rapide, a free-breathing 1000cc V-Twin, to an astonished motorcycle world.

This fearsome object would easily top 100 mph, and it was soon dubbed "The Snarling Beast" by one of its test riders. Unfortunately, the press also dubbed it "The Plumber's Nightmare" because of all the arachnid-like external oil lines; critics further noted the clutch slipped because it was overwhelmed with all that torque and power.

At this point, after 78 were sold, World War II drew a merciful curtain upon the Rapide's shortcomings and Vincent went into war production, building

things that exploded on purpose: artillery shells and land mines. During those dark years, Vincent and Irving plotted an improved post-war Rapide.

And here's where Herb's engine comes in. It's the very first works prototype engine, 1X, long believed to have been scrapped. And it almost was.

That first B-Series Rapide was much ridden and photographed by the press, who approved of its cleaned-up engine, whose external oil lines had been replaced by raised "veins" cast into the case covers. In place of the weak old proprietary clutch was a clever two-stage unit with lightly sprung discs operating a set of brake-shoe-like grabbers in a drum. The traditional diamond frame had also been eliminated by using . . . no frame. The Brampton fork was simply attached to a sturdy oil tank bolted to the top of the cylinder heads, and the unique A-frame swingarm pivoted off the engine cases, with spring boxes almost hidden beneath the seat. What you had, essentially, was that schoolboy's dream: a big hairy engine with two wheels attached.

But once the adoring press finished with it, that prototype bike didn't get much in-house respect. The lads at the factory used it for bashing about town, and then the British military decided they needed a fast assault boat to attack enemy coastlines and had Vincent build 1X into a hot Lightning race-spec engine for testing. Nothing came of this, but the poor engine got its transmission band-sawed off and a new set of contemporary case numbers (468) tacked on to the existing number 1 (which led to some confusion later). Then, the beast was left to languish under a workbench.

After that, the engine was sold off, installed in a later frame, and used in various hillclimbers and racebikes—with a Norton gearbox bolted on. And this is how Herb found it in England, a bitsa Lightning-spec racebike with straight pipes and later Girdraulic fork. He thought it deserved to go back into an early Series B chassis, replicating as closely as possible the bike shown in those 1946 magazine photos. And that's what we have here. Not the first complete Series B Vincent, which has long since been parted out into the cosmos, but a proper setting for its original engine, now fully rebuilt, of course.

So, on a warm Texas summer morning, we trailered the Rapide farther out into the Hill Country, and I took a ride on it, all duded up in 1946 riding gear (although this is two years before I was born, so I have only the photos). Herb, his son, Brian, and mechanic Mike Beck bump-started the bike, as I was suffering from a case of purple BSA Single kick-start knee at the moment, and I headed off down the road.

One ride on a Vincent reminds you why people put up with the expense and vintage eccentricities of these bikes—and why I sold everything to buy one of my own. They feel compact and light, with a low center of gravity, and the engine has a relaxed, almost liquid-smooth V-Twin gait and shuffle that make you want to motor down the road and off into infinity. It has great, easy torque, plenty of power, and light, agile steering from the Brampton fork, while the rear suspension really works, soaking up bumps in a way that must have seemed unbelievably civilized in this hardtail era.

And the view over that black tank with gold leaf lettering, while watching the fork work, is one of motorcycling's great pleasures. It feels and looks as if there's remarkably little bike beneath you, considering how much visual mass and heart-stopping charm that engine exudes from a side view—and how willingly it accelerates. It's exactly the right size for a motorcycle, with an ideal (and adjustable) riding position.

Out of respect for the value of this bike—and my own cowardice and recently healed ribs—I didn't push it too hard in corners, but the general characteristics are intuitively natural turn-in and good stability in fast turns. Brakes? Better than almost anything from the era—and for about 20 years thereafter—but if you're headed into a blind downhill sweeper at 65 mph, you should probably know where the road goes in advance. Surprises are not entirely welcome.

When we finally put the Rapide away toward evening and were about to head out for some great Texas barbeque (not that I don't like motorcycles), Herb offered us a bonus ride on another of his finished project bikes, a 1932 HRD Python Sport, a 500cc Single with a four-valve Rudge engine—in hot "Ulster Tune" competition spec. If the Rapide was intended to have historic patina, this one was restored so perfectly you almost hate to stand too close. Like the Les Paul Custom in *Spinal Tap*, perhaps you shouldn't even look at it.

This bike came at a pivotal point in Vincent history, as Phil Vincent had finally been convinced to abandon his unconventional early frame design, which was heavily triangulated and had an awkward frame tube slashing across the side of the engine. In its place came a more "normal" diamond frame, but still with his excellent rear suspension. At this time, he was also having trouble with J.A.P. (John A. Prestwich) engines and was trying out the more sophisticated

Rudge Python unit. This period lasted only briefly, until Rudge quit supplying engines, and Vincent and Irving designed their own.

And the Python is a pretty exquisite engine. It has four valves located radially in a bronze (sometimes iron) head, dual exhaust ports that empty into a pair of gracefully swept-back Highgate "silencers," and an Amal carb with the slide body turned sideways for more tank clearance. (Well, why not? Should work.)

Herb's started first kick, idled smoothly, and had plenty of midrange grunt. Compared with the Rapide, however, the old Single is a little more of a vintage contraption to ride. But only in that the Burman gearbox is a slower-shifting unit and the Blumfeld brakes are less effective. Did I call them brakes? More like a butter-injection system. The harder you squeeze, the faster the bike goes, just like my old Triumph 500. Luckily, it handles quite nicely, which helps when you're sailing through corners a little faster than intended. Overall, a charming, perfectly serviceable bike with great visual balance and mechanical presence.

I didn't ride this one hard at all, as it's already sold to a wealthy collector (redundant, perhaps) and on its way out the door. But bikes like this aren't lovingly restored so we poor deprived moderns have something to ride hard. We have new bikes for that.

We like the old ones not because we need transportation, but because we love history—and the beauty that comes from imagination and fine craftsmanship. Which, luckily for us, were sometimes borne of past frustration with other brands.

Index